Experience, Meaning, and Identity in Sexuality

James Horley • Jan Clarke

Experience, Meaning, and Identity in Sexuality

A Psychosocial Theory of Sexual Stability and Change

palgrave
macmillan

James Horley
University of Alberta
Augustana Campus, Camrose
Alberta, Canada

Jan Clarke
Associate Professor of Sociology
Algoma University, Sault Ste. Marie
Ontario, Canada

ISBN 978-1-137-40095-6   ISBN 978-1-137-40096-3   (eBook)
DOI 10.1057/978-1-137-40096-3

Library of Congress Control Number: 2016944118

© The Editor(s) (if applicable) and The Author(s) 2016
The author(s) has/have asserted their right(s) to be identified as the author(s) of this work in accordance with the Copyright, Designs and Patents Act 1988.
This work is subject to copyright. All rights are solely and exclusively licensed by the Publisher, whether the whole or part of the material is concerned, specifically the rights of translation, reprinting, reuse of illustrations, recitation, broadcasting, reproduction on microfilms or in any other physical way, and transmission or information storage and retrieval, electronic adaptation, computer software, or by similar or dissimilar methodology now known or hereafter developed.
The use of general descriptive names, registered names, trademarks, service marks, etc. in this publication does not imply, even in the absence of a specific statement, that such names are exempt from the relevant protective laws and regulations and therefore free for general use.
The publisher, the authors and the editors are safe to assume that the advice and information in this book are believed to be true and accurate at the date of publication. Neither the publisher nor the authors or the editors give a warranty, express or implied, with respect to the material contained herein or for any errors or omissions that may have been made.

Cover image: © Oleg (RF) / Alamy Stock Photo

Printed on acid-free paper

This Palgrave Macmillan imprint is published by Springer Nature
The registered company is Macmillan Publishers Ltd. London

Contents

1	Introduction	1
2	The Nature and Implications of PCT	35
3	Understanding Multiple Sexualities	71
4	Social Influence on Sexual Constructs	89
5	Power Relations in Sexuality	105
6	Interpreting Sexualized Bodies	125
7	Sexual Commodification: Pornography, Prostitution, and Personal Constructs	147
8	Sexual Offenders	167

9 Changing Sexual Interests, Identities, and Behaviours	193
10 Final Considerations	225
Further Reading	245
Name Index	281
Subject Index	291

1

Introduction

We are sexual beings, or at least we can be. Even though virtually all of us are born with sexual organs, what we choose to do or not do with our genitalia is up to us. This ability to choose appears unique to human sexuality. We have the ability to decide how to act sexually depending on our understanding of the situation, our role in it, and our current desires. If we do not see that sexual behavior is appropriate or necessary on our part for whatever reason (e.g., lack of desire, vow of abstinence, something in the situation is askew), we can avoid any type of sexual involvement or action. We are bound neither by instincts nor innate drives to reproduce, to engage in sexual behavior for the sake of pleasure, or to behave sexually in any way. Throughout our lives, there are innumerable reasons why we act in a sexual manner or refrain from any behavior that could be interpreted as sexual in any way. We will develop a position here that cognition is much more important to human sexuality than sexual physiology. Cognition and language, two related abilities that we tend to possess in spades, are fundamental to our sexuality and to all sexual behavior. While cognition, or at least one aspect of it, will be discussed throughout this book, language will be considered to a much lesser extent. A brief word on language—a system of verbal, manual, or written signs and/or symbols used to communicate—might be useful here to help to introduce our position on sexuality.

"Male versus female," "virgin versus slut," and "heterosexual versus homosexual" are just a few of the contrasts used by contemporary English speakers to refer to various aspects of human sexuality. In many quarters, a contrast such as "straight versus bent," or the more frequently encountered today "straight versus gay", has replaced the "heterosexual versus homosexual" distinction; and in some academic circles, "constructionism versus essentialism" is used to distinguish particular theories or positions concerning sexuality. No doubt such contrasts have been useful in the cause of making sense of human sexual reproduction, sexual behavior, sexual differences and similarities, social roles and relationships, and other related matters, but they have been, and continue to be, confining in terms of interpreting sexuality. What happens if, instead of viewing social actors as either male or female, we begin to understand them as male or not male, and female or not female? How about changing "gay versus straight" to "gay versus not gay" and "straight versus not straight"? Imagine the world of possibilities created by a simple change in wording. But this is thought rather than a simple linguistic manipulation. We can interpret our sexual world in different, more complex and multi-layered, and, frankly, much more interesting ways by rejecting rigid or traditional means of categorization and considering, or inventing, novel ways of construing sexuality.

It is difficult, if not impossible, to argue that evolution and biology have no relevance to contemporary human sexual interests, desires, and behaviors. Collectively, we are the sum of all that has happened to us ancestrally up to this point in time, and our biological make-up determines what we are capable of within any given environmental context, and sets limits on what is possible. There is, however, a significant difference now between human and infrahuman sexual behavior, and such a difference needs to be taken into account in any satisfactory theory of human sexuality. Human evolution, if nothing else, has provided us with an incredible and unique advantage—the brain and central nervous system. To deny its evolutionary development is nonsensical, but to focus on the brain as the source of, say, sexual behavior is far too narrow. It is not brain structures or processes that account directly for the wide range of human desires, attractions, and responses. Taking the mind into account in a serious fashion is required or, if a computing metaphor is acceptable, an understanding of the software that operates within the confines of the hardware is essential. As humans, and unlike infrahuman species, we are free from biophysical markers and instinctual demands (Masters, Johnson, & Kolodny, 1988). Human sexual behaviors are not simply immediate responses to particular colours, smells, or sounds; sex among humans is not simply a case of instinctive or automatic responses to various stimuli. We have no overarching "biological imperative", although we may have personal, psychosocial imperatives related to sex. We take a vast array of contextual features, including both external and internal factors, into consideration before behaving in a sexual manner. It is not just the naked body of a desirable individual, however attractive, that elicits a sexual response from the human observer. After all, a sexual response is much less likely should a naked individual be pursued by a knife-wielding attacker, or sitting on a concrete floor of a grimy institution among other naked individuals, and we are experiencing anxiety due to the knife or the dirty place full of naked bodies. The setting or the situation is important to human sexual behavior —indeed, all human behavior. We tend to think, and interpret, before we act, although certainly not in every instance. Understanding what kind of behavior is required in a particular situation permits survival and adaptation and, while some may question the quality of our thinking both individually and collectively on many occasions, it is certainly a key human characteristic.

Our so-called sex hormones (e.g., estrogen, testosterone) play vital roles in sexual functioning, but they do not determine our sexual behavior—at least not directly. Testosterone, for example, is required by men in order to produce viable sperm cells, but it is present in both males and females because it is a releaser hormone (i.e., it promotes the release of epinephrine into the blood stream). Epinephrine or adrenaline increases blood flow, which provides more available energy to the body. What is done with the available energy, however, remains a matter of choice for both sexes. If we are in a situation where danger appears imminent, we may choose to run, to fight, or to employ some other strategy. Similarly, if we are in a situation where sexual contact appears imminent, we may choose to run, to engage in sex, or to engage in some other behavior (e.g., "Anyone for a game of darts?"). Regardless of the cues, and regardless of our serum testosterone or serum epinephrine levels, we will consider our options and choose what we think is the best course of action, which may or may not prove to be the best, depending on the outcome of the act.

Currently, few serious thinkers take an analytic unit such as sexual instinct very seriously when it comes to human sexuality. In many circles, unfortunately, we still embrace related notions like personality traits. Such units, if they refer to hard-wired and innate behaviors, are wholly inadequate in explaining the range and adaptability of human sexual responses, desires, and behaviors. So-called evolutionary theories, such as sexual strategies theory (Buss, 1994, 1998), which rely on traits are very limited in explaining human sexual variation. All evolutionary approaches, as Singer (1985) noted, including sexual strategies theory, suffer from the problem that they cannot be evaluated directly, and the support for theories that promote evolutionary or genetic arguments is flimsy at best. Studies that rely on autopsy differences in a single brain structure in a handful of corpses of people who died of different causes and were assumed to have a particular sexual orientation (LeVay, 1991), or on results from various "sexual strategy" surveys conducted on US college campuses over the past two or three decades (Buss, 1994), let alone one that relies on simplistic and static units like traits, or even needs and drives, should not convince a serious thinker of the adequacy of any theory. A dynamic unit that can capture both change and stability of desire and behavior appears to be a necessary component of any adequate theory that can account for human sexuality. Fortunately, dynamic units of analysis do exist in psychology.

One striking aspect of human sexual desire and expression is variety. The labile nature of sexuality across both the species and the lifespan of individuals must be accounted for by any adequate theory. Just as the timing of human sexual expression is virtually limitless, the range of sexual interests and behaviors performed by people is vast. Whether alone or with others, we engage in a wide range of activities that can be construed as sexual, and not all of these behaviors result in an orgiastic finale—although many do. Sexual practice—indeed, gender itself (see Weeks, 1995)—is much more complex than many once believed, and explanations require a corresponding complexity. With this in mind, if we adopt a simple, biological, hedonistic position that seems to be at the basis of some views of human sexuality (e.g., Buss, 1994), how are we to explain variations? Theories have been developed, including a few long-standing and rather intriguing efforts (e.g., Freund, 1990), but most have proved to be too general or sometimes too limited, too vague, or too descriptive to be of much use. How can we account for the complexity of this sexual expression at the appropriate level of analysis? This appears possible only if we consider all possibilities in terms of human sexual outcomes. In other words, people do not engage in sex for a single purpose such as reproduction. In reality, we do not engage in sex for reasons strictly of reproduction, physical pleasure, or any single purpose; rather, as meaning-makers, we engage in sexual behavior, and all behavior, in response to a broad and varied set of possible meanings of the actions. The meanings of human sexual behavior or the reasons for human sexual thoughts, feelings, and action are likely as varied and unique as there are individuals. For some individuals, sex may be only about reproduction and, for others, only pleasure, but sex can—and probably does—stand for much more for the majority of individuals. The purpose of sexual thoughts and behavior can be for expressing love, expressing hate, expressing disgust, wanting to fall asleep, needing distraction from regularity, needing regularity, confirming attractiveness, advancing a relationship, achieving intimacy, and many other understandings or reasons. A survey of university students (Meston & Buss, 2007) found 237 distinct reasons for human sexual behavior, including "Getting closer to God" and "Wanting to humiliate the person", and it is doubtful that teenaged undergraduates at one Texas university are all that experienced or sophisticated in sexual realms. It is possible, if not probable, that a single sexual act can have multiple meanings and purposes. We need to consider not only personal attitudinal and emotional factors, but also larger cultural and sub-cultural contexts (Masters et al., 1988).

It appears as if sexual expression and sexual orientation are far more fluid than fixed throughout the course of life (e.g., see Diamond, 2008). Kinsman (1991, 1996) has argued that sexual interest in same-sex and opposite-sex individuals waxes and wanes over time for many individuals to the extent that he is reluctant to talk of dominant individual sexual orientations, and he is certainly unwilling to ascribe significant genetic or biological roots to such notions as "homosexuality" or "heterosexuality". We plan to address these and other issues about sexuality in this book by engaging in an ambitious project. We will present a rather unique theory that, we believe, can account for the rise, development, change, and stability of sexual desires, interests, and identities. Contrasts such as "gay versus straight" form not only a means of interpreting sexuality or making sense of sexual actors, but part of a much broader process by which all people make sense of or construe experiences in the world and, as such, come to form personal and social identities. Everyone appears to develop a unique, yet related, system of bipolar contrasts that is the fountainhead of all behavior, not just sexual behavior. Our chosen social science theory, personal construct theory (PCT), places an emphasis on the manner in which we describe, explain, predict, and eventually come to control our experiences and our everyday lives (see Kelly, 1955, 1963, 1970). The theory has at its core a very dynamic unit of personality analysis, the personal construct. Personal construct theory appears to us to be a helpful approach for both understanding sexuality and assisting those whose sexual encounters and experiences are not what they, or others, hope that they could be.

We intend to present an expansion of this theory but, before attempting to develop what began as an individual, psychological theory into more of a psychosocial theory, we need to lay some groundwork. At least a couple of topics seem necessary to include in an introduction to a theory of human sexuality. First, we will discuss briefly the terminology across disciplines that will be encountered in this book, and elsewhere for that matter, in reference to sexuality topics. This appears essential because, as mentioned, and as we will argue, language is important. Second, we will provide a brief historical overview of sexuality research and theory over the past two centuries. While this historical sketch will be both brief and somewhat selective, it will provide some context for the effort that we will make in the second chapter to describe in detail PCT and our theory and position, which we will elaborate in subsequent chapters.

Sexuality Terms and Constructs Across Disciplines

While this book presents a theory of sexuality rooted in PCT that is largely informed by psychology, we will also draw on constructs from social theories and concerns from social movements. Clarity of the language of sexuality cannot be taken for granted within disciplines, let alone across disciplines. At a fundamental level, the biological and physiological meanings connoted by many contemporary psychological terms can be at odds with the historical and social contexts that are subsumed under sociological terms. The territory where these two disciplines overlap is of the most interest and value to our purposes, although we feel the need to identify distinct cross-disciplinary differences in the language of sexuality. With active debate about gender and sexuality issues in different media, for instance, the language of sexualities has become seriously confused in general media, social media, and beyond. At this point, we take the opportunity to compare some psychological and sociological meanings of key terms and concepts that we use throughout this book. Our discussion of the language of sexualities is intended to encourage discussion concerning multiple meanings of sexuality terms and constructs, although we will clarify our use of them as we attempt to speak a shared language of sexuality in the context of this book. To avoid the awkwardness of a glossary, what follows is a discussion of a selection of terms that we highlight, because they can be interpreted in different ways based on differing disciplinary perspectives. We intend to avoid confusion with terms we use repeatedly throughout the book by showing the range of meaning of these terms and by indicating how we interpret the meanings for this project. In some instances, these distinctions are clear-cut but, more often, there is considerable debate in either the psychological or the sociological literatures, and often both, that is briefly outlined to set the debates in context.

In the social sciences, "sex" is a contested term, with quite different descriptions from different perspectives. Unravelling the different meanings of "sex" is critical, because the term is the focus of a wide range of psychological and sociological theoretical work, particularly in the multidisciplinary area of gender studies. The connection of sex to nature, often placed in contrast to gender as nurture, is an understanding that has become both clearer and more muddled with the expansion of research interest in sexuality. Weeks (1996), for example, reflects the many meanings of sex in sexuality studies by claiming that "the term refers both to an act and to a category of person, to a practice and to a gender" (p. 13), whereas Humm (1990) claimed that early second wave feminist theory "defines sex only as the biology of a person—whether he or she is male or female" (p. 201). Second-wave feminist theorists (e.g., Oakley, 1972) and symbolic interactionists (e.g., Goffman, 1977) initially described sex, even sexual categories, as variations on the physiological expression of biological differences, usually based on a binary or oppositional framework of male versus female. This was a way of drawing out biological distinctions between females and males, admittedly binary, which were then linked to socialization and even social organization. Studies of sex roles (see Hochschild, 1973) tend to address the social and cultural influences on the expression of social roles assigned to women and men based on biological sex. Even though questions of maleness and femaleness have been studied based on sex roles for many aspects of social and cultural life, critical analysis of the use of sex roles as being biologically determined have become more nuanced and critical. Critiques in feminist sociological literature exposed how social relations were often assumed to be natural male or female sex roles, yet were in reality largely shaped by social policies (e.g., parenthood) or capitalist practices (e.g., paid work), or led to stereotyping as a means of patriarchal control of females throughout their lives (Millet, 1970). In gender studies, the question of sex as biologically determined is continuously challenged, and taken to an extreme with some poststructuralist perspectives that focus on how sex is produced socially and culturally, not simply biologically. Butler (1990), Westbrook and Schilt (2014), and many recent poststructuralists argued that both sex and gender are produced socially and culturally, implying there is nothing natural about being sexed male or female. While we respect the importance of these debates, we will not be drawn into them; and, to avoid confusion, we will treat sex, at least in terms of male contrasted with female, as a biological construct. In addition, we use the term "sex" to mean doing sex, having sex, or indicating a range of intimate physical interactions.

It is striking how sex and gender have become blurred, if not entirely confounded. "Gender" has become a term that the media embraces in all its forms, but it has also become dominant within the social sciences (Haig, 2004). Today, gender is too often used to describe only biological sex—male and female—so that, at times, the social context of sexuality becomes invisible and hidden. Not surprisingly, "'gender' has been criticized as a prudish way of avoiding the word 'sex'" (Scott & Marshall, 2005, p. 241). The subtleties of masculinity and femininity, as one chooses how to express and identify oneself sexually, are lost when accounts reinforce biological sex. Social relations of experiences of masculinity and femininity, which a general audience may embrace, are used to tempt the general public to say "gender" and to think "sex".

Even though Margaret Mead's (1935) cultural–anthropological work in traditional societies acknowledged the cultural shaping of sex, a focus on gender came to the forefront in the 1960s and 1970s. As an early acknowledgment of what later would be described as "gender", Simone de Beauvoir (1949/1974) described woman as the "other" to man, basically taking for granted that women are dependent on men to frame their identities unless women actively choose to shape their own identities for themselves. Collins (2004) continued this analysis in a contemporary context. "It is important to stress that *all* women occupy the category of devalued other that gives meaning to *all* masculinities" (Collins, 2004, p. 187). Adding gender to earlier debates about sex acknowledges that people are more than physiologically and biologically determined by their sex, or their male or female biology; instead, people actively participate in the shaping of feminine and masculine behaviors in the social and cultural contexts of gender. This use of gender in feminist theory was an important theoretical and empirical distinction, which allowed the analysis of everyday social relations of expressing and behaving in masculine ways (e.g., dominant, aggressive, rational) and feminine ways (e.g., subordinate, passive, emotional) that are not necessarily linked to one's sex as male or female.

"Gender role", first used in the social sciences in the mid-twentieth century, was a term created and employed to separate understandings based on biological and physiological interpretations from understandings that take into account historical and social contexts that are also linked to human agency and social change. Early research on gender focused on gender roles in an attempt to understand how one learned to express masculinity and femininity appropriately in different social and cultural contexts. This area of research revealed the way that doing gender, or gendered behavior, is so much a part of socialization that it is almost invisible and can appear to be natural rather than largely nurtured. Gender roles tend to be prescribed in most cultures and learned through socialization. While parents may have goals of encouraging their children to be comfortable expressing themselves as both feminine and masculine in different circumstances regardless of their sex, peer groups beyond the family (e.g., schools, social media) often reinforce rigid expressions of femininity for girls and masculinity for boys. Learning, or the internalization of the masculine and feminine attributes of gender roles, becomes the process of gendering (Oakley, 1972). While gendering (Oakley, 1972), gender roles (Money, 1955) and even doing gender (West & Zimmerman, 1987) may reinforce attitudes and behaviors linked to biologically determined sex categories, a feminist perspective on understanding gender attempted to challenge narrow assignments of masculine and feminine behaviors that did not reflect the way women's lived experiences are shaped in complex ways by social and cultural contexts. Anderson (2005) summarized this situation concisely: "Whereas early on gender was conceptualized as a social role, there is now a more complex understanding of gender as a social reality" (p. 441).

Since gender includes how individuals make meaning of masculine and feminine behaviors, it also involves how individuals choose to express themselves in terms of gender identity. Turning gender roles into gender identity is a very real strategy that describes many peoples' lives, but the distinctions between the two are poorly articulated and often misunderstood. Gender identity is less connected with the internalization of masculine and feminine attributes than it is with a subjective sense of how one feels about expressing gender, and what identity a person adopts (Goffman, 1977; Mackie, 1983).

Masculinity and femininity are terms that can be used very generally in everyday usage but we use these terms to refer to particular attitudes and behaviors. Regardless of often being gender-stereotyped, "masculinity" and "femininity" do have meaningful distinctions in gender theories that are relevant to our discussion of sexualities. Gender theories tend to understand "femininity and masculinity as relational terms, each gaining meaning only through the existence of the other" (Weeks, 2011, p. 50), and do not necessarily link masculinity with males and femininity with females, because they can be expressed as attitudes and behaviors regardless of sex. Theories, whether psychological or sociological, that are influenced by Darwinism and evolutionary theories tend to see "masculine" as expression of males and "feminine" as expression of females in binary, normative, and static ways. To avoid this essentialism, we refer to "masculinity" and "femininity" as relational terms, similar to the usage in a wide range of gender studies.

The experience of heterosexuality, in reference to sexual relations with members of the opposite sex, is taken for granted when sex and only sex is assumed to drive people's lives. Such an ideology of heterosexuality, or heteronormativity, structures many societies so firmly that heterosexuality can appear to be unquestioned and entirely natural. By adding gender as a means of analyzing the multiple expressions of masculine and feminine behavior, however, feminist theorists argued that heterosexuality can no longer be the assumed norm. Rich (1980) exposed this assumption by identifying compulsory heterosexuality as the process by which heterosexuality is the assumed norm everyone must conform to in societies in different cultural contexts.

Inevitably set against heterosexuality as norm, or heteronormativity, that is often assumed and not named, homosexuality becomes the named deviant other. In the late nineteenth century, the term homosexuality was used initially to describe sexual attraction to, and physical involvement with, a member of the same sex in an attempt to use of a more neutral, less derogatory, language for same-sex relationships (Weeks, 2008). This attempt at a neutral term for same-sex intimacy was short-lived when homosexuality became recast as negative, particularly by sexologists, when the claims of science were reinforced by medicalization. Medicalization can also reinforce stigmatization and, to counter this, activists in the gay liberation movement in the 1960s attempted, ultimately with success, to change everyday usage from "homosexual" to "gay" to describe same-sex male relationships (Weeks, 1986). This was a political process by activists who recognized the power of language in negatively labelling any sexual orientation that stood outside the limits of heteronormativity (Kinsman, 1991, 1996).

The term "sexual orientation" is actually an interesting and relatively recent addition to the language of sexuality. It seems to have won a battle fought both professionally and publically with the term "sexual preference", a favourite among researchers at the Kinsey Institute for Sex Research (see Bell, Weinberg, & Hammersmith, 1981), after the original "sexual outlet" (Kinsey, Pomeroy, & Martin, 1948) was abandoned. Champions of sexual orientation, or psychosexual orientation, included John Money and his colleagues at the Johns Hopkins Sexual Behaviors Unit, who used the term throughout the 1960s until it eventually became adopted widely. One example of its success is in the *Diagnostic and Statistical Manuals (DSM)* of the American Psychiatric Association. In *DSM-II* (APA, 1968), there is no mention of either "sexual orientation" or "sexual preference"; yet, within five years, in the third edition of the nosology (APA, 1973), "sexual orientation" is used throughout, notably in the section entitled "Identity Disorder" and under "Ego-dystonic homosexuality". "Sexual orientation" was preferable to the Johns Hopkins researchers and the APA, where the medical connection is clear, probably because of its connotation of long-standing, underlying stability due to genetic or biological factors. "Sexual preference", on the other hand, with its connotation of temporal instability and choice, may have seemed more acceptable to sociologically oriented professionals or even treatment specialists. Ultimately, however, it was pushed aside in part for political considerations (i.e., not wanting to offend gay and lesbian communities due to the connotation of active choice). As noted by Kauth (2005), "sexual orientation" may be the term of choice now, but it is rarely defined by researchers and, when a conceptual definition is provided (e.g., Worthington, Savoy, Dillon, & Vernaglia, 2002), all underlying assumptions are not necessarily explicated. Epstein, McKinney, Fox, and Garcia (2012) explained that researchers studying sexual orientation, like themselves, had to accommodate a wide range of sexual orientation labels that "people actually report: mostly heterosexual, mostly straight, fluid lesbian, stable lesbian, stable non-lesbian, and so on" (p. 1377). Because both sexual orientation and sexual preference carry such baggage and problems, we will limit our use of both terms. Besides, as will become clearer in the next chapter, we regard sexual orientation, sexual preference, and similar terms to be unnecessary to a clear understanding of sexuality.

One important term found in a wide range of works on human sexuality is "sexual identity". It can be interpreted in many ways. As Weeks (1995) wrote, sexual identity "is a strange thing. There are people who identify as gay and participate in the gay community who do not experience or wish for, homosexual activity. And there are homosexually active people who do not identify as gay" (p. 196). The act of claiming a sexual identity can be taken for granted among heterosexuals, although the acknowledgment of a straight identity by heterosexuals can be a political position that acknowledges a range of sexualities. In contrast, claiming a non-heterosexual identity as variations of gay, lesbian, bisexual, transgendered, queer, or LGBTQ identity can be a critical transformative process of acceptance and coming out. The terms gay identity and queer identity also reflect a reclaiming of language because both these terms had been used as derogatory terms for same-sex identified men, and sometimes women. In the gay liberation of the 1960s, the term "gay" tended to include men and women. By the 1970s, "gay" referred more explicitly to men in same-sex relationships; women had claimed "lesbian" to describe their women-identified sexual identities. By the 1980s and 1990s, "gay" and "lesbian" identities had become limiting, as these did not reflect the wide range of sexual identities people claimed. The term "queer" is another reclaimed term, first used prior to the 1960s to refer to being homosexual, but replaced by "gay" by the gay liberation and gay rights movements. Most recently, "queer" is being seen as "referring to the rise of new forms of lesbian, gay, bisexual and transgender militancy in the late 1980s" (Weeks, 2008, p. 144). "Queer" has become an inclusive and political term that even includes allies, people who support queer politics but do not otherwise identify themselves as having a queer sexual identity.

Since the 1990s, the terms "transsexual" and "transgender" have been used to describe forms of gender nonconformity. "Transsexual" has biological underpinnings. The term is rooted in the mid-twentieth century clinical practice of treating a person who feels trapped in the wrong body, using sex change through sex reassignment surgery as a psychological and physical solution. While "transsexual" is still used specifically as a clinical term, since the 1990s in LGBTQ communities the umbrella term of transgender has become "inclusive of transsexuals, cross-dressers, and other gender variant people" (Williams, 2014, p. 233). "Transgender", used since the

1970s, initially described gender nonconformity that did not include those who identified as transvestite, or someone who dressed at least on occasion in the clothing deemed appropriate by consensus of the opposite sex, or transsexuals (Weeks, 2011). The focus was gender identity as opposed to genitalia. Transgender people consider gender-variant identities and queer communities as particular concerns, and "transgender" was a term originally suggested by the community members themselves (Williams, 2014). "Transgender" and "trans" are terms that are changing in scope as the community develops and expands. They are linked to social and cultural contexts and also cover a wide range of experiences of non-conforming gender identities, and are effectively undoing gender binaries as part of this process. To avoid confusion, when we use "transsexual", we refer specifically to individuals who have used sex reassignment surgery to change sex. We use "transgender" and "trans" as more general terms to cover issues of gender nonconformity in a contemporary context that is still changing.

As a critical insight from feminist social theory, patriarchy and patriarchal relations have a particular meaning in the context of human sexuality. Patriarchy is "a system of male authority which oppresses women through its social, political and economic institutions" (Humm, 1990, p. 159), and refers to the social structure in most societies that is based on male dominance as a core value and lived practice. Patriarchal social relations include not only the daily intended or unintended assumption by men that woman are subordinate, but also the consequence of this assumption in groups and communities and, beyond, in the social structure of societies where patriarchal relations become embedded. Patriarchal relations, for instance, are evident in the way that public policy is created by predominantly male decision-makers, and also in the role of male church leaders and doctors in the reproductive rights of women; yet, these decisions have consequences on women who have seldom had the same input. This is one way that not only is women's sexuality controlled, but also self-surveillance is structured to maintain compulsory heterosexuality (Rich, 1980), as a standard and invisible daily practice in patriarchal societies.

"Social construction" and "constructionist" are terms used in such different ways in psychology and sociology that we will be specific about our use to avoid confusion. "Personal construct theory" is a constructivist theory, but we use this term sparingly and carefully to refer in particular to

PCT; and we avoid other uses. This is not an easy choice, because "social construction" is a term that has a precise meaning in some social theory perspectives. For instance, Berger and Luckmann's (1966) understanding of social construction in interpretive sociology is "the relationship between man, the producer, and the social world, his product, is and remains a dialectical one… *Society is a human product. Society is an objective reality. Man is a social product*" (p. 61, italics in original). This starting point (i.e., humans construct societies and themselves) was developed in many contemporary social theories, including ones that concentrate on the sexual realm (e.g., Gagnon & Simon, 1973). In sociology, there is often a special interest in understanding the intersections between individuals, their communities and institutional/societal structures as socially constructed and interconnected; in psychology, while there are similar concerns in some social–psychological circles, there is more concern with the individual as the locus of the construction of reality (for more details, see Stam, 1990, 1998). We will employ the term "constructivism" to refer to all positions that embrace the view that knowledge or understandings flow from human creation, while "social constructionism" will be used to refer specifically to those theories that emphasize the social origins of ideas and objects.

Terms related to or contrasted with constructivism can also create confusion. "Essentialism", in reference to "givens" or "essences" that cannot be disputed, can be used to contrast "constructivism", although "determinism" (e.g., biological or technological), especially in sociology, is more likely to be used to describe aspects of what others might call essentialism. We will try to limit our use of essentialism and related notions in this book to avoid confusion but, where employed, it will refer simply to theories or positions that state or imply that sexual "biological givens" exist that cannot be disputed or dismissed (for a brief but useful discussion, see Wilkerson, 2007).

The Recent History of Sexuality Studies

Halperin (1989) might be correct to state that sex "has no history. It is a natural fact, grounded in the functioning of the body, and, as such, it lies outside of history and culture" (p. 257). However, if the reference here is to genitalia, a bio-evolutionary history might be said to exist in our distant past; and if the reference is to sexual functioning or sexual acts, surely a social history of particular sexual expressions might exist. Halperin (1989) is correct to state that a history of sexuality certainly exists insofar as it represents an "appropriation of the physical body and its physiological capabilities by an ideological discourse" (p. 257). We are not interested in tracing sexual relationships in the Hellenistic period, as Halperin (1989) does so admirably, in showing how sexual relations had much more to do with social status and power than any modern thinking such as "homosexual" versus "heterosexual". Neither are we interested in arguing for a personal construct history, as Brickell (2006) has done with symbolic interactionism in an analysis of the life of a nineteenth-century New Zealand man who was held in a psychiatric facility because of his sexual desires for another man. We are, however, interested in tracing briefly the science, especially social science, of the past century or so that has come to focus on human sexuality. Whether we term this "sexology" or "sexuality studies" or use another similar term does not matter to us, although we recognize that it may well matter to other researchers and clinicians for a variety of reasons. "Sexology" is our choice if only because it is concise.

With the emergence of clinicians in psychiatry in the Western world in the mid-to-late nineteenth century, some of those who dabbled in scientific theorizing about the nature of both normal and abnormal sexual expression, religion and moral philosophy lost their positions of domination with respect to interpreting and commenting on sexual matters to "sexual science" (Foucault, 1978/1990). Religion and philosophy, however systematic and rigorous they may have been, were replaced by more empirical and "objective" disciplines such as medicine, particularly psychiatry, biology, psychology, sociology, and even law. Much of the work of vital importance to this project concerned documenting the pathology of all forms of sexual divergence. The history of this work has been written well by a number of science historians, notably De Brock and Adriaens (2013), who produced a very detailed and accessible history. The groundwork for reducing all minority sexual practices to pathology can be traced to earlier times (see Aries, 1982/1997; Foucault, 1982/1997), but De Brock and Adriaens focused their attention on the past century and a half, when the project of psychiatry and allied disciplines became a clear and steady effort to wrest control of sexuality from practitioners of religion.

Together, practitioners in these disciplines concerned with human sexual function and behavior contributed to a new science called, by some, "sexology". Although the first use of the term appears to be in a book by Willard (1867), she refers more to a systematic study of sex differences and ideal sexual relations, very broadly defined. Willard's work includes a serious dose of sexual morality and utopianism, with an added touch of Christianity, so that no one could mistake the writer as a godless scientist. The current use of the term "sexology" refers to all aspects of human sexuality, and the discipline is typically dated to the early decades of the past century.

The Emergence of Sexology

Conducting sex research and theoretical work was dangerous work, at least professionally, even into the twentieth century. There are examples from the 1920s and 1930s in the USA where academics lost their positions because of their involvement in sexuality studies. A professor in sociology and one in psychology at the University of Missouri in 1929, for example, were dismissed by the institution's board for their involvement in a marital/premarital sex survey sent to students (see Bordwell, Gray, Thurstone & Carlson, 1930; Nelson, 2003). The situation improved in the USA by the 1940s, at least judging from the publication of one rather crude sex survey conducted in New York City bars by Maslow (1942), but risks remained for anyone venturing into this area.

According to Bejin (1982/1997), the origin of modern sexology can be traced only to "the 30 years following the First World War" (p. 182). This is a rather broad time period, and it includes a number of developments. Certainly the important work of Hirschfeld in Germany has been viewed as an origin of sexology, to say nothing of the claim (Mancini, 2010) that Hirschfeld spearheaded the first social movement opposing the repression of sexual minorities or those not part of the heterosexual majority. Also, Kinsey's survey research in the United States has been trumpeted by some (e.g., Bullough, 1998) as marking an important first in sexological research. Rather than nominate any single individual or development as the originator or origin of sexology or sex research, we choose to present a brief historical overview of some of the key developments and contributors from our perspective.

Richard Krafft-Ebing was a German nineteenth-century psychiatrist. He has been described as an early sexologist (Sauerteig, 2012), but he worked on issues other than sexual issues, particularly neurasthenia (see Hauser, 1992), so he is perhaps best viewed as a proto-sexologist at best. Without a doubt, his lasting legacy remains a text on abnormal sexuality, *Psychopathia sexualis*. Not only did Krafft-Ebing borrow the Latin title of the book from a much earlier publication (Kaan, 1844), but he borrowed the notion of sexual instinct from Kaan, a Russian physician intrigued by sexual variation and perversion. In his book, Krafft-Ebing (1886/1935) eventually presented more than 200 case studies of abnormal sexual behavior in detail. He seemed especially interested in masochism among straight men which he attributed to "feminine traits of character… [and this] renders it intelligible that the masochistic element is so frequently found in homosexual men" (p. 212). His views on abnormality appeared to depend largely on German and Victorian views of acceptable sexual behavior (Brecher, 1969). Whether discussing homosexuality, fetishism, or masochism, however, Krafft-Ebing (1886/1935) always relied on a simple explanation (i.e., sexual problems are hereditary, and reflect a perversion of the normal sexual instinct). In this way, Krafft-Ebing's work is very long on voyeuristic description and short on trenchant analysis and explanation. This may help to explain why, as noted by Hauser (1992), he never did gain much attention in the world of English-speaking psychiatry, and gained only rather limited attention among German-speaking psychopathologists.

Henry Havelock Ellis has been described as the "first of the yea-sayers" among modern researchers into sexuality (Brecher, 1969, p. 3) by virtue of his relatively positive views on sexual activity and even sexual minorities. Ellis was a British physician who made an important contribution to thinking in sexuality (Weeks, 2000), although his work seems to have been better received in North America and continental Europe than in his native land (Ellis, 1901/1906; Goldberg, 1926). Despite being trained as a medical doctor, Ellis referred to himself as a "psychologist", as did his contemporary Sigmund Freud who received medical training. Ellis is perhaps best known for his extensive, six-part series on sexuality, *Studies in the psychology of sex*, a set of books that seem to represent more of an anthropological perspective than a psychological one. The *Studies* series covers a wide range of topics, but Ellis' work on sexual inversion or homosexuality is noteworthy. According to Ellis (1910/1913), sexual inverts (i.e., all individuals whose sexual interests are inverted or directed towards members of their own sex) suffer from a disorder of an unknown origin that involves a deviation of the normal sexual instinct. Interestingly, despite a genetic account of this deviation, Ellis did point out some environmental aspects of inversion (e.g., same-sex school experiences), and he also noted some positive attributes of inverts (e.g., heightened artistic sensitivities and abilities). The final volume in this early series on sexuality (Ellis, 1910/1913), which appears to have been a late addition, given the original plan for only five books (see Ellis, 1901/1906), dealt with a number of topics relevant to sex and society. Topics such as family life, sexual morality, chastity, prostitution, and venereal disease are to be expected, given that his work was appearing in the early twentieth century; but the rather enlightened, and enlightening, discussions of the positive aspects of nudity, and tips on how to please a sexual partner, are somewhat surprising. A section on eugenics was an unfortunate choice for a final chapter, at least insofar as a lasting impact and legacy of the work is concerned. While somewhat even-handed when discussing eugenics, Ellis was clearly enthusiastic about the new "science" to control reproduction and regional populations.

Another early contributor to theories and research on sexuality—indeed, perhaps the first to offer a comprehensive, coherent, and formal psychosexual theory—is Sigmund Freud. Less well examined and understood than his theory is how Freud became interested in sexuality. Freud's earliest biological research on eel gonads likely did not betray an abiding interest in sex (Gay, 1988), but his studies in Paris, on and off from the mid-to-late 1880s, can be seen as the origins of his views on sexuality. Freud's main reason for postgraduate work in Paris was to study with the famous and charismatic French neurologist and psychiatrist, Jean Martin Charcot. Freud was so impressed by Charcot that he named his first-born male child after him, and Jean Martin Freud was a very odd name for an Austrian boy in the late nineteenth century (Freud, 1958). Charcot's research and therapeutic efforts centred on hysteria, regarded as a poorly understood psychiatric disorder affecting, mainly, women. Hysteria, as the

Greek root implied, had a clear sexual component, although the nature of sexual aetiology was unclear, at least since the ancient view of a wandering womb, detached and striking women's internal organs, was dismissed. Freud's later clinical efforts with so-called hysterics would help to form and to develop his views on sex and psychopathology, but his immediate influences in Paris of the 1880s came via certain writings in French pathology (Masson, 1984). According to Masson (1984), Freud acquired the books of a number of French pathologists responsible for documenting the physical and sexual abuse of children, especially young girls, and may even have attended their lectures. Although not widely reported, their work would have been shocking for those who were made aware of it, and Freud may well have pondered the effects of sexual abuse on survivors. Certainly by the mid-1890s, Freud had developed an explanation of hysteria that incorporated some presumed psychopathological effects of sex assault. In his so-called "seduction hypothesis" (Freud, 1896/1962), he argued that a cause for hysteria is prior, but suppressed, sexual assault. His hypothesis was dismissed immediately, perhaps because it offended the Victorian sensibilities of the times, and also because it seemed implausible, given what was seen as a very high rate of hysteria among women at the time. The dismissal led Freud to re-examine his views. Within a relatively brief period, he altered them to consider the childhood fantasy of sexual involvement, rather than actual sexual activity and abuse (see Freud, 1905/1975). Whether or not Freud's abandonment of his original seduction hypothesis represents a cowardly denial of the "truth" of sexual abuse and its impact can certainly be debated (see Masson, 1984). But, by embracing the importance of sexual fantasy in early childhood, Freud was on the road to developing one of the most elaborate and challenging, if at the same time controversial, psychosexual theories of the early twentieth century. Freud's (1905/1975) initial views on sexuality, although described as a theory in his brief book with four revisions, consisted of three essays that were sketchy, initial musings rather than detailed descriptions and explanations, and psychoanalysis emerged as a completed theory only in the mid-to-late 1920s. Simultaneously highly influential and contentious, psychoanalytic theory requires a more detailed description and critique, and this will be presented in the following section.

Although many early psychoanalysts remained loyal to Freud's teachings, some disciples broke with Freud over a variety of topics. The Freudian emphasis on sex was a major bone of contention. A few psychoanalysts defected over too little concern about sexuality. One relatively early defector was Wilhelm Stekel, who believed that Freud was too cautious in attributing many different acts to sexual motives. He (Stekel, 1924/1943) argued that problematic behaviors such as theft, fire-setting, and compulsive gambling all had abnormal sexual developmental roots.

Another early psychoanalyst who eventually went his own direction after agreeing with Stekel about Freud's timidity regarding sex was Wilhelm Reich. Reich came to psychoanalysis in 1920, and he quickly directed the sexual component of the theory into unimaginable areas (see Reich, 1942/1961). Reich's discovery or creation of orgone, a "primordial cosmic energy" (Reich, 1942/1961, p. 361) that lacked mass, represented a scientific footing for a study of psychosexuality, or so he believed. He argued that everyone needed a supply of this sensuous energy, and he even developed a machine, not unlike a contemporary iron lung, to store orgone and treat those he deemed deficient. He called this machine the "orgone accumulator". Reich emigrated to the USA to establish an institute in New York but, following a dispute with a branch of the US federal government regarding his orgone accumulator, he was incarcerated. No doubt his socialistic views compounded his legal problems at a time and place where left-leaning individuals were regarded with suspicion if not enmity. Reich died in a US state prison in 1957.

One of the first, if not the first, sexual investigators who also lobbied for increased tolerance of sexual minorities was Magnus Hirschfeld, a German-Jewish physician who moved to Berlin in the 1890s to devote his career to sex therapy and sex research. Hirschfeld believed that homosexuality was simply another variety or aspect of human sexuality, a rather radical position for a medical professional of the late nineteenth century (Mancini, 2010). He viewed people as originally bisexual, although most lost their desires for same-sex relationships. He embraced a biological view of sexual development where development, even morphology, was driven by the gonads and endocrine agents. Hirschfeld was a firm believer in Bloch's (1906/1909) understanding of sexual science and, like Bloch, included in his studies the social sciences as well as the natural sciences and medicine.

Beyond a general belief that the endocrine system provided the basis for homosexuality, Hirschfeld's ideas about the causes of homosexuality seemed to vary wildly throughout his writings over the years, and he "never really came to a satisfactory formulation, probably because none of what he said could really be proven" (Bullough, 1994, p. 66). Hirschfeld conducted a number of sex surveys in Germany, and he became a tireless advocate for the rights of sexual minorities. After founding a number of societies and journals dedicated to sex research and treatment, he founded the Institute of Sexual Science in Berlin in 1919, a research-based organization that included a large library and archive relevant to matters sexual. The timing and placement of the institute were unfortunate, and Nazi sympathizers destroyed the institute offices and materials in 1933, forcing Hirschfeld to settle in France, where he died two years later.

Among the first non-European contributors to sexology was Katharine Davis, a rather remarkable American who held a PhD in political economy from the University of Chicago but who contributed to a number of areas of research and practice in the early twentieth century (see Deegan, 2003). Davis (1929) conducted a mail survey of more than 2000 women in the USA during the mid–to-late 1920s on sexual experience and attitudes. Although the survey cannot be seen as representative of all women in the USA during the 1920s, Davis and her team did make a concerted effort to recruit a good sample, and they did include questions that, for the time, were viewed most likely as very provocative. They asked, among other questions, their respondents, who were about half married and the other half never married, about frequency of masturbation, "sexual feelings" (i.e., arousal or desire), intercourse, and same-sex involvement. Relatively large numbers of American female respondents reporting common and relatively high frequencies of autoerotic stimulation and lesbian activities should have raised eyebrows, if not outright fear and loathing, in some circles in the USA at the time, but there seems to have been relatively little notice taken of the work. Perhaps the research was seen as a woman asking other women about "womanly issues", and consequently it was not taboo or even all that interesting, but it deserves more attention today. Davis should be recognized as among the first to conduct serious and extensive sexual investigations outside of Europe. Unfortunately, her work is rarely mentioned today.

The first American sex researcher of any significance according to most historical accounts (e.g., Bullough, 1998) is the US biologist Alfred Kinsey. Kinsey was a zoologist and, in particular, a taxonomist who got into human sex research rather accidentally and late in life. While teaching biology at the University of Indiana, Kinsey was approached to teach an informal sex education course for married or soon-to-be-married students. After teaching sex education for a while, Kinsey found that he was asked some questions that he did not know answers to and, after some research, he concluded that no one else knew the answers either. He shifted his research focus from finding and categorizing gall wasps to finding and categorizing people in terms of their sexual desires and sexual behaviors. No doubt this research had some personal interests; according to his biographer (Jones, 1997), Kinsey had sexual desires for—and, later, sexual experiences with—both women and men. Kinsey and colleagues (e.g., Kinsey et al., 1948; Kinsey, Pomeroy, Martin, & Gebhard, 1953), despite some serious methodological difficulties (e.g., convenience or "snowball" sampling), did demonstrate in a series of detailed surveys in the mid-twentieth century that middle America was not nearly as homogenous in terms of sexual desires and experiences as many believed it to be. The practices and fantasies of many Americans were much richer than even many so-called experts anticipated.

Dr. Kurt Freund was a Czechoslovakian sexologist who eventually left his native land to continue his work in Toronto, Canada. Freund's research and clinical work was driven by what he termed "courtship disorder", a largely biologically based disruption of normal sexual desires that produced a wide range of sexually deviance. From his base at the Prague Institute for Sexual Science, Freund was credited with the largest biological study of the homosexual constitution due to his research in the 1950s (Herrn, 1995). Freund and colleagues compared various bodily aspects of groups of gay men, comparing the results between the groups and also to male heterosexuals. While they found no differences among homosexual groups, they did find the gay men "are somewhat lighter and have a significantly 'larger penis' than heterosexuals" (Herrn, 1995, p. 44). His main claim to fame, however, might concern the advancement of methodology in sexology. He developed a means to measure male sexual responses, penile plethysmography (see Freund, 1991), that involved monitoring blood flow to the penis during arousal. After first finding a way of reliably measuring and recording circumferential changes in the penis during erection, Freund (1991) eventually found a way of examining both changes in penile girth and length.

John Money was an American-transplanted New Zealander with a doctorate in psychology who has been described as one of the most significant contributors to sexology in the last half of the twentieth century (Goldie, 2014). He was one of the first to work with hermaphrodites, or intersex individuals, promoting their causes in medical settings where patients seldom had voices. While Money (1955) is credited frequently as the first to distinguish between sex and gender (e.g., Bullough, 1994), or at least the first to use the term "gender" in a scientific publication, the term seems to have been used previously by other psychologists. Bentley (1945), for example, used the term in a developmental psychology article 10 years earlier. As Bentley (1945) wrote in his detailed study of development during childhood, "gender (which is the socialized obverse of sex) is a fixed line of demarkation {sic}, the qualifying terms being 'feminine' and 'masculine.'" (p. 228). Money, however, very self-confident to the point of impressing others as an arrogant know-it-all, and a successful self-promoter, did employ many neologisms, although those were not always his own creations (see Goldie, 2014). After explaining that he borrowed "gender" from philology—a dubious claim given not only Bentley's prior use but the use of "gender" in nineteenth-century literature by writers such as George Eliot—Money (1985) described how gender role differs from sex role insofar as sex role has a biological referent while gender role has a psychosocial referent. Money might be considered a pioneer in sexuality studies, in addition to being a fairly controversial figure. His consultation with the family of one young boy who had suffered an accidental penile amputation during a botched circumcision was criticized (see Colapinto, 2006) because Money recommended castration and raising the boy as female, not the last time that he made such a recommendation. Money introduced the notion of "lovemap" into the professional and everyday lexicon. Lovemaps for Money were templates for individual sexual interests and behavior based on genes or reproductive instincts that could be distorted by early childhood experience into deviant sexual expressions (see Money, 1984). Overall, while Money was a very successful publicist for scientific sexology as well as a successful self-promoter, the significance of his contributions to the field are debatable.

Michel Foucault, a French philosopher, has been called many things, everything from a poststructuralist (Callis, 2009) to a social constructionist (Spargo, 1999), but he has rarely if ever been described as unimportant. His writing has been credited with being a central influence on the subsequent emergence of queer theory and queer studies (see Spargo, 1999; Weeks, 2000). Foucault's analysis of sexuality from a social–historical perspective focused on the use of power by various scientific disciplines to categorize and to marginalize anyone who was not interested in pursuing traditional, reproductive, heterosexual practices. He argued that by turning "sexual sin" from a religious concern to a scientific concern, disciplines such as medicine gained even more social power, as it could control the behavior of a significant number of citizens, by labelling them "dysfunctional" or "deviant". An important insight from Foucault (1976/1990) is the link between sexuality discourses and power relations. Through a detailed sociohistorical analysis of different forms of discourses or texts, Foucault demonstrated how sexuality is shaped by policies and practices designed as forms of social control—both formally and informally, intentionally and unintentionally. Instead of seeing power in terms of social structures that impose policies and practices on people, he understood power as a form of social relations in which we are embedded. This occurs from discourses that impact us from without, and the way we then claim or embed those discourses internally, so that external control, from without, becomes a form of self-regulation, from within. Regardless of whether policies are imposed on us or not, the power relations that shape sexual practices then become embodied or embedded, so that they can be taken for granted.

Ken Plummer, a British sociologist who founded the journal *Sexualities*, was struck by the change in stories about individuals' sexual experiences—from near-silence in the mid-twentieth century to the public telling of many sexual stories in the mainstream media by the end of the century. He drew on symbolic interactionism and interpretive sociology to inform his analysis and presentation of randomly selected life-history interviews. Plummer's (1995) book, *Telling sexual stories*, included vivid details of peoples' lives, often early in life, when a critical event in a person's everyday life was understood as a turning point that influenced later sexual experience, interests, and practices. Since his work involved people with a range of sexual interests, but not in therapeutic or clinical settings, Plummer demonstrated how some individuals think about sex lives and sexuality within their particular social contexts. Taking sexual storytelling out of a clinical setting was an important project that exposed the diverse ways that individuals, when given the opportunity, frame their life stories around their understandings of sexuality.

A number of unique and important theories of sexuality emerged from both early and recent work in sexology and beyond. Many of these theories have significant shared aspects with others, while others are very sketchy at best, so we will not even pretend to provide an exhaustive survey here. A brief description of a few noteworthy theories of sexuality from a variety of disciplinary perspectives appears necessary in order to set the stage for an overview of our theory of sexuality.

Theories of Human Sexuality

Freud's innovative theory intended to explain human development and developmental failures, psychoanalytic theory, is an interesting and at times infuriating attempt to blend biology and psychology into a psychosexual account of change and stasis. Despite all of its problems—and there are far too many to list, let alone discuss, here—psychoanalytic theory did view everyone as sexual beings from birth; it was one of the first theories of its kind to do so, if not the first. Infants are characterized, according to Freud, by polymorphous perversity; in other words, they have a very plastic or malleable sexual expression that is driven by instincts or instinctive urges that are constrained by social conditions, especially familial ones. For Freud, sexual instinct, a constructive instinct that promotes life, involved far more than mere reproduction; and he described a set of stages and periods in which the direction and satisfaction of urges determined later tendencies and behaviors. Freud was certainly not the first to discuss childhood sexuality, but—like Moll before him (see Sauerteig, 2012), and in contrast to Krafft-Ebing (1886/1935), who saw childhood masturbation and sexual experimentation as a forerunner if not cause of subsequent sexual pathology—his inclusion of childhood sexuality in a systematic theory of development was significant.

The first stage in psychoanalytic theory, the oral stage of development, is characterized by energy being focused on the mouth, for not only sustenance but for the satisfaction of many desires. Manipulation of many things by the mouth produces pleasure, and Freud saw the mouth as the first erogenous zone, or centre of sensual delight. As he wrote (Freud, 1905/1975), anyone "who sees a satiated child sink back from the mother's breast, and fall asleep with reddened cheeks and a blissful smile, will have to admit that this picture remains as typical of the expression of sexual gratification in later life" (p. 43). After weaning, the erogenous zone shifts from the mouth to the anus, and the anal stage of development involves pleasure from the elimination, or not, of solid waste. Once again, familial experience, in this case revolving around toilet training, determined how the infant or toddler experienced pleasure. Around three to five years of age, following toilet training, the next erogenous zone is the penis, never again to shift. The concern in this third developmental stage, however, has nothing to do with adult sexuality but rather with pleasure from genital manipulation and forming a view of oneself as a sexual being. Such a task was accomplished, according to psychoanalytic theory, by facing and dealing with certain developmental challenges. For boys, such a step could only be accomplished by resolving what Freud termed "the Oedipal Complex" (see Freud, 1940/1955). About this time, after observation and experimentation, young males recognize that they possess the same genitalia as adult males, notably their own father's penis. At the same time, they recognize their own mother as a "love object" (i.e., their love for their mother becomes a desire to possess mom alone), but they understand that fathers possess mothers. Such a situation leads to "castration anxiety"—the fear that the father, a large and powerful individual who is willing and able to defend his possessions, especially wives, can eliminate any boy's prize possession, his phallus. In order to avoid such a possibility, boys come to accept their fathers' dominant position within the family, come to identify with them, and thereby possess their mother in a roundabout manner. Girls, on the other hand, have a very different problem, "the Electra Complex". This develops from the recognition of their own lack of a phallus. Desiring one, through "penis envy", girls form a close bond with the closest powerful male who has one, dad, to resolve the problem. Unfortunately, mom already has dad; so, the young girl, not willing to alienate her mother, begins to bond with her mother in order to, like her brother, experience vicarious possession of the opposite-sex parent. This tumultuous period, lasting only a couple of years, is followed by a latency period, which is not really a developmental stage, but more of a recovery and consolidation phase of childhood, where all that has been experienced before is cemented into place. Finally, at puberty, both males and females enter the genital stage of development, where adult sexuality comes to dominate, but only through "negotiation" with other social expectations such as understanding and accepting adult social roles. Also, love begins to emerge as a necessary offshoot of genital pleasure, so that through work and love there begins a socially required balance between broader obligations and the personal desire for sexual satisfaction. While desirable, progression through all four stages is far from expected; indeed, depending on familial or social circumstances, there may be no movement through the stages.

A social psychologist, Daryl Bem, offered a rather different explanation of sexual orientation, one that blends aspects of biological essentialism and environmental constructionism. For Bem (1996), there are six aspects that must be taken into account in any adequate theory of sexual orientation: biological variables, childhood temperament, activity and playmate preferences (whether sex-typical or sex-atypical), feeling toward same and opposite-sex peers (whether similar or different), differential arousal to same and opposite-sex peers, and attraction (sexual or romantic) to same- and opposite-sex peers. According to this theory, genetics does not have any direct impact on later sexual preferences or sexual orientation, but does produce temperaments or activity preferences that lead to sex-typical or sex-atypical behaviors. These behaviors eventually lead to "non-specific autonomic arousal" (p. 330) of dissimilar peers and, eventually, eroticization of these peers. The precise process by which eroticization of "exotic" or dissimilar peers occurs is not clearly described, although Bem offered some suggestions. Another large stumbling block is presented by the notion that childhood behaviors perceived or labelled "aggressive" and "passive" can be attributed to genetic factors. It also seems to fall short of explaining non-binary sexual interests (e.g., bisexuality, asexuality, sexual sadism). Regardless of its problems and limitations, this theory does make a brave attempt to explain both heterosexuality and homosexuality in terms of biological and environmental forces.

Based on symbolic interactionism, sexual script theory was introduced by Gagnon and Simon (1973) and developed (Simon & Gagnon, 2003) over the years since, sometimes in the face of detailed critiques (Frith & Kitzinger, 2001). Sexual script theory, sees meaning as emerging from social interactions, but focuses on interactions that come to be understood as sexual. While meaning arises from interaction, it does not necessarily determine future interaction—individuals actively interpret meanings of interactions in the light of their own symbolic processes. For sexual script theorists, socially derived sets of conditions or sequences produce common understandings of sexual interactions and, in effect, provide any interaction with its "sexual meaning". Scripts, transmitted generally through socialization or other social processes, exist at three different levels: a macro or cultural level, an intermediate interpersonal level, and a micro or intrapersonal level. For Simon and Gagnon (1984, 2003), individuals may receive scripts from others but they, as individual agents, are also script writers or "re-writers". Schank and Abelson (1977) developed a similar notion within social psychology, but their understanding of script emphasizes the cognitive processing of stereotypical sequences of social events. The differences here, while apparently minor (but see Frith & Kitzinger, 2001), do distinguish the two terms, and Simon and Gagnon (2003) maintain that their sexual scripts are more consonant with social constructionism than cognitive social psychology. Research informed by script theory is ongoing and, among other advances, it has resulted in a Sexual Scripts Scale (Bowleg et al., 2015) for examining particular types of sexual scripts (e.g., sexual initiation scripts).

Storms' (1980) work on theories of erotic desire and preference led to the development of a somewhat unique erotic orientation theory. Storms (1981) proposed that the human sex drive is conditioned around puberty by the presence and nature of erotic stimuli and sexual fantasy. Homoeroticism and heteroeroticism are each dependent upon exposure to both social relationships and sexual material that produce sexual desires and sexual fantasies for same-sex or opposite-sex individuals. Masturbatory sessions using material and fantasies, as well as sexual experiences with peers, tend to cement a particular orientation in place.

Storms argued that sex differences, with males entering puberty later than females but showing a sex drive earlier, account for a higher rate of homoeroticism among men than women.

Herrn (1995) presented an interesting overview of the history of biological theories of homosexuality. As he saw it, there were four basic types, such as theories based largely on heredity and others based on endocrinology, dating from the beginning of sexual science. All types seemed to count on science to "treat" the perverse, although Hirshfeldt and some other activist–scientists believed that social justice could be achieved through science, a point that Herrn established as a false one. While their influence has waxed and waned over time and place since they were first proposed, biological theories of sexuality have never disappeared and, indeed, appear to again be on the rise. There are a number of proponents of "scientific", "evolutionary" theories of sexuality and human sexual desire, and one of the foremost is Buss (1994, 1998) (see also Buss & Schmitt, 1993). Buss (1998), a psychologist interested in social and personality processes, has proposed a sexual strategies theory to explain human mating strategies and sexual desires. Sexual strategies theory posits that men and women have developed very different mating strategies over time because of evolutionary concerns. Men, constantly attempting to contribute to the gene pool through mass distribution, are much more promiscuous and more concerned with quantity in coupling; women, on the other hand, with limited resources for siring offspring, pursue more quality, long-term relationships with partners best able to support and to protect fewer offspring. Despite a sweeping story, and claims of survey support for aspects of the theory (e.g., men do appear to be more promiscuous than women, at least at the moment), there seems to be little concern for non-reproductive, non-heterosexual desires and sexuality.

Another recent biological account of sexual orientation was presented by LeVay (1993, 2011). LeVay (1991), a neurobiological researcher, conducted postmortem analyses on the brains of three groups: men assumed to be gay, men assumed to be straight, and women of unknown sexual orientation. Despite the assumptions, the AIDS-related cause of death for all the "gay men" and only one of the women, and the rather small numbers involved (i.e., 41 cadavers in total), LeVay concluded that there were obvious differences in cell groups within one part of the hypothalamus, a small mid-brain organ, between gay men and straight men. Since this preliminary study, LeVay has advanced a biogenetic theory of sexual orientation that relies heavily on evidence garnered from a variety of sources and studies in neurology, psychology, and psychiatry. LeVay is convinced, and hoping to convince others, that sexual orientation is determined *in utero*, although his explanation of the genetics involved in the production of sexual orientation rather lacks in specifics. It explains for LeVay why some gay youth are able to state with assurance that they have always felt different and have known that they were gay from a very young age.

The emerging fusion theory is a fascinating and compelling developmental account of human sexuality. After examining the coming-out stories of sexual minorities, and even considering some stories of awareness of heterosexuality, Wilkerson (2007, 2009) argued that sexual identity and sexual orientation are due largely to daily, contextualized decisions based on our interpretation of personal experiences. For Wilkerson, sexual desire and sexual identity owe little to genetics and biology but rather emerge from experience. More specifically, emerging fusion points to the constant choices involved in the interpretation of necessarily ambiguous experience, where desire and identity are the result of finding meaning within the personal and social encounters an individual has over the entire life course. A sense of self as a sexual being emerges over time after a focus of desire and interpretation of experiences eventually leads to fusion and clarity. According to Wilkerson (2009), we should view sexual orientation, a form of enduring desire, as due to choices made to interpret ambiguous daily experience, although he is careful in describing sexual orientation as due only in part to conscious choice.

These theories and others do provide food for thought about human sexuality. None of them strikes us, however, as providing the last word on sexuality, and further theoretical efforts appear required. We are prepared to offer a relatively novel theory based on an existing theory of personality dating from the mid-twentieth century.

PCT and Sexuality: Our Position in Brief

Our main intention in this book is to provide a theory of sexuality and sexual development based on the acquisitions and use of personal constructs, the means by which we interpret experience and predict future events. While this theory is essentially a psychological theory and a cognitive one in particular, it includes developmental and social–psychological aspects. We do not intend to provide a theory simply of heterosexual development, similar to Worthington et al. (2002), nor do we intend to present a theory relevant just to homosexual development, like Cass (1979). We would note here, however, that theories are not models, and far too many models are simply collections of factors within circles connected by lines, sometimes with arrowheads. We are concerned with a coherent, concise, formal theory of human sexual development. Sexual development, we argue, is similar, though with some differences, whether we are concerned with the sexual majority or sexual minorities. Our concern is to be inclusive, by presenting a parsimonious theory that addresses all aspects of human sexuality.

One of our minor intentions is to expand the social aspects of the existing theory of personal constructs along the lines of some previous work. Proctor and Parry (1978), for example, argued that individual psychology is an insufficient basis for an adequate psychological theory, and they presented a case for the social origins of constructs. More recently, Horley (2008) argued that social power within PCT must be seen as more than simply "in the head". These and other developments need to be taken seriously and incorporated into the theory in order for PCT to explain a wide range of phenomena, especially phenomena of a sexual nature.

We believe that a constructivist-based understanding of human sexuality will open doors, and minds, to a much more positive and tolerant context for everyone, and it might also suggest and promote more useful intervention strategies when required. Such a theory has guided our research, teaching, community involvement, and clinical interventions with respect to sex, gender, sexual abuse, and domestic violence. It is not that we reject all aspects of the existing theories of sexuality—indeed, a number of theories contain rather useful insights, but they require a broader and more systematic framework to support and to integrate the various components. We offer this framework in the rest of this book, following a brief overview of our main argument.

People are born with genitalia, although not necessarily an unambiguous set, but sex can be seen as much more than genitalia, and in this sense we are not even born with "sex" *per se*. We are certainly not born with gender, and we have no preprogrammed set or sets of sexual desires or preferences. The process by which we acquire sexual desires, interests, fantasies, thoughts, feelings, goals, and preferences is learning, although not learning a set of behaviors. We acquire constructs, or bipolar means, both verbal and nonverbal, by which we interpret the ambiguous events and actors that we encounter constantly. Constructs allow us to interpret events, and make sense of the ambiguity of the world we inhabit (Wilkerson, 2007)—not only an outer world but an inner one as well. Just as significantly, if not more so, constructs permit us to anticipate events, which can lead us to feel a sense of control, and sometimes real control, over events before consequences overtake us. Constructs do more for us on a personal level. They give us a sense of who we are via reflection and interpretation concerning our own actions, external and internal. In other words, they provide us with a sense of selfhood, a personal identity as well as a social one; they provide us with a sense, however transitory, of our own sexual or non-sexual nature. Our constructions of our selves may be as limitless as imagination in theory, but they are tied to real events and actors, including ourselves; and as we develop an organized construct system, our further use of it leads to change as we consider new events, but also to a certain dependence on our existing set of constructs.

As we have more and varied experiences, our constructs constantly change, are replaced, become more central, and may even become dysfunctional—if not downright dangerous—to ourselves and other individuals. Our constant choice in terms of our constructions of events does not mean that we are always correct or adaptive in terms of the constructs that we select. We are, however, condemned to live with our choices and the consequences of our choices. In terms of sexual desires and behavior, our choices can prove harmful to ourselves and/or others and, while we can always stop and try to alter our sexually relevant constructs, changes are neither quick nor easy, despite the rare possibility of epiphany and sudden, overall "correction". Like some current and earlier theorists (e.g., Wilkerson, 2009), we see sexual desires as chosen, although the choice must be considered a set of choices over the long term.

Self-validation is a key process in employing constructs that we apply to ourselves, whether related to sexuality or not. In terms of our sexual selfhood, it is inherently satisfying or pleasurable to validate our existing constructs, or in some cases to discover new constructs that open new and exciting possibilities; but, sometimes, the pleasure of validation means that we cement problematic constructions into place. Viewing oneself as "pervert" or "sexual predator" can be difficult enough but, with mounting evidence of perversion or predation that reinforces the use of such constructs, we become locked into a pattern of sexually problematic behavior whereby further pain is indeed pleasure. In this way, some individuals follow a path that can only end badly, but they often feel powerless to stop the final act. We believe that there are ways of assisting those who become lost in a sexual sense, but the techniques clearly differ from many psychotherapeutic practices employed today. Often, the approaches are diametrically opposed to common ones in use, such as theatrically based ones where individuals are encouraged to act roles that they see as useful ones, but they are best pursued in the light of PCT. We intend to pursue and to expand these theoretically-based topics and concerns, as well as some others, in the following chapters.

2

The Nature and Implications of PCT

Background and Overview of the Theory

Sixty years ago, George Kelly, a clinical psychologist from the USA, published two volumes that introduced a theory of personality that he called PCT. While Kelly (1955) offered a theory of personality rooted in clinical practice, he also described a philosophical perspective at odds with the prevailing intellectual climate in psychology, as well as a methodology that attempted to blend individual-analytic richness with statistical rigour. The theory was presented very formally and in detail, and consisted of a postulate and 11 corollaries. Although at variance with the dominant psychology of the 1950s, especially radical behaviorism, PCT was a theory connected to American pragmatism, particularly the work of Dewey (1916) and James (1890), of the late nineteenth century and early twentieth century (see Novak, 1988, for more on the relationship between PCT and pragmatism).

Over the six decades since the publication of this work, PCT has come to claim an international following, but the numbers are small, and the following comprises mostly clinical and counselling psychologists (for a history of the development of PCT, see Neimeyer, 1985). Although it predated and

© The Editor(s) (if applicable) and The Author(s) 2016
J. Horley, J. Clarke, *Experience, Meaning, and Identity in Sexuality*,
DOI 10.1057/978-1-137-40096-3_2

contributed to psychology's cognitive revolution of the 1960s, PCT seems to be regarded today as more of an intriguing novelty within psychology, one worthy of a week of discussion in an undergraduate theory course, or of a brief reference to technique in a methods or clinical course, but little beyond. A number of factors, such as the dominance of behaviorism in mid-twentieth century psychology and the recent rise of more biomedical perspectives and evolutionary psychology, account for the relative lack of attention given to this unique and, we believe, important theory. Various general reviews of the literature relevant to PCT are available to anyone wishing to examine the existing work (e.g., Bannister & Mair, 1968; Bonarius, 1965; Walker & Winter, 2007), and reviews of PCT work exist also in more specific areas or subdisciplines of psychology, such as clinical psychology (see Epting, 1984; Landfield, 1971; Landfield & Epting, 1987; Winter, 1992a) and forensic-clinical psychology (Horley, 2005a; Houston, 1998). Reviews and analyses of PCT work beyond the social sciences, such as philosophy (Warren, 1998), are available. There has been a decided emphasis in PCT on abnormal and clinical topics, especially empirical versus theoretical contributions. This is hardly surprising, given Kelly's involvement in the establishment and expansion of clinical psychology in the USA (Neimeyer, 1985). The contributions of PCT to abnormal and clinical psychology are noteworthy and considerable (e.g., see Epting, 1984; Winter, 1992a), but they will not be discussed in depth here (see Chapter 9 for more assessment and clinical description). A brief introduction to the clinical side of this approach, however, does appear necessary.

Kelly (1955) championed what he called a "credulous approach" to psychological assessment and treatment. If mental health professionals want to know what is happening with a client, the client should be asked directly. This is not to ignore the importance of therapeutic interpretation in terms of making sense of what we are told, and it certainly does not suggest that every statement from a client be taken at face value. A direct method of questioning, however, is of utmost importance according to Kelly. A client's perspective must be requested and respected, avoiding the over-interpretation and hubris that comes from a "doctor-knows-best" position that appears implicit, if not explicit, in many psychotherapeutic camps. More will be said about this approach (see Chapters 8 and 9), and about some of its implications, but the credulous approach was very much out of step with behaviorism and psychoanalysis—both very dominant perspectives in psychology during the mid-twentieth century. As is the case with his entire theory, Kelly's view of psychological and personality assessment was, and remains, at odds with mainstream perspectives. The field of personality assessment, for example, tends to be divided among objective techniques, such as the Minnesota Multiphasic Personality Inventory, and projective techniques, such as the Rorschach Inkblot Test. Kelly (1958a), however, viewed both types of test with a jaundiced eye. His preferred approach was, appropriately, neither objective nor projective. He developed a number of different assessments, most notably the repertory grid technique, or rep grid. This matrix-based technique, which is a methodology, and not a specific, standardized technique, allows a clinician to examine a very limited number of a client's personal constructs. While procedures and formats differ, the common format of rep grid elicits construct pairs and asks the individual being assessed to compare and contrast various role elements, such as oneself and other individuals (for more discussion of this methodology, see Chapter 9).

Over the past decade or two, there has been a noticeable drift within PCT towards research on so-called disorders such as "psychopathy" and "post-traumatic stress disorder". This is a regrettable development, and out of step with Kelly's original direction for PCT. Denying the existence of such disorders and reifying them at the same time are incompatible enterprises, and the use of psychodiagnostic labels is rather contrary to effective psychotherapeutic practice within PCT (Horley, 2011). This trend in PCT research and clinical work likely speaks to the power of the dominant medical model in psychology and psychiatry, but it is not how personal construct theorists and therapists should proceed. However clumsy it may appear, we will refer to psychiatric diagnoses only in quotations.

Unlike most clinicians and personality theorists, Kelly (1955, 1958b, 1963, 1969, 1970a) explicitly formulated the epistemological assumptions underlying his approach. His principle of constructive alternativism asserts that reality—and, according to Kelly, there is indeed a real world that we all must come to understand to some extent—does not reveal itself to us directly; rather, it is subject to as many alternative ways of interpreting it as we ourselves can invent. In this way, we can explain the rich diversity of human experience. Moreover, according to Kelly, all of our current representations of events are anticipatory in function. In order to predict our future experience, each individual develops a unique personal construct system and attempts to accommodate it to the unknown, or at least not completely known, structure of reality. This system of constructs, including complex subsystems, is ordered hierarchically insofar as some constructs (superordinate ones) subsume other constructs (subordinate ones). In other words, the use of "good", as one pole of a superordinate construct, implies that the event is also "positive", "constructive", etc. (i.e., whatever the poles of subsumed constructs are). A construct system affords the underlying ground of coherence and unity in the ongoing experience of each person; in fact, a construct system is the sum total of any individual, psychologically speaking.

Although any particular sequence of events lends itself to a variety of different interpretations, some ways of construing probably prove more useful for anticipating similar events in the future. As events do not directly reveal their meanings to us, it must be the anticipatory constructions or hypotheses which we impose on them that endow them with whatever significance they may have in relation to our own behavior. Thus, constructive alternativism carries specific implications in terms of how human behavior relates to both internal and external stimulus input. He explicitly argued that "one does not learn certain things from the nature of stimuli which play upon him, but only what his cognitive framework permits him to see in the stimuli" (Kelly, 1955, p. 75). From the perspective of PCT, people have the capacity to represent and to anticipate events, not merely to respond to them, and each individual is personally responsible for choosing the specific constructions of events that will inform his or her actions.

In developing and presenting PCT, Kelly (1955) avoided explicitly any distinction between psychological scientists and the subjects of their inquiries. He asserted that all persons are scientists. As scientists, we attempt to describe, to explain, to predict, and to control events; in other words, we all seek to understand experience and to anticipate the future, whether we are professionally trained scientists or not. In this way, Kelly applied a constructivist model of scientific activity to the explanation of all human behavior. The reflexive nature of this theory is obvious, because Kelly attempted to explain his personal behavior as a clinician and a theorist, and not just his clients' actions. Each individual not only constructs his or her own hypotheses for anticipating events, but also evaluates and, possibly, revises them in the light of the results of behavioral experiments based on these hypotheses. Of course, the final arbiter of each experiment is the real world because, again, none of us has any direct access to objective reality—just to our representations of it. Kelly (1970b) viewed all behavior as experimental, with our personal experiments providing validation, or not, for current constructs and, thus, serving as the basis of future construction.

In terms of the implications of constructive alternativism, several authors have dealt specifically with the epistemology of the philosophical position. In an early analysis, Mischel (1964) considered Kelly's position in terms of the distinction between rule following and causal explanations of behavior, and showed how PCT entailed a rule following explanatory system. Mischel also addressed its implications for psychological assessment. Major contributions to the philosophical foundations of PCT appeared in Bannister's (1970) edited book. Here, the theory was examined as a perspective bearing close resemblance to several formulations, including those by Wittgenstein (Shotter, 1970), existentialism (Holland, 1970), and common language philosophers (Leman, 1970). Little (1972) compared and contrasted the philosophical assumptions of PCT with those of psychoanalysis and behaviorism. He suggested that the "person-as-scientist" model is unnecessarily restrictive as a guide to inquiry within the field of personality, a point with which Yorke (1989) would agree, but for different reasons. In addition, a "person-as-storyteller" metaphor has been suggested as more appropriate (Horley, 2008). While the merits of these variations or alternative models could be debated, little would be gained from doing it here. Besides, the egalitarianism inherent in Kelly's model is both clear and admirable.

The Nature and Organization of Personal Construct Systems

To reiterate, all human experience involves interpretation according to PCT. As Wilkerson (2007) argued, everyday events do not come with clear-cut meanings. Ambiguity characterizes everything that we encounter, and we tend to expend serious energy making sense of our daily transactions. Similarly, for Kelly (1955, 1963, 1970a), all of us, lacking omniscience, employ constructs to predict and to understand the daily events that comprise our lives. We can only interpret and attempt to make sense of our personal experience, whether the experience is proximal (e.g., a stray dog approaches along the roadway) or distant (e.g., we read about a war raging in Yemen). The means by which we break our flow of experience into "chunks" is abstraction; and we use our own, somewhat unique, and somewhat shared constructions as we search for themes or recurring messages among the events, things, and people that we consider as experiential chunks. These personal constructs are bipolar lenses through which the world is viewed. "Up–down", "friendly–unfriendly", "male–female", "night–day", "good–bad", "tall–short", and "black–white" are but a few of the examples of construct pairs we employ. The poles of a construct pair are not necessarily diametric opposites, although some problems with interpretation arise as construct poles become increasingly non-orthogonal or unrelated. Kelly (1955) argued that direct opposition in construct poles provides optimal interpretative ability. This is not to suggest that we necessarily or should view the world in strict, "black versus white" terms. Indeed, as we age, we likely do come to view events in more complex ways, when "black–white" is differentiated into "black–not black" and "white–not white", which permits us to recognize shades of grey, if not many colours (Kelly, 1955, 1970a). Ancient thinkers, both Eastern (Taoist notion of yin-yang) and Western (Greek law of opposition), demonstrated awareness of bipolar construction although they tended to view opposite characteristics as inherent to the world around them.

We necessarily employ many thousands or tens of thousands of different constructs in order to construe and to reconstrue our experience, whether the interactions we have are with people and objects or with the internal biophysical world of our individual bodies. We need to make sense of experience in order to discern patterns or to formulate hypotheses, as any good scientist would, about the nature of things and coming events. Like scientists, we are constantly attempting to describe, to explain, to predict, and to control our life experiences. Although Kelly (1955) himself argued that we tend to be tantalized by the future rather than concerned with the past—hence his emphasis on prediction and control rather than description and explanation—there is a case to be made for more human variation in terms of temporal orientation, with the past as more of a focus of construal as we attempt to describe and to explain significant personal experiences (Horley, 2008).

However many or few personal constructs we may possess, they are not all equal in terms of importance, or at least level of use. Our constructs are arranged, according to Kelly (1955), in a complex hierarchy or, more specifically, within complex hierarchies. Some construct pairs exist at a higher ordinal level with respect to others. A more superordinate construct pair, such as "good–bad", might be used to understand people's behavior, perhaps as part of what we might see as a moral system, but by employing such a construct pair we might also be viewing a "good person" as "honest", "hardworking", and "God-fearing". In other words, all subordinate constructs are implied or taken for granted when a superordinate construct is applied. Our construct systems, too, are composed of various subsystems, or arrangements of hierarchically ordered constructs that may or may not have any relationship to each other. A lack of relationship, for Kelly (1955), is not a problem; indeed, a certain degree of psychological fragmentation is likely in any healthy person. From a PCT perspective, we are not so aware or concerned with cognitive consistency on a daily basis as some psychologists would argue, and this allows us to go about affairs that may involve a certain degree of psychological incompatibility (e.g., a deeply committed Christian who is also a deeply committed astrophysicist).

Our personal constructs, in a sense, form the building blocks of human consciousness. They permit us to interpret life experience and to figure out what might befall us should we attempt any particular course of action. Construing a brick wall as hard as opposed to soft, or even illusory, allows an individual to avoid injury or worse by restricting attempts to walk into or through a wall. They are behind all of the behavioral experiments that we may choose to perform at any time. Should an experiment fail, a construct pair might be discarded entirely, or it may simply be used with a different set of elements. Unfortunately, we may also persist with the same construction and enacting the same behavior, yet hoping for a different result (i.e., a common definition of "crazy" or "loony"). In this way, constructs come and go, although most of us probably retain a set of relatively consistent constructs because we have found that, over time, they have proved their worth in our personal experiments and we need them, perhaps regularly or just on a rare occasion, in order to understand events. Therefore, PCT is a theory about psychological stability and change in that it allows us to explain both personal consistency and inconsistency. Our constructs and construct systems are constantly undergoing revision based on various experiential cycles presented and discussed by Kelly (1955). Such a discussion would take us too far afield at this time, but suffice it to say that PCT takes a very dynamic stance with respect to psychological processing. We are active, constant, and typically creative construers of our life experiences.

A couple of qualifications about the nature of personal constructs seem required. First, PCT is not simply a theory about language use or psycholinguistics, and trying to force it into such a limited box, as Peck (2015) attempted recently, should be avoided. Not all constructs have verbal labels or linguistic referents and, even if this were possible, we should not mistake a word for its underlying referent. Infants are able to make some sense of experience without employing verbal labels, as do some animals, especially great apes. Probably an aspect of appearance, a smell, or a sound can represent a construct or can invoke the unnamed construct. All of us likely employ some constructs that defy verbal labels, although most adults are likely able to access words that come very close to the underlying construct. Nonverbal constructs, or constructs that defy any verbal or linguistic label, may be understood as "intuitions", "feelings", or "just a sense", yet they still permit us to make sense of events, or the people and things that comprise the events in our everyday lives. While one person might describe an undesirable individual as "creepy" or "obnoxious", a second person might avoid the same individual but describe their avoidant behavior as due to "a vibe" or "a feeling that I can't describe in words". In short, not all of the ways that we make sense of our experiences need to be translated into words, although this might be our most common means of framing or describing our constructions.

Second, and related to the previous point, PCT is not simply a theory about cold and rational thought. Kelly (1955) was loath to distinguish between "affect" and "cognition", a very traditional distinction within psychology, because he did not want to create a false distinction. He certainly did not want his theory to be known as a cognitive theory, yet he no doubt anticipated correctly that this is how it would be viewed, and indeed it has. Within PCT, "affect" is bound inextricably with construal processes. Although the exact nature of affect has not been developed in detail within PCT, both Kelly (1955) and McCoy (1977, 1981) have described it as a companion to, or a consequence of, construal processes. Specific affective experiences have been described by each writer. Kelly (1955), for example, described guilt as a result of dislodgement from core role constructs, or an experience that is the result of acting counter to how a person perceives himself or herself centrally (e.g., behaving cruelly while construing oneself as kind), while McCoy (1977) defined happiness as the awareness of the validation of some core constructs. Within PCT, affect or emotion refers to construct transition, a dynamic process, rather than a psychological state, a static entity.

All of our personal constructs can be applied only to a limited range of events, people, or things—or "elements", to use the terminology of PCT. Some constructs, for example "good", might be used to interpret many elements, including people and things, but cannot be applied to every possible element. We might speak sensibly about "good friends" and "good trees", yet have difficulty describing "good prime numbers". For some of us, goodness as a construct may have very narrow applicability—we might, for example, only apply the term "good" to certain individuals who believe in a very narrow set of beliefs, such as a set that we subscribe to, whereas trees can be best seen as "useful" or not. Sometimes—or perhaps very frequently, for some individuals—we are able to employ constructs to make sense of a very limited range of elements, with no others ever allowed near such constructs. While such impermeable constructs might be adaptive in some circumstances, they might lead to a very rigid and narrow frame of reference. On the other hand, if we have a large number of constructs that include a very wide range of elements, we might be able to construe efficiently, but perhaps only in a superficial manner. To a great extent, a PCT perspective does not make categorical judgments about structural aspects of construing, because it depends on the specific conditions that an individual is dealing with as to the suitability of style and type of construal patterns. Even a preemptive thinker, a person who only tends to see people as "good or bad" and events as "this way or that way", who we might condemn generally as simplistic or rigid, may prove to be highly successful in social situations. In times of war, during certain business meetings, and during conflict situations in a dangerous prison setting, there can be no tolerance for the shades of gray or moral relativism that might result from complex constructions. He or she who hesitates may be lost, and simplistic consideration of alternatives might facilitate quick and successful decisions. It really depends on the many factors—environmental, interpersonal, and intrapersonal—that impinge on us during any event.

When it comes to the assignment of an element to a construct pole, often there is little variation for many of us. A person is "tall" rather than "short", and that is the end of that. At times, and for some of us more than others, however, there can be considerable vacillation. Elements can shift quite easily from one construct pole to the other. Consideration of events from diametrically opposed positions can be a fruitful exercise. For Kelly (1955), this is a matter of loose construing, and it is neither pathological nor normal in and of itself. Loose construing likely aids in creativity, although perhaps only in the presence of a degree of tightening, but it can be at the basis of significant confusion and, over the long run, probably at the basis of serious thought disorder. Tightness alone is likely maladaptive, unless someone lives in an unchanging world; and it has been implicated in a variety of psychological difficulties, such as "major depression" (see Space & Cromwell, 1980). An ability to both loosen and tighten our constructs probably separates the genius from the mad person.

As Winter (1992a) noted, there has been relatively little research into construct content compared to construct structure. There are, however, good reasons to examine the specific constructs that an individual employs. Some work (e.g., Horley, 2008a; Horley & Quinsey, 1995) has been done with sexual offenders' constructs, and this will be discussed later. In a general sense, it may be important to see what types of constructs are employed by certain individuals or groups of individuals. According to Kelly (1955), optimal construing involves construct poles that tend toward orthogonal relations rather than oblique relations. In other words, logical opposition is better to sort elements on a construct pair versus something less than complete opposition. When construct pairs display less than a 180-degree relationship, they are described as "bent". On occasion, when an individual's construct pair shows no apparent connection whatsoever, it is necessary to question the person to find out the particular meaning of terms, because the construct terminology may be very idiosyncratic and may mean something very different to the actor than the observer. Sometimes, however, given no distinct meaning, and given no mistaken attempt to combine two different construct pairs, some construct pairs are just very oblique. Aspects of construct content related to psychological problems, such the use or avoidance of constructs related to emotion, have been linked to various problems (see Winter, 1992a, for a summary).

Choice and Experience in Personal Construct Theory

The broad camp of constructivism appears to be extremely concerned with issues related to meaning, language, choice, and experience (Raskin, 2002; Stam, 1990). As a constructivistic theory, PCT takes such issues very seriously; indeed, an important strength of PCT from our view is its central concern with choice and personal agency. People are active construers of their own experience, and they have the ability to choose for themselves construct pairs, their own placement within the construct, and specific behavioral experiments. This invokes the notions of will and willpower, lost and forgotten within much of twentieth-century psychology. A PCT position on willpower, however, is not based on willpower as thing, such as a personality trait (c.f., Fitch & Ravlin, 2005), but as process. What we are able to do, we are able to undo; what we are able to construe, we are able to reconstrue. This does not mean, however, that all construction proceeds along normal or adaptive lines. Invalidation of constructs may appear to require the removal or at least reconfiguration of construction but, for some of us—or, perhaps, all of us, some of the time—we resist removal of invalid constructs for a variety of reasons. In the long run, this can lead to detachment from consensus reality and serious pathology, although such a discussion appears beyond the scope of our present concerns. Suffice it to say here that there are clearly good and bad scientists, with good ones able to revise theories in light of new information or new data from personal experimentation.

According to Kelly (1955), a person chooses for himself or herself "that alternative in a dichotomized construct through which he anticipates the greater possibility for extension and definition of his system" (p. 64). However, this theoretical corollary has been amended by Horley (2008) to include "extension and/or definition of his or her system", because there are times (e.g., wanting oneself to be remembered as a martyr for a cause through suicide or extreme self-sacrifice) when an act freely chosen for optimal definition results in ultimate system constriction (i.e., death or serious injury). What PCT is concerned with here are the psychological reasons for particular acts. While this might be referred to as motivation, Kelly (1955, 1958b) chose quite consciously to avoid such a term. With respect to PCT, to live as human is to construe—it is impossible to be a living, breathing human being, at least one not in a vegetative state, and not be motivated. Also, if everyone is motivated to do something constantly, the notion of motivation has no real meaning. This does not mean, however, that we are unable to express concerns about any individual's or group's reasons for doing what they do. The importance of asking and examining responses to motivational questions has been accepted by many investigators, but examined by relatively few.

Construct system extension is likely the main reason for selecting one act or behavior. Since all behavior is experimental, a tentative trial to observe whether an outcome is acceptable or not, such as having sex with a prepubescent child, or being bound during sex, could allow an individual, as normatively strange as it may seem, to experience intimacy or potency. It depends, ultimately, on the individual's prior experience and employment of personal constructs—our individual axes of meaning. The extension to an individual's construct system, or psychological processes, does not require any degree of social acceptability, although social demands undoubtedly shape an individual's possible construal of an act before, during, and after the experience. Experience of potency or virility might then lead to confirmation or formation of such self-referents, such as "fearless" or "sexual adventurer". In this way, a personal construct system is extended by adding or amending core role construction.

Definition, for Kelly (1955) and PCT, refers to more explicit and clear self-definition. The act or repeated acts of forcing another individual to have sex could lead to a more refined sense of self. Whether the self-referent would include a "negative" label such as "pervert", or whether it would lead to a "positive" label such as "virile", is a function of the actor's thinking at the time and the immediate social input that they receive. Once adopted, a construct, whether pervert or virile, determines not only future behavior but future construal patterns and subsequent construct choice. In this way, a channelization of construction occurs. The path might prove to be a *cul-de-sac* eventually, where the individual is cornered figuratively by his or her own constructs. Seeing no other option, such an individual might choose suicide in order to maintain a personal definition as, say, strong versus weak or persecuted versus tolerated. Once again, the meaning of the act is defined personally, not normatively. From the outside, suicide might always appear "irrational", but from the inside of a single individual's construct system, it might be the ultimate in rational solutions to an otherwise inescapable predicament.

One problem with the idea of choice and agency is the question of freedom or, really, the question of limits on freedom. These limits on freedom may be placed by lack of awareness and conditioning. Certainly, when he uses the term "choice", Kelly is not suggesting that individuals have access to all pertinent information before choosing a course of action. The limitations on cognitive processing and stated versus actual reasons for behavior are very clear (see Nisbett & Wilson, 1977). We simply cannot know everything about ourselves and the world around us to state categorically and correctly why we choose one act over another. Also, once chosen, we must accept the consequences of an act, and these consequences clearly limit future freedom. An individual does appear free, for whatever conscious or less-than-conscious reasons, to enact and re-enact a wide variety of behaviors. Why, however, would any individual choose the actions repellent to the majority? Why would a person act in a manner that appeared to be self-injurious and injurious to others? The answer, ultimately, is a personal one, in that it depends on his/her own experience and past efforts to construe personal experience, and is related to self-perceived construct extension and definition. Physical injury or humiliation can be self-confirming and, hence, very positive. Being physically injured and/or humiliated during what one construes as a sexual act can confirm one's identity as a sexual masochist. The pain, in effect, is pleasure for that individual. In the same way, a normative painful or negative label like "molester" or "rapist" can, when reinforced by the experience of sexually assaulting individuals, or even being told that one is such a creature, provide reassurance in terms of self-identity (see Horley, 2008, for more details).

From a philosophical perspective, the preceding discussion of choice, freedom, and meaning might be reminiscent of certain forms of existential thought (e.g., Sartre, 1956). Such a connection has been discussed by Holland (1970). Kelly (1955) dismissed any connection between PCT and existentialism, but Holland (1970) noted that, apparently, on more than one occasion, Kelly admitted that he had no real understanding of existentialism. It certainly appears that Holland was correct about the correspondence of certain features of PCT and existentialism.

According to PCT, the particular labels that we apply to ourselves are known as "core constructs", with the particular ways of construing ourselves in a social context as "core role constructs" (Kelly, 1955). Core role constructs take on an importance that non-self constructions do not share. The ways that we adopt to view ourselves in relation to others, which can be viewed and described in terms of values (Horley, 1991, 2012), are difficult to change. Violation of core roles, such as acting in a way unbecoming of a "loyal gang member" or a "caring daughter", produces guilt, and the experience of imminent, comprehensive core change in general will result in threat and, likely, resistance (Kelly, 1955; Winter, 1992a). Core constructs, and core role constructs in particular, are not readily altered.

A careful consideration of the nature of human experience appears essential to understanding the human condition. Wilkerson (2007) understood this, and he argued that experience is inherently ambiguous—it demands some form of active interpretation, and sometimes reinterpretation, to be understood and appreciated. Within PCT, experience is afforded a prominent position within the theory, with a theoretical corollary devoted to it, but it carries a somewhat different meaning than commonly understood. According to Kelly (1955), experience is comprised of "the successive construing of events" (p. 73). This requires some explanation. Events or episodes are void of meaning in and of themselves. We take or make meaning from our encounters with the physical and social world via our construct systems, so that there is no experience without construction. In this way, our interpretation, conducted in a constant, iterative process, is the essence of experience. The process of construal and reconstrual allows us to refine and to alter our constructs which, as mentioned, does not necessarily mean that we are becoming smarter or better scientists; it simply means that our complex systems of constructs vary over time via experience. More will be said about what might be termed "downward construction spirals" in later chapters.

The Individual and Society in Personal Construct Theory

Embracing PCT as a theory to explain human sexuality would clearly support the saying "Sex happens between the ears and not between the legs", although what happens between the legs is certainly not inconsequential. Even physiologically focused accounts of sexual arousal (e.g., Basson, 2002) recognize the primacy or initial impact of "sexual interpretation". We could also add, as we will argue, that sex is between an individual and society. The connection between individuals and their social contexts is not all that apparent in the case of PCT. For someone schooled in sociology and education, Kelly (1955, 1970a) was strangely silent on social matters. Given Kelly's profession (clinical psychologist) and the primary activities of most psychologists drawn to PCT (individual counselling and psychotherapy), the individual nature of PCT is probably not very surprising. This does not mean, however, that the theory is anathema or unsuited to concerns about the social world. Epting et al. (1996) and Leitner et al. (1996), among others, have argued that PCT has the potential for an account of the social that far exceeds contemporary theoretical contributions. While they may well be correct, any such potential has not been realized to date.

Jahoda (1988), Burkitt (1996), and others have pointed out that personal construct theorists have not adequately considered the social world. In the language of PCT, social elements appear beyond the range of the convenience of PCT. According to Jahoda, PCT has, at least until the late 1980s, had little concern for a real world inhabited by real social entities. This is a fair critique. Many contributors to PCT have attempted to address the social using PCT as a foundation in a variety of formulations. Notwithstanding the efforts of Bannister (1979), Duck (1973, 1979), Horley (1991, 2012), Procter and Parry (1978) and Stringer (1979), the social–psychological and sociological aspects of PCT have not been developed or examined fully.

Burkitt's (1996) valid and important concern about the origin of construction, whether individual or social, has never really been addressed. Kelly (1955) and other PCT theorists have said little about the origins of constructs, although Procter and Parry (1978) pointed to the family as an important source of constructs in early life. The origins of self-referents, whether positive or negative, undoubtedly lie in personal experience. The social environment (e.g., family, peer groups) is responsible no doubt for many of the initial application of these descriptions (see Mead, 1934/1977). The old, anonymous schoolyard chant "Sticks and stones may break my bones but hard words will never hurt me!" seems less about expressing a truism and more about fending off the words that even young children realize can cause harm. The harm is not always a social harm, such as loss of social status, or a nasty title that can lead to social isolation; it often occurs as the acceptance of a label that "seems to fit" and alter the personal identity of the butt of the verbal assault for the worse. Without doubt, we rely on others to suggest constructs for us, and not just ones to make sense of "social" events but ones that we can and perhaps should apply to ourselves. People seem quite willing, and likely always have been willing, to apply terms or labels to us, because of our behavior, appearance, or assumed internal characteristics. Every individual can probably recall numerous instances when they were called "ugly" or "fool", perhaps "gorgeous" or "brilliant", by others without invitation. Whatever the particular circumstances, the use of labels by others can lead to the internalization of such labels, at least in a form understood to the individual. The acceptance of such labels may be instantaneous or very gradual, but their impact and durability appear unmistakable. We define ourselves through the feedback or appraisals we receive from other people (Mead, 1934/1977), and sometimes that information is positive in a normative sense and sometimes it is not. There are likely times when we quite consciously adopt a consensus-defined negative descriptor. If we are part of a subcultural group or gang, especially as a child or youth, we might accept a negative label. "Killer", in most circumstances, would be construed as undesirable, but to a youth who has participated in a homicide and has a desire to please friends in a particular deviant peer group or street gang, such a term might be viewed as an honourable title, one that required a display of great courage and skill to earn. It is often those around us who define terms for us, whether normatively or non-normatively. It is important to emphasize that PCT is not a theory about social labelling, although it has been proposed as a partner for sociological labelling theory in order to account for the internalization of "negative" social labels that lead to deviance (Scimecca, 1977). Such a project has not been embraced wholeheartedly by deviance or labelling theorists within sociology or criminology to date, although we would endorse such an effort and wish the project success, with the caution that PCT has explanatory power well beyond criminology and deviance studies.

Perhaps frequently, those who provide potential core role constructs, and begin the process of construct redefinition or reassignment of self with respect to these notions, are well-intentioned professionals (Horley, 2011). Some labels provided by professionals, such as "schizophrenic", are adopted with little knowledge of their general meaning. The individual who accepts such a label from an authority figure such as a mental health professional might not even ask about the meaning of the term, perhaps to avoid the appearance of ignorance, yet will do their own research into the definition and implications of the term. Personal investigations might take them to other individuals so labelled, or to confidants who may have little understanding of the term themselves. Quite interestingly, a few individuals who question the nature of their diagnostic or formal labels are quite prepared to accept that the label is a professional construct applied by another that does not really describe them. "Symptoms" can disappear relatively quickly when the possibility is raised that the label is someone else's construction and might be misapplied. Some symptoms may well be, in a sense, extensions of the diagnostic process, whereby an individual concludes that, if the label is to fit, the various symptoms must be present. While this may occur in a minority of cases, it certainly raises important questions about the impact of the traditional psychodiagnostic process (see Honos-Webb & Leitner, 2001; Raskin & Epting, 1993).

Social power is another factor rarely considered from a PCT perspective. Just as he was unconcerned with social class (Procter & Parry, 1978), Kelly (1955) was unconcerned with social power. Rowe (1994), however, did use PCT to view power as "the ability to get other people to accept your definition of reality" (p. 29). Leitner, Begley, and Faidley (1996) described power, following Rowe, as "the ability to influence another individual's construct system" (p. 323). On the surface, these similar views of power may appear adequate from a psychological perspective, but they fail to consider variations of power and power relations. In a very important respect, they miss the basic ways that power is wielded in everyday social interaction. Perhaps an occupational hazard for many psychologists, especially PCT-influenced psychologists, is mistaking thoughts rather than actual aspects of events as all-important. All too often in contemporary psychology, real people and processes are obscured by psychological referents and processes. PCT, to account for social relations adequately and become a truly social-psychological theory, needs to take very seriously a very basic component in the theory, elements, and the nature of different types of elements. Specifically, there has been significant consideration of the nature of personal constructs but, with a few exceptions (c.f., Husain, 1983; Horley, 1988b), very little consideration of the nature of what constructs are applied to (i.e., elements). Kelly posited a real world populated with real people, but rarely does PCT accept and consider the attributes of elements, let alone the all-too-real attributes of elemental interstices. While there is a wide variety of possible elements, our concern here is with social elements (i.e., people, social groups) exclusively.

Power, as a relational characteristic between all social elements or actors, is very distinctive not only because it bridges the gulf of social grouping level (i.e., individual versus collective), but it appears to bridge the gap between social elements in a literal sense. Power defines the relationships among social elements. The conduct of people is very much determined by such aspects, and the determination does not just refer to the construal processes of the actors. While considerations about construct validation (see Epting et al., 1988; Leitner et al., 1988) are pertinent, they may have little to do with the nature of a social interaction. If two individuals meet on a street, with one producing a revolver and demanding valuables from the second, the various constructions of the assault victim undoubtedly mean little to the person holding the gun so long as the behavior (i.e., giving up valuables) is accomplished. All that can usefully be questioned in such a situation is the meanings of certain terms (e.g., what might be construed as valuable to the assailant), the intent of the gun-wielding individual (e.g., whether a simple robbery is the real purpose of the encounter), and other similar considerations. While the gun *qua* power is in play, the relationship, however brief, is directed by the will of the gun's possessor. In most everyday social interactions, another person's constructions are secondary, if relevant at all, to more primary considerations like obtaining goods and services, whether through the use or abuse of power (see Horley, 2008). Power, therefore, is a term applied to a relational characteristic that is real. If power were illusory in an ultimate sense, as Rowe (1994) would have us accept, it would be silly to speak of powerful and powerless people, as she does. Perhaps the most appropriate construction of people and power would be those who dupe versus those who are duped. While this falls far short of acceptable—if nothing else, it does not allow us to develop or to elaborate PCT—it does remind us of one aspect missing in many discussions of power. How do we account for voluntary acceptance of directions that are not in our own interest? Can we be duped, either individually or collectively? The answer is "Of course" and, according to some theorists, it happens quite regularly. The Marxist notion of "false consciousness" refers to the cognitive distortion involving social contradictions and the denial of class interests due to ideology from extended exposure to propaganda (Eyerman, 1981). False consciousness describes a situation where we can and do deny ideas and actions that are in our own interest in favour of ideas and actions that we accept but are actually in others' interests. Sartre (1943/1956) presented a similar notion, "bad faith", or lying to oneself. Strictly speaking, bad faith refers to the paradoxical situation whereby, through a conscious and free choice, an individual denies his/her ability to make a free choice; more broadly, however, bad faith can be seen as the denial of beliefs and actions that are in one's own interest. Through propaganda and other sources, we can certainly, at times, be persuaded to accept that which is harmful to our own interests and not resist others' attempts to get us to do their bidding.

Sexuality and Personal Construct Theory

Efforts to Date

There has been some work on sexuality done by personal construct researchers, clinicians, and theorists; unfortunately, the work until now has been limited. Among the research, clinical efforts, and theoretical contributions to date, three main areas of concern seem to emerge: research and theory in general sexuality studies, sexual therapy, and research and treatment of sexual offenders.

Much of the PCT research into sexuality in general appeared in a special issue of *Journal of Constructivist Psychology* in 2005. Here, Cross and Epting (2005) provided a rather compelling, if very incomplete, account of understanding the identities of sexual minorities. Cross and Epting argued that the use of restrictive sexual categories is not limited to the heterosexual majority, and members of sexual minorities need to keep a loose or open view of themselves and others like them. A personal understanding of being gay is central to self-integration and self-acceptance. Bridges and Neimeyer (2005) presented an understanding of sexual relationship development involving four subsystems (viz., eroticism, gender, interpersonal bonding, reproduction) that required a similar understanding for couples in successful relationships to grow together. With a lesbian couple experiencing obstacles in their ongoing relationship, they demonstrated how problems limiting closeness in relationships can be overcome by examining and reconciling differences between partners' perceptions of the relationships between the various subsystems. Finally, Barker (2005) presented an interesting analysis of the development of a polyamorous identity in social surroundings and conditions that are hardly conducive to such sexual pursuits. She also outlined her approaches to working with such individuals in clinical settings.

Sex therapy is another area where there has been some PCT research and clinical work done. Winter (1988, 2005) described cases where PCT-based therapy demonstrated efficacy in addressing psychogenic impotence and other sexual problems. The thrust of the treatments involved exploration of core constructs as well as clients' views of ongoing relationships. Winter (2005) argued that, despite limited research on efficacy, PCT be used more often by sex therapists because of its holistic approach and technical eclecticism. Sewell (2005) likewise suggested that PCT can be a useful theory for understanding and treating sexual dysfunction by connecting PCT's "experience cycle" and the sexual response cycle discussed by Masters, Johnson, and Kolodny (1988).

Research and clinical work with sexual offenders has proceeded along a number of lines. Houston (1998; Houston & Adshead, 1993) has reported some research on sex offender treatment group evaluations using PCT methodology, as well as describing various PCT-inspired treatments of sex offenders. Chin-Keung (1988) and Horley (1988; Horley & Quinsey, 1994, 1995; Horley, Quinsey, & Jones, 1997) have described research and treatments involving child sexual abusers. Horley (2000a) emphasized PCT work in a review of sex offenders' cognitions, and Horley's (2000b) discussion of the formation of an abnormal sexual identity among sexual offenders. We plan to expand significantly some of Horley's (2008) initial thoughts on sexuality in general presented in a book that was concerned for the most part with the assessment and treatment of sexual offenders using PCT tools and ideas.

The Developmental Shaping of Sexual Desire

Leaving aside issues concerning experience *in utero*, human infants are clearly construing beings. All of us may be born with a number of hard-wired reflexes that aid in survival, but these innate responses are typically lost in the first few weeks or months of life to be replaced by learned behaviors. While it is far from certain that infants acquire constructions as part of their early life experience, and necessary studies are certainly hampered if not curtailed completely by babies' lack of verbal ability, it seems likely that they do indeed learn rudimentary ways to sort events and context-encased elements. Such preliminary constructions are no doubt transitory, preverbal or nonverbal, and likely prone to invalidation, but they would account for any infant's progression from "one unanalyzed bloom of confusion" (James, 1890, p. 496), which must characterize early life, to a more stable state, which involves less anxiety. Also, it is worth noting here that Kelly (1955) avoided any inherent or pre-existing ego or any related notion (c.f., Freud, 1905/1975; James, 1890) as an integrator of thought—our collection of constructs, verbal and nonverbal, that have any self-reference give us a sense of who we are as unique individuals.

Many of the early, rudimentary constructs, we would posit, involve some aspect of what could be termed "sexuality" or at least sensuality. Moll, Freud, and others were correct to point to childhood sexuality. If we were like our distant infrahuman ancestors and operated solely or largely on preprogrammed olfactory, visual, or auditory cues concerning sexual interest and behavior, puberty, with its accompanying shifts in sex hormones and so-called "sexual maturity", might be the source or starting point of sexual life. We are, however, constantly trying to make sense of ourselves and others around us in terms that can be construed, broadly speaking, to be sexual. First attempts to discover the nature and uses of genitalia through "playing doctor" or other early childhood encounters, never mind via infantile masturbation (Freud, 1905/1975), are not just manifestations of childhood curiosity but can be seen as important developmental aspects of an emerging sense of separateness and selfhood. We are able to understand how we are the same, yet different, from family members and peers. Along with such intentional play or active discovery come unintended outcomes. On occasion, such "playing doctor" scenarios are interrupted by others (e.g., older siblings, parents, nonfamilial adults) who may be appalled or amused by their discoveries. Any and all nonverbal and verbal responses (e.g., shrieks, smiles, exclamations of "Naughty!" or "Wonderful!") can and likely are noted and possibly internalized by the young experimentalists. As Mead (1934/1977) pointed out, we come to see ourselves through the reflected appraisals of others and, parenthetically, Meadian symbolic interactionism appears similar in many ways to PCT, perhaps owing to their shared pragmatic roots (Butt, 2001). To use the terminology of PCT, the appraisals of others are expressed as constructs, or more specifically as single poles of construct pairs. Repulsion, a slap, or a "Bad!" cry from a parent, in response to discovering their beloved four-year-old sitting naked with a naked playmate and pointing to genitalia, is capable of sending a clear message to the young child in the form of a potential personal construct. The nature of the message, of course, depends on many factors (e.g., existing self-constructs, thoughts-feelings about parent, thoughts-feelings about the situation), but the message-construct has the capability of becoming internalized and marking the child's development, for better or ill, for years to come. Everyday experience is made up of many thousands of such "choice points" for all of us, young and old, and it is very difficult to know what will be a significant encounter and what will simply be sloughed off as being of little cognitive-affective impact or none.

Older siblings likely play an important role in the acquisition of constructs, especially sexual constructs, early in life. Research (e.g., Blanchard & Bogaert, 1996) has shown a relationship between birth order and being or becoming gay, with younger males in families with multiple older brothers showing an increased likelihood of homosexuality. Much of the interpretation (see Blanchard & Bogaert, 1996; LeVay, 2011) seems to centre on biological factors, such as increased estrogen in the amniotic fluid of later-born males, rather than social factors, but an explanation involving social factors appears much more parsimonious, not to mention compelling, given the very debatable view of estrogen as a "feminizing" agent and testosterone as a "masculinizing" hormone. The idea that later-born males, especially young and impressionable ones, look to older brothers for feedback and a sense of identity seems much more clear and compelling than that exposure to female hormones *in utero* leads to effeminate or gay male behavior after birth. If older brothers, as they often do, use disparaging terms such as "queer", "weirdo", or "sissy", however innocently, sensitive younger brothers can accept and internalize such constructs rather easily. No doubt the impact, if not tyranny, of familial labelling is responsible not just for an increase of gay younger males but all sorts of issues for younger children (e.g., children's over-inflated sense of their importance in the world), although this is not to say that labels from younger to older siblings are never internalized.

In addition to what might be seen as normal aspects of growing up, such as being taunted or insulted by siblings, non-normative experiences such as childhood trauma might be expected to influence construction and identity formation. One non-normative factor to consider seriously is child sexual abuse. A number of studies have pointed to long-term impairment of sexual function and personal identity due to early abuse, especially among females (e.g., Meston, Rellini, & Heiman, 2006), although the findings are not entirely consistent. A recently published study by Bigras, Godbout, and Briere (2015) attempted to examine a complex relationship between childhood sex abuse, negative sexual outcomes in adulthood, and a set of intervening variables comprising what is known as self-capacity disturbance. Self-capacity is seen as the ability to maintain successful relationships, maintenance of a stable and positive personal identity, and the ability to control negative affect or emotion. They found as expected that their mostly female respondents aged roughly 30 years who reported child sexual abuse did indeed show more interpersonal conflicts, identity disruption, and affective dysregulation than those who did not report prior abuse. What they were then able to show is that interpersonal conflict and identity disruption predicted sexual anxiety and, negatively, level of sexual satisfaction. While this cannot be taken as support for a causal relationship given the retrospective design employed, we might expect that such a relationship does exist. We would suggest that the self-capacity variables are simply constructs, and perhaps entire construct subsystems, that have been adopted in order to make sense of the early childhood trauma. This does not mean that one is condemned to live with any negative consequences of trauma, because any such experiences can always be reinterpreted in the future; indeed, as pointed out by Bigras et al. (2015), their respondents seemed to indicate that the effects of their abuse were limited after roughly 20 years post abuse.

Peer groups, too, are an important source of sexual identity construction, and peers may be the most important source of constructs for some individuals, especially during adolescence. In a recent study, Iuduci and Verdecchia (2015) used semi-structured interviews with 34 self-identified gays and lesbians to examine "their personal life stories" (p. 743) and their personal, informal theories of homosexuality to discover the role that homophobic labels play in sexual identity development. Not surprisingly, they discovered that the use of negative labels of gays and lesbians, particularly by friends during their adolescence, seemed to have a marked impact on slower self-acceptance as gay or lesbian by their respondents. No doubt their gay and lesbian interviewees embraced or accepted negative core constructs regarding homosexuality that took them years to alter or at least to accommodate within their understandings of themselves.

Giles (2006), Wilkerson (2007), and other sexual theorists have argued against both socially constructed sexual desire and biologically essential desire or inborn sexual instinct. Both Giles and Wilkerson have presented very viable alternatives to social constructionist and essentialist accounts of desire that share a common thread of existentialism. For Giles (2006), his phenomenological explanation of desire explains sexual desire "as having its origin in the nature of the awareness of our gendered human condition" (p. 225). While we could quibble over the use of "gendered" here, certainly awareness of sexual body parts and sex-related biochemicals does appear to shape in a very fundamental manner our sexual interests and desires. From an early age, but throughout life, we interpret the utility of body parts, especially prominent or mysterious ones like genitalia, as well as internal sensations like energy that results from biochemical agents such as testosterone. The development of sexual desire, or even a lack of sexual desire, appears dependent on the particular and changing constructions of what or who is exciting, pleasant, etc. for us at any point in time. Although we would not suggest that there is any single outcome of our constructions of body parts and sensations, such as Giles' (2006) view that gender always leads to a sense of incompleteness and a desire for experience of another gender, there are no doubt dominant social themes and directions, such as heteronormativity, that direct constructions in one direction over other possibilities (see Chapter 4 for more details). The sense of ourselves as desirous of others or certain activities leads to a sexual self-identity, although there is no reason to believe that the process of identity formation occurs in a stage-like manner, as posited by Cass (1979), Freud (1905/1975) and other theorists.

An emerging sense of ourselves as sexual beings, or not (more on this possibility later), seems to depend on many experiential factors. The primary consideration, in general, is the present formation of an individual's construct system—in other words, the characteristics of current constructs are vital to acceptance or rejection of new, potential constructs—and especially the sexual subsystem, should it exist. Personal construct theory has relatively little to say about the nature of development, except that it is characterized by construct differentiation (Kelly, 1955).

Differentiation points to not only increasing numbers of constructs but also increasing complexity in terms of organization. We can, typically early in life, realize that we can recognize or understand colours or shades of grey—not just visually, but in the broadest sense—by avoiding a black-versus-white view of the world. A more differentiated, complex perspective would split the contrasting construct poles to create two constructs, namely, black versus not-black, and white versus not-white. This gives us possibilities such as grey versus not-grey, emerald versus not-emerald, and so on. As differentiation occurs, and it may not occur for everyone—PCT has largely ignored issues such as developmental delays, but see Lewin's (1935) understanding of differentiation within the "feeble-minded"—we tend to see events, things, ourselves, and other people in more nuanced manners. This can produce a more complex and more "mature" sense of our sexual selfhood. It is entirely possible that at least some children have a well-developed and understood sense of their own sexual desires by a very early age (Wilkerson, 2009). While such desires are open to reconstrual, and for most of us they will be re-evaluated and altered at times throughout our lives (Kinsman, 1996), they may well be relatively set long before puberty occurs. Hence, it is quite possible, if not probable, that a child might "know" that he is gay at a very early age (LeVay, 1993, 2011), or even that she is straight (although, given heteronormativity, it is less likely that such a realization will be remembered), without obligatory biogenesis. Childhood "crushes" may simply be intense feelings of love or "really liking" another individual in a nonsexual manner, but a crush can certainly be construed as revealing an early same- or opposite-sex sexual attraction long before puberty.

Halperin's (2010) entertaining and insightful book "How To Be Gay" points to one social mechanism whereby everyone can "acquire" sexual orientation. Gay culture no doubt exists, just as straight culture exists, and the socialization processes by which one learns to be gay or straight are similar. Lessons being learned, however, are not specific behaviors *per se*, but rather constructs that permit a wide range of behavioral expressions that will be recognized or interpreted as gay or straight by others, at least those socialized or astute to recognize the key expressions or behaviors. While Halperin mistakes gay culture in the USA for universal gay culture—given the spread of American culture worldwide these days, he may well be right soon—he argues convincingly for the cultural transmission of "gayness" via particular experiences and lessons. We would add that being gay or having and enacting gay desires are founded on possessing constructs or values (Horley, 2012) that support such desires and, while these constructs that may include "likes camp–doesn't like camp", there is no necessary set of "required constructs" that will invariably lead someone to become gay or straight. The complexity of construct system development ensures such an outcome, and some discussion of construct system and subsystem development is required here.

Kelly (1955, 1963, 1970a), as mentioned, presented his personality theory as a single, fundamental postulate and 11 correlates. The fundamental postulate of PCT states that "[a] person's processes are psychologically channelized by the way in which he {or she} anticipates events" (Kelly, 1955, p. 46). In other words, people, as dynamic organisms, attempt to predict the outcome of real events by adopting a set of constructs that are organized into a flexible, modifiable network. True, this postulate refers to psychology, and it is in fact a psychological versus a sociological or geological theory first and foremost, but this should not be viewed as an entirely limiting aspect of the theory, because every theory has its limits. A key notion here is channelization, or the manner by which the process of everyday interpretation via constructs allows us to make sense of events, especially in terms of looking to the future, but is limited by the content and choice of particular constructs and their connections to other constructs within the entire network. Channelization can be understood using a river metaphor, where water from the source cuts a path through the landscape depending on the terrain and composition of the soil. Such a metaphor, of course, misses one crucial element of our humanity, agency. We are always able to choose or to reject a construct depending on our estimate of its ability to lead to more elaborate interpretation and/or more complete self-definition. Our construct choices, however, while evaluated in terms of their immediate elaborative and/or self-definitional outcomes, do not always consider the overall shape or direction or nature of the network of constructs and the behavioral aspects of the system or subsystem. For example, if an individual sees broad-mindedness versus narrow-mindedness as a better way of seeing himself and a particular group of close friends, and one immediate payoff of such a construct is consideration of non-normative sexual involvement, this can combine with prior constructs and their implications to produce a view of him or herself as different from many others, including the group of friends, as perhaps gay, queer, into sadomasochism, or whatever. In other words, we may choose our constructs, but we cannot necessarily choose where our entire system may lead us. In this way, choice limited to what we may term "sexual constructs" is not a choice as, say, choosing pants to wear for the day. Green pants versus brown pants may be selected in the morning because they are more stylish or fit better with other clothes of the day versus clashes with clothes, but the conscious choice of which pair of pants to put on is probably based on a limited, defined set of constructs with a limited outcome. It might, however, have long-term implications if it were to impact a core construct, such as stylish versus a slob. A more ephemeral choice, involving a choice of a notion such as broadmindedness, may well have system-wide implications, the immediate results of which are very difficult to determine, and not many of us monitor such choices all that carefully at any time. Thus, while we may describe coming to the realization that we are indeed gay or straight as choice (Wilkerson, 2007, 2009), it is not like choosing clothing insofar as it is a channelized choice which involves many prior decisions, many prior construct selections, and many event anticipations. This is not to suggest that we can never amend our constructs, subsystems, and overall system, but the effort to do so is difficult and fraught with anxiety. We may decide one day that, for example, being straight is not really what we were led to believe it was, and so would like to be queer. Getting to queerness, however, is not at all a clear path psychologically speaking; and if we make a mistake in replacing constructs, the result might be disaster in terms of our ability to figure out what might happen to us. "Best the devil we know than the devil we do not" is likely the policy that guides many self-improvement projects. In this way, changing sexual identity, or orientation or preference, is not to be taken lightly and is a very complex, long-term project involving serious self-reflection and perhaps significant social support, but more on this effort in a subsequent chapter.

From a personal construct perspective, human sexuality revolves around personal identity and the validation of personal constructs related to sexuality for an individual. What we are not saying here is that sexual behavior is necessarily selfish; instead, sex, whether autoerotic or involving one or more partners, ultimately concerns an affirmation of an individual actor's construction of the sexual event. This may be the affirmation, for example, of selflessness, insofar as someone views a particular sexual encounter as a demonstration of his or her own selfless giving. It is true that we may benefit collectively from sexual encounters for any number of reasons, but the sexual act is essentially an individual one based on the views and the interests, desires, or concerns of individual actors. This proposed mechanism can be referred to as self-validation (Horley, 2008). Self-validation—the cementing or reinforcing of a particular understanding of an individual with reference to himself or herself—is a powerful process that can help to explain some rather puzzling aspects of sexuality. We will present two examples briefly in the sections that follow.

Understanding Bondage-Discipline-Sadism-Masochism (BDSM)

Bondage-discipline-sadism-masochism (BDSM) seems to befuddle many observers (Baumeister, 1997). How, for example, can inflicting pain be pleasurable? How can being whipped or simply bound in a masochistic encounter be a sensual delight? Unless one subscribes to some position that people can be wired incorrectly (LeVay, 2011), where painful stimuli like being slapped or whipped are actually perceived "erroneously" as pleasurable, basic hedonistic assumptions of many positions make anything "aberrant" very difficult to explain. Coming from a personality trait and biological perspective, Wismeijer and van Assen (2013) attempted to dismiss the issue entirely by arguing that BDSM is not aberrant at all and, in fact, BSDM practitioners are more psychologically healthy than non-practitioners. Their support, however, in the form of an internet survey including measures of five personality traits, is not the only attempt to justify or to promote BDSM by employing traits (see Rye, Serafini, & Bramberger, 2015), and a measure of psychological well-being with a large sample of volunteer, self-described regular BDSM practitioners smacked of "a fix" when they compared their responses to a "control group" recruited from an internet subscription to a women's magazine. The comparisons, largely women versus the majority male respondents of the BDSM group, were recruited by being told that they were taking part in a study of "secrecy" that no doubt led to a very select group of individuals, many of whom might have been tortured for years by a burdensome secret. Inflicting pain or being pained, even if it is "mere" emotional suffering via humiliation, cannot be neatly redefined as the epitome of psychological health.

Certainly there have been some serious attempts to avoid hedonistic or biopathological explanations. After a series of careful, extensive studies of self-identified "sadomasochists", Cross and Matheson (2006) concluded that power was at the basis of sadomasochistic desires and behaviors. Similarly, Langdridge and Butt (2005) described an "erotic power exchange" account of BDSM, where the exchange of power is viewed as the basis of the sexual excitement, although the authors do not explain how power is necessarily erotic or sensual, nor do they consider that only a minority of BDSM practitioners or "players" actually share power or roles (Faccio, Casini, & Cipolletta, 2014). Lindemann (2011), in a rather interesting study and analysis of dominatrices who seemed to view their work as "therapy", relied on what they saw as a reverse Foucauldian explanation, observing that "BDSM practitioners comprise a group that has mobilized a particular reverse discourse in response to its historical oppression" (p. 168). Unfortunately, not all clients of dominatrices are men, and in fact it is debatable as to whether many dominatrices are truly convinced that their work is therapeutic or would even report such an explanation, or rationalization (see Febos, 2010). Baumeister's (1997) account is perhaps the best known recent attempt within psychology to explain masochism, despite raising more questions than it answers. According to Baumeister, masochism is a deviation from "the normal operation of the self" (p. 137) insofar as most of us pursue encounters that do not focus on humiliating, insulting, or powerless situations; and he describes masochistic involvement as an escape from the self, or the overly rational self of daily life in Western countries, with pain as a form of narcotic. Unfortunately, this general explanation seems to avoid answering particular questions about who uses masochism to escape and when such escapes would occur, and perhaps even a question such as "Why don't we all engage in masochistic encounters from time to time?" Such attempts beyond the typical explanations that fall back on some unspecified pathology, whether psychological or due to some biogenetic failure, are ultimately unconvincing. From our perspective, all attempts to explain BDSM to date have failed because they have neglected to account for the meaning of the BDSM experience to participants as well as the way it impacts participants' understandings of themselves.

Viewing individuals as operating from a position of self-validation can help to explain the wide variation of human sexual interests and expressions, including BDSM. If we can adopt a more flexible position whereby an individual agent is viewed as an active construer of his/her own world, pleasure and pain become very subjective and very personal. Clearly, even a soft caress of the cheek is not in and of itself pleasant; it depends on the situation and the relationships between those involved. An unwanted touch, however gentle, can sting like a whip. If so, why cannot the reverse be true as well? The crack of the whip, or even the cut of the knife, might well be perceived by the recipient as the ultimate in sensual delights. Both context and construal are key factors. A cut on the cheek or leg from a razor appears to be an event that causes injury, draws blood, and appears irritating and unpleasant regardless of the circumstances. If, however, the cut comes during a BDSM role-playing encounter staged by two individuals keen on mutual pleasure, either as part of a long-term sexual relationship or a brief affair lasting a few hours or even minutes, the resulting sensation may well be much less irritating if not downright exciting. Most BDSM encounters do appear to be well scripted or discussed in advance (Faccio et al., 2014). In fact, compared to an accidental cut during a morning shave, a planned "bloodletting" during a costumed "play" or "scene" may be very exciting by contributing to the authenticity of the "action". How an individual construes the nature of any situation considered sexual and one's role in the action is important, as is one's overall view of oneself and any other players in the encounter. Being tied up and punished by a stranger or an abuser may be extremely unpleasant, if not traumatic; whereas, being punished by a lover or dominatrix may be arousing not just due to the increased blood flow but due primarily to the psychological stimulation. Arousal and excitement can, for example, result from a perception that the "pain" is justified because one is "bad", if only temporarily. A long-term view of oneself as unworthy or unacceptable in some fashion may well provide a backdrop for the perception of continual pain and humiliation as quite acceptable if not pleasurable. It may also be that, as part of a generally overall positive view of oneself, the pain is perceived as pleasure if an understanding of oneself as sexual explorer, liberated, or adventuresome. The pleasure, here, is the result of self-validation insofar as an individual views himself or herself as flawed, unworthy, domineering, liberated, a cutting-edge sexual adventurer, or whatever is supported and extended by acts within the encounter. The resultant self-knowledge or affirmation of current self-understanding is inherently pleasant or satisfying. Pain, including inflicting pain, is indeed pleasurable if it provides more self-validation or increased knowledge of one's identity, a "true self" or a "real me" in a limited and constructed sense. Rather than an escape from the self, masochism and sadism represent quite the opposite: they represent a confirmation and extension of the self.

Asexuality via Self-Validation

Like BDSM, asexuality appears to confuse and to confound many observers. Not to be confused with celibacy, a state or temporary period of self-selected or other-imposed abstinence from sexual activity (Abbott, 1999), asexuality refers to a lack of interest in sexual activity, at least involving other individuals, and it appears to involve recognition, if not active elaboration, of a particular self-image or identity. Is it possible that a sexual encounter, or a long series of sexual experiences, can result in no self-validation? If so, what is the result? A lack of self-validation and an accompanying lack of pleasure without a doubt can, and likely, does occur; and the outcome might be varied, depending on the individual actor. Such a result might be construed or felt as frustration, and it may produce sexual experimentation involving different kinds of partners and circumstances. It may also result in a termination, perhaps only temporary, of attempts to find pleasure and satisfaction. In some individuals, likely few and far between (Bogaert, 2004), the result may be a conclusion that they have no response to or interest in further sexual exploits. Indeed, they may well have decided prior to any sexual experiences, successful or otherwise, that they have no interest in sexual interactions with anyone with the possible exception of themselves. Such a state might be viewed by others as pathological, perhaps qualifying as an extreme case of hypoactive sexual desire disorder (APA, 2013). Research, however, suggests otherwise. Self-identified asexuals report less sex-related anxiety or distress than those diagnosed as having a hypoactive disorder (see Brotto, Yule, & Gorzalka, 2015). Those who identify as asexual appear to be very diverse, and the term "asexual spectrum" (Chasin, 2013, p. 407) has been used to describe the group, although a term like spectrum could be employed in the description of any sexual grouping, majority or minority. Asexuals include those who have no interest or desire for any sexual activity, those who merely tolerate sex to maintain relationships with sexually active individuals, and those who have no attraction to other individuals but who engage in autoerotic activities (Houdenhove, Gijs, T'Sjoen, & Enzlin, 2015). Asexuality appears to be more of a distinct sexual identity or a sexual orientation, albeit a null one, with a distinct "coming-out" experience for many who identify as asexual with an existing community or communities of individuals who identify as asexual, even if not all are sure what the identity entails (Houdenhove, Gijsa, T'Sjoen, & Enzlin, 2015). Asexuality, insofar as it challenges existing sexual binaries or black-and-white constructs related to sexuality, does appear to have a "radical potential" (Chasin, 2013, p. 405). Certainly, as Chasin (2013) has done, we can question whether asexuality is necessarily a lifelong disposition, orientation, or identity. For some individuals, however, it may well be.

One source of problems when attempting to make sense of asexuality is Storms' (1980) theoretical analysis that presented asexuality as one quadrant among four mutually exclusive "sexual" categories. Same-sex attraction, opposite-sex attraction, and both-attraction made up the remaining three. While this may appear on the surface a simple yet effective way of interpreting sexuality and sexual theories, the categorical nature, which limits the possibilities to four, presents problems. A more dimensional view of sexuality might be an improvement, or at least a way of expanding categories. A number of researchers and theorists, notably Bogaert (2012), have followed Storms with limited success. Bogaert's view of asexuality is decidedly biological: despite some serious avoidan' of questions of "aetiology" (Bogaert, 2012), the causes of asexuality t' to be left to unspecified genetic origins, much as we "know" that "homosexuality … is partly genetically based" (p. 149), although Bogaert leaves the door slightly open to some non-specific, non-biological possibilities. It seems, however, much more straightforward and parsimonious to ascribe the cause of such a state to psychogenesis, or psychosociogenesis, rather than biogenesis. Here, PCT comes to the rescue.

Sexual identity, even an identity denying a sexual component, is likely comprised of one or more construct subsystems. The nature of constructs in such a subsystem, however, is not necessarily recognizable normatively as "sex construction" because, again, the final arbiter of a sexual construct is the individual. Someone might, for example, view "being a good son" versus "being a bad son" as an important sexual construct because, being raised by parents who emphasized filial obedience in all areas, including sexual teaching, as key aspects of goodness. Most other men, however, assuming they embrace such a construct, might not establish any connection whatsoever between "good son" and sexual acts. Again, the nature of the individual's system has the final say.

Sexual identity is relatively stable for most of us most of the time, although Kinsman (1996) appears correct when he argues that sexual identity tends to be relatively fluid for many individuals. Certainly Gamson and Moon (2004) agree that sexual desire is fluid throughout the lifespan. Diamond's (2005, 2008) important work on stability versus fluidity of sexual identity has demonstrated that, at least for adolescents and young women, both stability and change are characteristic of self-described sexual identity. In a recent survey involving nearly 200 young Americans (specifically, aged 18–26 years) who self-identified as sexual minorities, Katz-Wise (2015) found that 64% of women and 52% of men reported changing gender attractions, with about 15% fewer for both women and men reporting corresponding changes in sexual identities as a function of fluid attractions. Often, the perception of stability is simply due to a static view of sexual descriptors, or even ignorance of alternatives due to rigid definitions or constructions (see Callis, 2009). Sin (2015), after conducting a novel study of immigrants crossing the Canada-USA border and claiming refugee status based on sexual minority persecution, concluded that, rather than challenge sexual binaries, bisexuality tended to entrench existing binaries, at least in this limited legal situation, insofar as bisexuals were viewed as "somewhat gay" and denied claims of entrance to the USA based on sexual minority persecution.

Various factors appear to promote a labile identity. Baumeister (2000) suggested that women's sexual identities are more fluid than are men's insofar as they exhibit higher "erotic plasticity... {where their} sex drive can be shaped and altered by cultural and social factors, from formal socialization to situational pressures" (p. 348). While he may be correct, at least for many Western women at the present time, the reasons for such a difference are far from clear. Developmental changes can lead to a changing view of oneself as a sexual being. An obvious change, such as the significant ones that typically occur at puberty, can certainly cause serious reflection and possible major shifts in sexual identity, particularly when a clear or solid sense of sexual selfhood is lacking. Adolescence is often seen as a time of sexual experimentation, although sexual experiments likely occur throughout the lifespan, where new and adventuresome sexual encounters and relationships may occur. Other factors, such as psychological distress or psychosocial dislocation, may result in a massive shift in construct system that affects constructs key to sexual identity as well as many others. Clearly, sexual assault at any point throughout the lifespan often has a profound impact on sexual identity and sexual behavior (e.g., Abbott, 1999; Beitchman et al., 1992; Mezey & King, 1989), and the sexual effects on both male and female victims appear similar. While it would be foolish to suggest that asexuality or avoidance of sexual contact following sexual trauma are necessary, such effects are common and well documented (see Abbott, 1999).

From the early 1980s, to explain both normal and abnormal sexual desires, Money employed the notion of lovemaps, or brain-based templates that prescribe normal reproductive sexual behavior, but are open to corruption early in life (e.g., Money, 1984). It does seem likely that we all do have templates that operate to identify one individual, sequence of actions, or general context as "the one", "arousing", or "perfect" from a sexual perspective. But—rather than begin with some form of reproductive instinct, which may be characteristic of most infrahuman species, but again seems to be a distant evolutionary memory for humans, given our brain structures and consequent abilities to adapt via interpretation—it seems more compelling that the templates actually form during the course of our encounters with the world, and are the result of a complex array of constructs that permit multiple interpretations of any manner of people, things, or events. Sometimes, "the one" becomes just any ordinary and uninviting individual after one misspoken word, or in the light of day, just as a long-term "just friendship" can become something much more extraordinary following a certain mundane experience. It appears that the countless constructs that we possess and use constantly permit us to carry many templates beyond the perfect lover, sexual companion, lifelong marital partner, or similar relationship. "Perfect teacher", "perfect leader", and "perfect friend", with an endless list of other perfect roles or people, seem available to anyone and everyone depending on the intersection of the constructs that make up subsystems related to the particular role or category. Sometimes someone or something seems like the perfect fit for us because of their perceived qualities, even if we are unable to put a finger on each and every way that the person or place might be identified as perfect; remember, not all constructs have verbal labels. It may also be the case that not all of us have any perfect or ideal "lover template". Some individuals may see themselves as perfect, or at least difficult to match up against, and many more might have no such set of constructs, perhaps rendering the idea of sexual involvement or desire too distant or undesirable (Bogaert, 2012). The possibilities seem as boundless as there are individuals in the world.

3

Understanding Multiple Sexualities

[handwritten: a linguistic coding or cage — is this not always going to be present(?)]

The language that we invent to describe experience tends to shape the experience. This is very clear with respect to human sexuality. To date, in part due to religious injunctions which still exist in many parts of the world, our languages of sexuality have been limited (see Weeks, 2011). The ways in which we describe our sexual selves to others, and think privately about our identities and desires, are often impoverished. How, for example, would a mid-30s man describe himself based on a series of same-sex relationships during his teens, a 10-year exclusive relationship with a woman, and bondage fantasies involving older, sexually ambiguous partners? Due to a host of reasons he might choose straight, but he might also select bisexual. Currently, an expanded list might include queer and BDSM-curious, but the choices are limited, and any term or set of terms selected might even be disputed. With respect to English, we operate with a relatively restricted terminology for sexual identities, desires, and experiences that can lead to confusion, anxiety, and even social conflict. This restricted use of language at times lags behind the dramatic changes in the sexual world that have occurred since the 1960s, although Scott's (1998) research would suggest that the so-called Sexual Revolution was anything but revolutionary in terms of impact on sexual

© The Editor(s) (if applicable) and The Author(s) 2016
J. Horley, J. Clarke, *Experience, Meaning, and Identity in Sexuality*,
DOI 10.1057/978-1-137-40096-3_3

values and ethics. There were certainly some effects, and these social changes were well summarized by Weeks (2007):

> In little more than thirty years, before the baby boomers had reached middle-age, the sexual world had been irretrievably transformed, and attitudes toward marriage or non-marriage, to childbearing or non-parenting, to female sexuality, to family, to sexual unorthodoxy, all had changed fundamentally. (p. 59)

Even though our language changes to accommodate social change, we hope to press change further and faster by suggesting that a personal construct perspective accommodates a much broader range of options. Since PCT accepts that individuals may name their personal experience, and encourages it—and does not expect them to be bound to rigid sexual categories—it can take into account the fluidity of sexuality. It can provide important insights into sexuality, because of the wide range of constructs that can account for the way that individuals interpret their experiences, reflect on social interactions, make sense of their actions, and attempt to predict their futures. In this chapter we specifically focus on what we call multiple sexualities, or the wide range of sexualities and changeable sexual interests, and what a PCT perspective offers as a means of interpretation and analysis.

The Present, Limited View of Sexuality

Many sexuality researchers and activists acknowledge the limitations of binary analysis that create rigid categories for understanding experiences of sexuality, and some attempt to deconstruct the heterosexual/homosexual binary to get beyond the limitations of this traditional framing of sexualities. This acknowledgment of the need to go beyond rigid binaries is apparent in recent social science writings from feminist, symbolic interactionist, queer, and trans perspectives (e.g., Brickell, 2009; Butler, 1990, 2004; Lorber, 1996; Plummer, 2003; Stryker, 2008; Weeks, 2011, 2012). Even though these different perspectives deal with similar topics that appear to overlap, all too often they do so in isolation and sometimes

3 Understanding Multiple Sexualities

at odds with one another. At present, there is inconsistency in the way that sexualities are understood when addressing diversity, social context, and the wide range of possibilities for experiencing and interpreting sexuality. We would suggest that PCT offers an option to get beyond this impasse by providing a consistent manner of understanding and expressing a variety of interpretations of sexuality without relying on or even spurring the production of a series of different, incompatible, and internally inconsistent mini-theories and models.

The issue of multiple sexualities addressed here concerns how individuals understand a diversity of sexual identities at a personal, community and political level. Contemporary life in many Western countries has meant a change in social and personal identity insofar as sexual identity is not fixed or given at birth; rather, it "is something you make for yourself, as a reflexive project of the self" (Weeks, 2005, p. 62). This places the focus on how an individual understands and describes sexuality, how they engage with others based on perceived personal sexual identity, how sexual politics influences the personal and public claiming of sexualities, and the development of language to describe sexual interests and identities.

In a contemporary context, the desire to reinforce and confirm one's sense of sexual identity by fitting into a defined category is hardly surprising. Whether to conform to the comfortable space of being heterosexual or live within the much less comfortable spaces of non-heterosexual and non-binary sexual identities, considerable effort is put into identity-naming to fit oneself into one box or another, though seldom into more than one. Claiming a sexual identity is often encouraged as a way to gain confidence and be out as non-heterosexual, to find a place to belong. At the same time, the process can leave a person open to different forms of victimization and stigmatization, from labelling to outright discrimination (McIntosh, 1968). While the academic and activist project of deconstructing binary sexual identities, particularly heterosexual versus homosexual, has been evident since the 1970s in the social sciences, the framing of sexual binaries remains surprisingly intact in many areas of psychology. As just one fairly recent example, a study of sexual arousal patterns among bisexuals using a very small volunteer sample recruited via one Chicago "alternative newspaper" concluded that most bisexual men look more like gay or straight men in terms of penile arousal (Rieger,

Chivers, & Bailey, 2005). The authors, in other words, dismissed bisexuality as a distinctive and separate sexual orientation. While more than two orientations may seem hopelessly complex or threatening to some people, recognizing multiple sexualities—many yet to be created and named—might help to free many individuals now and in the future from the straitjacket that is constricted construing.

In an effort to transcend the pain and stigma of labelling that occurred with the medicalizing and psychologizing of sexualities, collective efforts to change the language of sexualities was a way to gain personal confidence and to address collective needs through political action. Such efforts appeared important, and much needed changes to the ways sexualities were described. People need language and categories, or constructs, in order to claim a sexual identity, often as a transformative part of the coming-out process that reinforces difference but also develops communities of people marginalized as sexual minorities. This claim of sexual identity, locating oneself in a community and confidently taking political action, was very much a part of the gay and lesbian rights movements in many countries, particularly in the late twentieth century. More recently, Callis' (2014) critical analysis of nonbinary sexualities reflects the concern for sorting out sexualities that are seen as outside the heterosexual/homosexual binary. The shift away from limited categories of sexual binaries to more diverse sexualities is traced succinctly by Callis (2014). She pointed out that "by the 1950s the modern sexual binary was firmly in place" (p. 66); by the 1980s, self-identified bisexuals claimed name recognition and space outside the hetero-homosexual binary but within gay and lesbian organizations; and, by the 1990s, "GLBT" to mean gay-lesbian-bisexual-trans was used routinely in publications and organizations.

The use of sexual binaries contributes to a basic form of analysis which sets up the dominant "one" versus the subordinate "other". This analysis is commonplace in terms of sex inequalities, often drawing on de Beauvoir's (1949/1974) early feminist insight that women lived their lives as the dependent "other" to men who barely took them into account in framing themselves. The most obvious situation of the "other" as a binary framework of analysis is pitting heterosexuality against homosexuality. As Johnson (2004) pointed out, "heterosexuality relies on homosexuality to provide it with its own borders" (p. 187), so that part of the meaning of each term is the assumption that the second term exists as contrast or reference point. Until the 1960s, heterosexuality was seen as the norm and accepted form of sexual practice, and stressed reproduction as primary focus with pleasure as just a secondary aside. These kinds of descriptions of heterosexuality, however, assumed a sexual binary which left homosexuality as the stigmatized, criminalized, and subordinate "other", always framed in reference to and seemingly on the opposite pole to heterosexuality. This distinction of the heterosexuality/homosexuality binary goes well beyond sexual practices in private spaces to an entire personal and political identity within society, which influences how an individual understands their sexuality and themselves. In the case of heterosexuality, gays and lesbians in the 1960s and 1970s successfully demonstrated that heterosexuality not only informed interpersonal sexual relations but also the norms and policies that structured societies (see the following chapter for further discussion). Identifying heteronormativity, similar to compulsory heterosexuality (Rich, 1980), provided a way to understand the effect of sexual binaries. What occurs not only involves stigmatization and criminalization of being the "other" as homosexual in a heteronormative society, but also the experience of how sexuality is embedded in the norms and social structures that inform public policies and private practices of individuals' lives. One of the limitations of depending on this sexual binary is that both heterosexuality and homosexuality are left as generalized universal experiences. People, however, do not fit so neatly into "heterosexual" and "homosexual" boxes. There is a wide range of how these generalized sexualities are experienced that is entirely missing from such a limited framing of sexualities. On the one hand, the heterosexual/homosexual binary seems like a succinct way to describe sexualities; yet, it is extremely limiting, because under each of these categories there are numerous ways individuals experience and describe their sexuality. This binary sets individuals up as "either-or", or on one side or the other, without taking the diversity of people's sexual lives into account.

Prior to the gay and lesbian rights movements, the understanding of heteronormativity or compulsory heterosexuality so firmly reinforced heterosexual identity that any nonheterosexuals were vulnerable to stigmatization and victimization (Weeks, 2007). Before the 1960s, most people who were comfortably heterosexual and in relative conformance with traditional family ideals in some form or another never necessarily questioned how they labelled themselves. They remained blind to the different sexual identities that might be around them or that they might embrace. Their heterosexual identity was not seen as problematic, although anyone claiming a nonheterosexual identity was basically challenged and silenced, if not institutionalized, as decidedly problematic. To combat such silencing, identifying the constraints of heteronormativity was one way that individuals with non-normative sexual identities claimed political space. While coming out as nonheterosexual may have often been encouraged, it also involved rising above labels and stigmas that usually came with claiming sexual identities (Johnson, 2004).

Surprisingly, even though gays and lesbians were the main critics of binary sexual identities, the way in which they became the homosexual "other" to heterosexuals produced another sexual binary, i.e., gay versus lesbian, a different guise but with similar consequences. In the 1970s and 1980s, gays and lesbians were initially not only one half of a sexual homo/het binary, but they reproduced a sexed binary as separate, rigid homo categories. With the binary of gays and lesbians, the sexed binary with female as "other" was reinforced, and the valued diversity of gays and lesbians was essentially obscured.

The relevance of social and cultural context for sexualities is evident in the development of Gay Pride events in North American and European countries in the 1970s. Initially an event for the gay community that commemorated the 1969 Stonewall Rebellion in New York City, this developed into Gay Pride and Pride marches and parades in cities across North America and even beyond (Staggenborg & Ramos, 2015). What started as small, marginalized, radical events in the late 1960s have recently become the most visible political and public claiming of an identity in countless urban centres internationally. With increased visibility and acceptance, these events are often called Pride or Pride Week, and represent sexual inclusiveness, with expressions of diverse sexualities and genders by numerous groups. Stryker (2008) rather cynically highlighted the confusion in San Francisco sexual politics, where homonormativity, which mimics the power relations of heteronormativity, is an issue. As she wrote:

> In this model of GLBT intracommunity relations, each identity is happily attracted to its own kind and leaves other groups to their own devices except in ceremonial circumstances (like Pride parades and other public celebrations of diversity), and whenever political expediency calls for coalition action of some sort. (p. 148)

While still fundamentally a political rally, these Pride events have become commodified as major tourist attractions. Regardless of this progress, many countries that do not acknowledge diverse expressions of gender and sexuality also continue to criminalize Gay Pride participants and organizers, attempting to silence nonheterosexuals and non-gender-conforming individuals and groups. Gay Pride events in different locations point to how confusing the relationship of sexual minorities to the state can be. While Pride parades and events are an important way to be "out and proud" where tolerated or supported by the community and the state (e.g., Canada, France), that same political strategy can lead to active silencing and incarceration where non-heterosexuality and non-gender-conformance is marginalized and criminalized (e.g., Kenya, Ukraine).

Queer theory is fundamentally about challenging sexual binaries and the social controls of heteronormativity (Valocchi, 2005). With this in mind, it appears to offer a way around having to deal with categories of sexual binaries and a way for individuals to claim their sexuality as open ended, changing, and even fluid: "Queer, as an identity and as a basis for a theoretical school, is an ambiguous fluid concept that can and does change" (Callis, 2014, p. 69). Even though challenging categories is fundamentally part of this perspective, achieving this goal is not necessarily straightforward or clearcut. Queer theory and practice both overlap and work at odds to one another by seemingly being inclusive for all nonheterosexual identities and exclusionary at the same time for all heterosexuals. Recently, queer theory and practice has led to an endless list of sexualities, particularly including transgendered persons (LGBT—lesbian, gay, bisexual, transgender—and even LGBTTIQQ2SA—lesbian, gay, bisexual, transsexual, transgender, intersex, queer, questioning, 2-spirited and allies). Strangely, these sexual categories seem restrictive, as one must fit into one of these identity slots, even though such pigeonholing is exactly what people self-identifying as queer aim to avoid. Perhaps this unintended rigid categorization is the cause of some tension and confusion, seemingly reflected in trans writer and activist Julia Serano's observation that "lesbian and gay folks who passionately critique heterosexism in society will dismiss bisexual folks because of sexual orientation" (Van Deven, 2014, p. 22). Queer communities may not be as welcoming for trans people as they had expected; yet, "in a contradictory environment simultaneously welcoming and hostile, transgender activists staked their own claims to queer politics" (Stryker, 2008, p. 147).

There seems to be a need for some way out of this conundrum, because it seems to aim to deconstruct sexual binaries; yet, at the same time, it creates equally rigid categories. Perhaps Callis (2014) offered a solution to the way that the homo/het sexual binary still holds firm as a hegemonic system of categorization. To understand nonbinary sexualities, she suggested the analogy of a "sexual borderland"—an in-between and liminal space, which is "a place of sexual and gender fluidity, a space where identities can change, multiply, and/or dissolve" (p. 64). Callis stressed that while the sexual borderland may appear to be exclusive to nonbinary sexualities, she imagined "individuals of all sexual identities react to the borderlands, by crossing them, inhabiting them, fortifying against them, or denying them" (p. 77).

Interestingly, bisexuality provides a window into the surprisingly, perhaps unintentionally, rigid categories used in current dominant but non-heterosexual identities. Bisexuality is far from being a new sexual identity, although it is often subsumed by heterosexuality in a variety of cultural contexts. One argument made about women who have changed their identity over time from heterosexual to queer is that claiming a bisexual identity is a way to avoid questions of whether they are heterosexual or lesbian (Rust, 2000). In a contemporary context, most gays and lesbians who struggle to acknowledge their sexual desires and to claim a gay or lesbian identity might be expected to value openness and tolerance of diverse sexual expressions. The paradox of binary sexualities as rigid and taken for granted, however, is that it leaves the homo/het binary as the fallback position for the organization of sexualities.

A further concern with the sexual binary of gay and lesbian is the way that bisexuals are seen as a problematic third category, neither gay nor lesbian, often constructed as indecisive and fence-sitting. Sin (2015) indicated that bisexuality should be viewed in a more positive light, and used the term sexual fluidity to describe the "capacity to be attracted to erotically and romantically partnered with either sex" (p. 415). Frequently, instead of seeing bisexuality as perhaps an obvious situation that shows how sexualities may be experienced in many ways, it is seen as opting out, or even as a transitional stage between more conventional heterosexuality/homosexuality options.

In the context of indigenous studies, there is a notion of sexual fluidity, although this particular term is not used, apparent in descriptions of indigenous communities prior to contact with missionaries and colonizers who imposed patriarchal binary sexual practices on them. Aspin and Hutchings (2007) analyzed the Maori Sexuality Project that described the ways that Maori sexual history was traced through historical accounts and art forms prior to European contact. This project attempted to understand and to reclaim a more fluid view of sexual practices prior to the European colonization of New Zealand by taking into account the spiritual and religious practices relevant to sexuality. Similarly, in North America, Cannon (1998) traced the changes in sexual practices that occurred with the implementation of the Canadian Indian Act in First Nation communities. The Indian Act provided a means of social control over the more open view of sexual practices among Canadian aboriginals through the imposition of rigid binary patriarchal structures. Interestingly, these studies of indigenous beliefs and practices indicate an area where the shift from fluid sexualities to sexual binaries is constructed by legislation and colonization imposed on indigenous communities. They may indicate, too, that a shift back to a more fluid sexuality is possible.

The recent literature on transgendered individuals and communities, even though the focus is gender nonconformity, adds confusion to the issue of sexualities by drawing on both essentialism and constructionism at different times, even both at the same time (e.g., Schilt & Westbrook, 2009; Stryker, 2008). From the perspective of trans people, there is a sense of constantly shifting sexualities, perhaps because both genders and sexualities are intentionally blurred with the breaching of the boundaries that usually delimit sexualities. Certainly any binary analysis appears rejected. With hegemonic heterosexuality in the background, however, descriptions of trans bodies still focus on what body parts are male versus female, and how such parts do or do not influence a person's self-perception (Schilt & Westbrook, 2009). Clearly, how those who identify as transgendered articulate their understandings of gender and sexualities provides insights into sexual binaries, and how undoing gender and fluid sexualities are experienced.

A Dimensional View of Sexuality

Personal construct theory provides a dimensional perspective on sexuality, unlike other so-called dimensional theories (Horley, 2008). Eysenck (1964, 1977), for example, presented what he called a dimensional approach to personality, criminal behavior, sexual behavior, among other psychological concerns. According to Eysenck (1964), there are two basic personality types or dimensions, extraversion-introversion and neuroticism-emotional stability. These two bipolar dimensions are neurologically and biologically based as well as present from birth. Criminals, including sexual offenders, are individuals high in both extraversion and neuroticism. Later, Eysenck (1977) added high psychoticism to his understanding of the personality dimensions of criminals. Such a view is a restricted, static, and dimensional view at best. Eysenck's approach is based very much on the personality trait, and represents a stable—but unchanging and deterministic—view of human psychology. The dimensional nature of PCT, based on a unit of analysis much more dynamic than the trait, includes stability and change in thought, feeling, and intentional behavior. Indeed, from a PCT perspective, we can interpret the three Eysenckian dimensions as professional constructs, rather preemptive and narrow ones at that, used to sort all individuals into neat categories. All PCT dimensions, in contrast to Eysenckian dimensions, are open to change, modification, and total replacement if required.

Within PCT, psychological space can be described best as consisting of a very large number of bipolar dimensional lines, or as the constructs stretched out and anchored by each pole. Given the nearly limitless possible constructs that most healthy adults possess at any given time, the number of active dimensions is extremely high. Some dimensions inhabit a very unique part of psychological space (e.g., used to interpret parts of carburetors in internal combustion engines) and will never come in contact with other dimensions. Various dimensions, perhaps more common, will not contact other dimensions either, because they are parallel to those dimensions, or they have different labels but are either identical to or unrelated to each other. Many dimensions, however, when in contiguous space and orthogonal to or having some vector that is at a slight angle to other dimensions nearby, can intersect with other dimensions. It is at the points of intersection, no doubt extremely common for most of us, that we can examine the relationships between elements in space for individuals, and rather interesting experiences can occur. When a new person is encountered as an element within a new experience, all constructs relevant to interpreting people are in play to provide some interpretation of the new individual. It may be, as happens to some of us regularly and others occasionally if at all, that the individual is deemed extremely attractive, dreamy, ideal, a prince, or a princess and we might label the experience "love at first sight", "lust at first sight", a transformative interpersonal interaction, a magical moment, or some other term or phrase to express a significant encounter. On occasion, there are individuals or events that are downright perplexing, and such people or events may be deemed rather mysterious and interesting or downright scary and threatening—it depends on our prior experiences and what constructs we have placed within our systems at the time of the experience. What is anxiety-provoking one moment is not necessarily so in the next, because we can learn from experience and incorporate unique and useful constructs to provide an understanding of the person, place, thing, or event, and thus eliminate the fear that comes from the realization that there are no constructs to provide an interpretation of the event. The event or person may still be recognized as unsavoury or a threat, but at least the nature of the threat is understood. There are as many possible outcomes as there are possible intersections of construct dimensions that apply to people or events, and in this sense the theory is very much a dimensionally based personality theory.

When it comes to the interpretation of our own or others' sexuality and sexual desires, which determines in part whether we can play a particular social role with others as well as the nature of the role, we are dependent on those around us, whether family members or other important social figures, to provide examples of available and acceptable labels as well as corresponding behaviors. This can be seen as an integral aspect of primary socialization, although it can be viewed more specifically as sexual or gender socialization. The words, or the potential constructs, such as straight versus gay, are important, but they are not all that is relevant to the development of a sexual identity. Our personal feelings and unique constructs that arise from individual experience also colour, if not dictate, the direction of sexual identity formation. As mentioned, being called "fag" or "sissy" on a single occasion by an older and respected sibling or peer might be a more powerful experience than years of being called "little man" or "tough guy" by parents or peers. The impact of any label depends, of course, on both the context in which it is presented and the construct system of the individual so labeled. An insult like "fag" might just as well result in rejection, such as a thought or retort like "You're the fag!", although sometimes the experience through doubt or unresolved feelings may mean that the experience may contribute to a later understanding of oneself as not straight or not like most others.

Sexual categories, such as gay and straight, probably are higher-order or superordinate constructs for many people. For most of us, they likely subsume sets of related yet subordinate notions such as effeminate, hypermasculine, and promiscuous. For others, however, whether one is gay or straight is less important and has fewer psychosocial implications than if one is loyal, reliable, or honourable. Once again, personal experience is of central importance. The personal nature of the constructs that we employ to provide meaning about our sexual selves, others' sexualities, or whether sex and sexuality have absolutely no importance to us can lead to a solid sense of who we are as a sexual being, or it can lead us to the view that we have no sexual desire. It can also produce a rather diffuse sense of sexual identity, perhaps due to a sense of isolation or confusion and lack of confidence about "fitting in". Alienation, depression, and a host of other negative thoughts and affective experiences can occur if one has a constant sense of being alone, strange, or freakish. While it may be little consolation to those who believe that such is true of them, it seems to be the case that in a very meaningful way each of us is alone, strange, and freakish in a personal world that we create—until we are able to come together with others who share some significant concern with us. While PCT is an individual psychological theory, it is not oblivious to, or at least should not ignore, the importance of community, or of communities that can help to alleviate the aloneness of existence and to provide a fuller sense of oneself in relation to others, sexually and beyond. Additionally, the nature and number of the communities or social groups that one could affiliate with regarding sexuality appear limitless. It is certainly not the case that the world of sexual dimensions is limited to one, two, or even 20. While we could argue rather cavalierly that the sky is the limit, there are probably practical, social limitations, after which claims to be of a particular exotic orientation would only lead to institutionalization or social rejection. Certainly, however, just as Chasin (2013) pointed out with respect to the asexual community, there are probably subtypes of many existing or soon-to-be sexual minority communities that may demand an equal status of their own because of perceived differences with an umbrella group or larger community.

The Pros and Cons of a Dynamic Dimensional Approach

Dimensionality may provide a number of distinct general advantages over categorical views. One advantage of such a perspective is that it seems to capture and to express a fluid view of sexuality. Sexual or erotic interest and involvement does not appear to be a fixed, monolithic entity, but appears to shift, depending on experience and perhaps periods throughout the course of life (Diamond, 2005, 2008; Katz-Wise, 2015; Kinsman, 1996). Viewing sexuality as limited and static may help professionals to make limited predictions about the sexual behavior of clients or research participants, but it likely misses the true nature of sexuality; and it is unlikely very helpful to individuals concerned with such matters as gender desire or sexual interest variation. Dynamic units like constructs that are constantly in a state of flux through revision and replacement are very hard to map and, thus, extremely difficult and frustrating to work with. On the other hand, much like the drunk searching for lost keys under a streetlight not because they were lost there but because it is an easier search than in the dark alley where the keys were lost, we risk conducting fruitless research and assessments by taking any easy approach.

A dimensional approach to sexual offending appears to express the nature of sexual deviation more precisely. If, as reported by a number of investigators (e.g., Abel et al., 1984), there appears to be an overlap between many sexual offenses or, in contemporary psychiatric parlance, many offenders display multiple paraphilias, it seems likely that offenders can slip easily between various deviant sexual desires. Rather than possessing a variety of discrete sexual problems, an individual could be viewed and described as moving more or less continuously, and perhaps effortlessly, along various continuous dimensions. The appearance of an increasing number of sexual deviations, at least according to the American Psychiatric Association (APA, 1968, 2013), may be just that—an appearance. A close examination of many of the cases presented by Krafft-Ebing (1886/1935) reveals that many of the behaviors attributed to those individuals classified as exhibitionists, for example, appear to have much more in common with other diagnoses. Krafft-Ebing, if not all psychiatric nosologists, forced square paraphilic pegs into round holes in order to facilitate a parsimonious nosology at the expense of an accurate reflection of the state of sexual affairs. Moving individuals or groups around in two-, three-, or even multi-dimensional space is not very difficult, and it may be advantageous if we accept that change via experience and insight is possible. It is very possible that such a view of sexual offending will increase the likelihood of such change given that, with the dominant categorical perspective, there is a tendency towards a more pessimistic and static view of offenders. Any change acknowledged is seen as limited. Presently, we treat or attempt to control the symptoms rather than aim for the root of the problem(s). Perhaps part of the problem is the stated or unstated assumptions that mental health professionals and the public hold concerning the long-term and congenital nature of sexual deviation. Sexual offenders, like all non-offenders, are trying to account for their own sexual behavior, however different from the norm; and if we force them to accept attributions of the offensive behavior as static and unchangeable, they will view their own efforts at change as futile. By embracing dimensionality, we avoid the tendency to think simplistically and preemptively about sexual offenders. When we use diagnostic labels like "paedophilia" and "exhibitionism", a trap is created that many, professionals and laypersons alike, fall into. Any diagnosis of paedophilia is a loose and confusing one, and a person diagnosed as a "paedophile" is viewed as "a paedophile and nothing but a paedophile". The assumed genetic/biological components of this condition reinforce the stability of constructs among those so labelled, and it creates what has been described as a self-fulfilling prophesy, although it can also be seen as validation of professional constructs and predictions. In a general sense, rather than understand sexuality as a set of discrete categories, psychiatric or otherwise, we might better view sexuality dimensionally, or in terms of multiple sexualities. An overarching view of sexuality might include a set of primary dimensions along which individuals could be placed and considered in relation to each other in order to simplify matters in normative comparisons so long as the true complexity of sexual desire and identity is not forgotten. If nothing else, a dynamic dimensional view would help to avoid any "hardening of the categories" (Kelly, 1969, p. 294), or a narrowness of focus that only allows us to refine and to alter our existing and perhaps defective constructions, and no doubt improve therapeutic efforts with respect to sexuality.

Without a doubt, dynamic dimensionality would not encourage or promote concise communication between mental health professions concerned with perversion, and concise communication is presented as a major benefit of present psychiatric nosologies. Given disputes over the real meaning of certain terms such as "paedophilia" (see Marshall, 2006), however, the issue of concise communication may be more moot than acknowledged presently. At any rate, precise communication appears to trump concise communication in most forensic-clinical circumstances. More broadly, it might become very difficult to communicate an individual sexuality, sexual identity, or orientation if PCT were to become more accepted professionally and beyond. Again, however, if gay or straight really fail to capture an individual's complex sexual makeup or unique set of desires, the idea of a much more cumbersome approach might be preferable if accuracy or a more complete picture is the result.

Perhaps most importantly, a dynamic dimensional approach to sexuality might address the problem of stigmatization of sexual minorities. An acknowledgment of the range of sexual expression has occurred structurally in many Western countries; yet, at the community and individual level, sexual identity labels still limit minorities from claiming acceptance and avoiding stigmatization. In a fascinating study of 60 Australian women who were married to bisexual men, Pallotta-Chiarolli and Lubowitz (2003) found that women involved in relationships that appear "normal" reported that they felt "outside heteronormative and gender-normative constructs" (p. 55). In many societies, heterosexuality has been critiqued as not only a sexual identity but also a series of structural norms and ideals. The diversity of sexual identities, however, also has forms of structural norms and ideals, although often at the margins of society within a community. Heterosexuality is criticized for contributing to the hierarchies of sexual identities; yet, other forms of hierarchy and marginalization occur in LGBTQ communities. For many people, claiming a sexual identity is the key to legitimization through a shared experience; yet, paradoxically, it can also contribute to the very labelling process that stigmatizes and alienates. Elimination of labels may be one way to eliminate stigmatization, although it must be acknowledged that claiming or reclaiming labels like gay, lesbian, and queer have provided many individuals effective political spaces for social change. There is a binary of same-sex versus opposite-sex relationships, especially in legal situations like marriage, yet trans individuals and other sexualities are overlooked in this binary. Although LGBTQ sexual identities are pulled apart into a diverse range, het sexual identities remain uniform and seemingly undifferentiated, except as het and asexualized allies. In theory, the "LGBTQ" identity aims at inclusiveness; yet, in practice, it divides people with different sexual identities and excludes heterosexuals, although it accepts them as allies. Some people may describe the changing nature of their sexual experiences and identities, yet they have to ignore this range of sexualities when slotting into the heterosexual/homosexual sexual binary. Why not permit them a language that would express to themselves and other individuals their own sense of sexual selfhood?

Our view of human sexuality is that it is highly complex, and reflects the overall psychological complexity of most people. True, there are probably some individuals who see the world, their worlds, in very limited ways. But such individuals may be simple by choice, or at least have been in such impoverished environments that complex construing is an extreme aberration rather than the norm, which makes the possibility of a broader and multifaceted view of themselves and others a remote one. By opening up our language of sexuality, we can reflect and promote the potential sexual options that can be created. It will likely result in freedom in sexual behavior, or at least in expanding vistas on potential ways of relating sexually.

4

Social Influence on Sexual Constructs

Social context, as mentioned in the Chapter 2, has been given relatively little explicit consideration in PCT to date. There is a formal recognition of social relationships in terms of the sociality corollary of the theory. The corollary states that, to the extent that people interpret the construction processes of others, they are able to play roles in social processes involving others (Kelly, 1955). This theoretical corollary has inspired an entire book to make sense of social processes, individuals, and related topics (see Bannister, 1979; Stringer, 1979), as well as numerous attempts (already mentioned) to sort out the social side of PCT. In addition, Kelly's commonality corollary—to the extent that one person employs a construction of experience similar to that employed by another person, their psychological processes can be seen as similar—seems to point to social factors to some extent. It remains unclear, however, what social processes and social context actually mean to individuals, self-identity, and especially to their understanding of sexuality. Additionally, the ontological status of various social factors is unresolved within the theory, which is odd and uncomfortable in a personality theory with clinical implications—social interaction and social conditions must be relevant, for example, to a psychotherapeutic encounter if only between

© The Editor(s) (if applicable) and The Author(s) 2016
J. Horley, J. Clarke, *Experience, Meaning, and Identity in Sexuality*,
DOI 10.1057/978-1-137-40096-3_4

two individuals. We feel the need here to consider the potential contributions to PCT, and especially a PCT-based understanding of sexuality, of sociology, social psychology (both psychological and sociological social psychology), and other social science disciplines.

Agency in Social Context

When considering human agency in the social sciences, a tension exists between individuals and larger social entities. Specifically, the question can be reduced to: Are individuals more driven by social structures that seem to constrain and force them to conform to roles and rules, or does agency, if recognized, free individuals to act with fewer constraints? From a PCT perspective, we are interested in how individuals make meaning of their everyday sexual experiences within an expanded understanding of social context that appears to have an impact on how construction of individual action occurs. This places us clearly on the individual agency side of an agency and social structure teeter-totter or seesaw, but the social structure side still provides tension or force. A useful starting point for considering the questions of agency and structure in the social context involves the way that people do make their own history or "herstory", but not necessarily under conditions of their own choosing. For instance, when in the 1960s women argued that they should have the right to control their own bodies—through the right to express their sexuality, with their choice of partners, and reproductive rights, including access to contraceptives and safe abortion practices—it was a seemingly straightforward agenda about control of their own futures. But even in most Western countries female activists could not have anticipated at the time that the state and the Church would apply the weight of their patriarchal power to block women from gaining control over their sexuality—a change that could transform women's everyday experiences—and that they would spend many years in challenges to achieve this goal. The many years of collective action by activists and social movement groups to get beyond these hurdles were certainly not under conditions of women's own choosing (Hamilton, 1996; Rowbotham, 1989). Nonetheless, social changes led eventually to advances in sexual and reproductive rights for most women in many countries, but by no means all. This kind of struggle highlighted for women that decisions about their bodies, their sexuality, and reproductive rights were not entirely their own actions or agency; instead, these were partially or entirely the domain of the Church and state. The changes in women's situations since the 1960s gave them opportunities to select and discard constructs, because they gained a different understanding of how they and others did or did not control decisions about their bodies, expression of sexuality, and reproductive rights.

To gain an understanding of social context, many social science perspectives are framed by the way individuals, groups, and communities interact with social structures. Social structures like family, education, work, religion, and media are all influenced by social relations like gender, race, ethnicity, sexuality, and class. From this angle, social structures and social relations are integral to the social context in which people live out their everyday lives, because they include the homes, schools, workplaces, playgrounds, community spaces, restaurants, and bars where social interaction occurs with others individually, in groups, or by watching from the sidelines.

A puzzle that has preoccupied many social scientists is: Who influences changes in social structure that lead to social change? Is social change driven by the actions of one passionate individual, or by a series of collective actions by a determined social group or committed social movement activists? Regardless of whether sparked by an individual or by groups—it is probably both—social change makes a difference to people's everyday lives. Accompanying any changes are new ways of thinking, involving new constructs, which in turn change the ways people make sense of themselves and their experiences. This process and the context in which our social interactions are embedded need to be acknowledged explicitly in PCT.

To clarify links between individuals, their everyday lives, social structures, and the meaning of individual agency versus collective agency, consider these examples. In many Western countries, was it individual athletes coming out as gay or the consequence of gay rights activism that led to gay men being tolerated and even encouraged to come out? Was it a woman individually demanding a workplace free of sexual harassment, or collective action by union members who identified sexual harassment as a workplace pattern that led to policy changes, so that those who experience sexual harassment at work can safely pursue mediation or legal action without the fear of being silenced? In both examples, whether social change occurred due to individual or collective action, or both, it led to a safer place for individuals to speak out, claim their rights, and influence how they see themselves and experience their sexuality. These examples highlight how the social context of athletes and women's workplaces involve not only the direct environment of our everyday lives, but also the larger context of the community and society in which we live. The different ways that social interaction links an individual to social structures influence how we make sense of our selves and sexualities. Seidman (2010) summarized the meaning of sex as social interaction in the following manner:

> If we approach the meaning of sex, its social organization, its rules and norms, and the divisions established between good and bad sexualities as products of social factors (economics, gender, public discourses, media images, family, science)—we will be forced to think harder about the politics and morality of sex. (p. 208)

The sociology perspective of symbolic interactionism, especially Goffman's (1959) version of it, is quite compatible with PCT, because of its focus on the perspective of individuals and on how they make meaning of their social world. Of concern are the ways that individuals interact, often symbolically, in their immediate environment and individually influence this direct social context. For instance, when out with friends at a bar, would you express your interest to a new member of the group with a non-verbal "look", then watch for another non-verbal "look" in response, perhaps some nod of interest, perhaps a shrug of disinterest? If so, you would both have some control over this interaction, and the symbolic nonverbal communication is probably mutually understood. To draw out subtle details of social interactions, qualitative ethnographic methods like life history interviews and participant observations are used for symbolic interactionist studies, which have a small sample size but extremely detailed data. We have drawn on many ethnographic studies in this book because of the rich details of issues like sexual identity and social interactions, usually in defined contexts and in ways that complement PCT approaches. A limitation of a symbolic interactionist perspective is that it tends to focus on the immediate social context, such as the room or community group, rather than larger social structural issues. What we are suggesting is that there is much to be gained by expanding the understanding of social context from the immediate surroundings, the domain of symbolic interactionism and PCT, to consider how other perspectives address larger social contexts in which our lives are embedded.

The link between social structure and human agency is described by Giddens (1984) who emphasized how "social relations are certainly involved in the structuring of interaction but are also the main 'building blocks' whereby the institutions of social systems are articulated" (p. 89). For Giddens, social relations are not seen in isolation; instead, they are informed by structural issues including rules about rights and obligations "relevant to persons having a particular social identity" (p. 98) seen as part of an individual's practical consciousness of daily social life. For instance, for a person in a workplace who wants to be "out" about his queer sexual identity, inequalities of gender and class may be relevant. This situation would be differently experienced if he is in a workplace where sexual inequalities and homophobia go unchallenged versus one where institutional practices have helped create a tolerant, diverse workplace. Giddens (1992) was also aware of how social changes in the 1960s onwards contributed to a decentred or plastic sexuality, meaning sex and sexual pleasure were freed from reproduction, which he saw as having radical implications for many women in the form of "a revolution in female autonomy" (p. 28).

If theory is a means to uncover more layers of analysis, adding a feminist analysis would be important. From a feminist perspective, the question of agency versus structure involves the addition of an analysis of patriarchy, or male dominance, as part of social structures that specifically marginalize and oppress women. For instance, this kind of analysis helps explain how male dominance is embedded in the social context of heterosexual families not because of the particular males in that family but because of the patriarchal structure of societies in which the men live has real impacts at the everyday level (see more discussion of power relations in Chapter 5). In these examples, human agency and social structure are interconnected, like the two ends of a teeter-totter or seesaw, in the way that sexuality issues are experienced and understood in different social contexts.

Private Troubles to Public Issues to Collective Action

To consider change over time in social contexts, "sociological imagination" (Mills, 1959) is a concept that describes human action and social change in terms of a shift from personal troubles to public issues. When a personal struggle like sexual violence begins to be experienced as not just one individual's private concern but as a pattern among many individuals, it shifts from being a private trouble and beyond the limits of one's personal life to being a public issue that is understood as being linked to social and institutional structures. With this shift, there is a possibility for collective action to make changes that may transform many people's lives. The early development of the antiviolence and shelter movements, first organizing rape crisis centres then creating safe shelters for women and their children (Walker, 1990), are examples of taking a private trouble hidden from public view and shifting it to a public issue supported by public or state funding. Obviously, when women became temporary residents in a women's shelter that was usually state-funded, they found themselves living in a place radically different, and much safer, than their own homes. In this situation, women's constructs probably changed, because instead of being victims of violence alone in their own home they were encouraged to see themselves as part of a larger pattern of violence in their community, including sexual violence, that other women in the shelter and elsewhere also experienced (Barnsley, 1985). In this case, the concept of sociological imagination helps to explain how individuals' everyday lives, including their sexuality, are shaped by private troubles and public issues in the social context that includes not only their family and friends but also the community in which they live.

Noticing the consequences of social context is part of the way individuals go about their daily lives, though we often take it for granted. Think of how we feel that the difference between a good job and a bad one can be a friendly and fair employer, or that the actors in our favourite movies influence who we think is hot and who is not, or that the demands of our virtual community interrupt everyday activities in our real-life world. Social analysis is often about finding openings where contexts that are taken for granted and invisible become visible so that the effects on individuals are more tangible. Social analysis can take invisible everyday interactions individuals may take for granted, and expose or make visible the consequences of these social relations on people's lives. One effective way to take advantage of openings that make social relations visible is to study strategies employed and actions taken by social movements, because they often expose hidden assumptions about social inequality, like systemic sexism, and develop strategies to promote social changes and changes in policies and practices that transform people's lives. Those involved in social movements actively work with others on group projects using collective strategies to contribute to social change, which often reach individuals' everyday lives. A contemporary understanding of social movements, particularly evident since the 1960s, involves organized collective action with specific goals, which often make personal troubles a political issue. The use of human agency to gain political goals is visible as activists' attitudes are changed during the collective process. Also, more relevant is the change in attitudes of other groups in society as a result of the strategies and successes of social movements.

Many changes that affect everyday lives are to improve social inequalities and human rights, and sexuality issues have constituted an important topic addressed by social movement actions. As a result, the social shaping of sexuality is evident in people's everyday lives at the same time as shifting attitudes are evident in the demand of groups and communities for changes to social practices, policies, and programmes in relation to sexuality. In terms of sexualities, access to contraceptives, decriminalizing of homosexuality, confronting sexual violence, legalizing same sex marriage, and legitimizing *in vitro* fertilization are all consequences of social movement actions and individual and collective agency. Looking beyond the individual to the ways in which social context influences daily lives provides insights into how a person's constructs change and how new ones are added.

Social Movements: Transformation of Sexual Attitudes

By the mid-twentieth century, the effectiveness of collective organizing by social movements was evident in the significant contributions they made to social changes, including the Civil Rights Movement in the USA and the post-World War II peace movements in European countries. Through their human agency, social movement activists contributed to social change by making the personal political—personal troubles that became public issues were taken into the political arena. There was an attempt to achieve social change at the community and structural level, and that change had an impact on individuals' personal lives and their sense of self. What is sometimes claimed to be inevitable change and progress, like equal rights, is the consequence of long struggles by activists in social movements and beyond. The importance of social movements addressing sexuality, including the contemporary feminist movement, and the gay, lesbian and other sexual movements, is that they have "challenged many of the certainties of the 'sexual tradition', and have offered new insights into the intricate forms of power and domination that shape our sexual lives" (Weeks, 1986, p. 17). Sexuality and social movements from the 1960s onwards were social spaces where new, and shared, personal constructs emerged due to social changes actively shaped from below, at the grassroots, by social movement activists and community participation. At that time, the social relations of sexuality were challenged, and existing unquestioned assumptions about gender and sexuality questioned. In this altered social context, individuals adopted new personal constructs, which then produced altered outlooks, meanings, and sexual identities.

The political actions of social movements in many Western countries were partly a response to changes implemented in the 1950s and early 1960s, after the turmoil of World War II and the upheaval of previously colonized countries that gained independence. In terms of sexuality, what is often called the Sexual Revolution took place between the mid-1950s and the mid-1970s, "though its parameters vary from country to country, and its character is defined as much by national peculiarities as by international trends" (Weeks, 1985, p. 21). The 1960s constituted an important turning point, in that it set changes in motion in attitudes towards sexuality that affected different aspects of the personal and social lives of individuals.

The dramatic changes initiated by the women's movement and the lesbian and gay movements led to possibilities of new identities and meaning (Weeks, 2005). The changes between the 1960s and 1990s were particularly transformative, as social movements contributed to living in a world in transition "in the midst of a long, convoluted, messy, unfinished but profound revolution that has transformed the possibilities of living our sexual diversity and creating intimate lives" (Weeks, 2007, p. 3). While the consequences may not have been revolutionary in the traditional sense of societal upheaval, they did transform the way sexual relations were understood in many countries in terms of premarital sex, same-sex relationships, access to contraception, and abortion rights. The transformations sparked by social movements resulted in dramatic changes in individual and group understandings of sexuality: "the revolution that emerged in the sixties was as much a change in attitudes about sex as it was a significant shift in sexual conduct" (Escoffier, 2003a, p.xiii).

The 1960s and 1970s were an interesting time in terms of the power relations of sexuality because the idealized assumptions of romance and love—leading to marriage and an ideal nuclear family, which were prevalent in the 1950s—were challenged (Rowbotham, 1989). After the upheaval during World War II in the lives of many people, particularly in Europe and North America, this family ideology had been reinforced to reclaim stability. Expected to conform to a traditional family life, and to particularly narrow views of appropriate sexual relations, many youth challenged the status quo by organizing collectively, so that the effect of "sexual and intimate revolutions of our time are largely the result of grass-roots transformations—literally the world we have made together" (Weeks, 2007, p. 4). While there may have been many individual changes people experienced in the 1960s that contributed to different sexual attitudes and behaviors, the more widespread changes, linked to the social context and challenge to the status quo by social movements, are more meaningful. Such changes in attitude about sexuality contributed to new constructs that were taken into account when construing sexuality.

Shifts occurred in terms of power relations between the generations, and between men and women. In Western countries, the 1960s was a time when youth reacted against their parents' generation in a far more radical way than in earlier generations. The influence of peer groups and the media cannot be overestimated in reshaping the social context and enabling youth to claim more power and rights, particularly more freedom to make their own decisions about sexual relations. Weeks also refers to shifts in terms of separation of sex from reproduction, and sex from marriage, and marriage from parenting, plus overall the "redefinition of the relationship between 'normality' and 'abnormality'" (p. 62). These are significant changes in the social context of people's lives, partially shaped by social movements, that contribute to new constructs that lead to changes in attitudes and behaviors based on sexual practices and identities.

The shift in power between generations and between men and women was likely most meaningful for women in the 1960s and 1970s. In the earlier labor, peace, and civil rights movements, women had expected to be treated equal to men. But they experienced the same sexism and patriarchal power relations that trapped them in traditional supportive and sexualized gender roles, and repressed their sexual and political identities, and left to form women's movements to claim their space and express their identities. Many of these women were involved in the women's movements of the 1960s and 1970s. Although many contemporary contexts set aside women's challenge to patriarchal relations as no longer relevant, it should not be underestimated.

Rowbotham's (1989) analysis of social movements links the personal and the political. "How we perceive our bodies in the prevailing culture and in the social circumstance which physically affect us is not unalterable; it is one way in which the personal is political" (p. 61). Making the personal a political issue was important in many Western countries in the 1960s, when windows of opportunity opened for social change for women. One of these windows offered women a way to organize in consciousness-raising groups to share and explore information about their bodies in terms of making sense of sexuality and reproduction. There was a desire to uncover knowledge about women's bodies, so that women could not only understand how to claim their sexuality more effectively but also gain some autonomy over decisions made about their bodies, whether for choosing contraception on their own terms or understanding their unique birthing and mothering experiences. The Boston Women's Health Book Collective (1973) was an example of how this interest extended to larger consciousness-raising projects like *Our bodies, ourselves*. This publication developed from an educational project that included vivid information from women's perspectives about their bodies, including their genitalia, sexual health, and childbearing, so they could start to take control of their own bodies and sexuality. This strategy was so successful that *Our bodies, ourselves* continues today, and has been translated into many languages, in more or less the original format, and still includes surprisingly contemporary information about bodies and sexualities not covered effectively elsewhere.

Along a similar line of sharing intimate details of women's lives is Ensler's (2001) *The vagina monologues*. This work, combining humour and pain, has been performed extensively to young women in particular as a form of consciousness-raising about the complexity of female bodies and sexuality, as well as naming the reality and pain of sexual violence. While *Our bodies, ourselves* and *The Vagina Monologues* use different strategies, they address some similar concerns over encouraging women to gain knowledge about their own bodies and sexualities. With women of all ages gaining more understanding of the details of their bodies and sexualities, these kinds of strategies gave women agency to make decisions about their sexual lives and anticipate consequences based on new constructs that changed their self-perceptions.

What may have started in the women's movement as an attempt to gain control over one's body and efforts to ensure access to safe contraception from doctors has led to a range of changes to our understanding and practices of sexuality. With these changes, women worked with different constructs that allowed them to imagine their futures as sexual women quite differently from their mothers and grandmothers. Just imagine what it meant to women and men to be exposed to views of sexual freedom while also being able to protect themselves from conception with reasonably available and increasingly reliable medical contraceptives. Rowbotham's (1989) comments capture this moment in time:

> So for the first time it became possible for millions of women to make love with men, knowing that it was unlikely they would conceive. This was an

extraordinary change with significant effects on women's consciousness. The next step was a newly confident demand from women for a technology which was not harmful to their bodies" (p. 63)

The freedom of changing sexual partners was one important consequence of contraceptives. But perhaps a more important one for many young women was the separation of sex from reproduction that also gave them the chance to experience sexual pleasure more freely inside or outside marriage: "The emphasis was upon women actively pursuing sexual pleasure unencumbered by marriage—that is, by economic or sexual dependence upon men" (Hamilton, 1996, p. 65). With this separation of sex from reproduction came more freedom for women of all ages in many countries. What cannot be ignored is that reliable contraceptives also gave women some freedom to plan childbirth and relieve the burden of the extended years of childbearing and childrearing that affects women and their families in many economic ways, including poverty.

The longing to separate sex from reproduction and marriage is not new, and has been lived out in many ways for centuries with a wide range of culturally specific tacit knowledge and contraceptive practices. What was unusual about the late 1950s and early 1960s was that "sex for the sake of pleasure was one of the most insistent, if often unexpressed, ideals of the sexual revolution" (Escoffier, 2003a, p.xxx). Also key were new technologies, pharmaceutical products, and medical contraceptive methods that offered women, in particular, the means to take control over their sexuality. This was a time when biomedical technologies enabled both sexual liberation and the medicalization of sexuality. Women who acknowledged their sexual freedom increasingly saw sexuality as being natural; at the same time, perhaps unintentionally, sexuality was increasingly becoming controlled by medical professionals. Even though seldom understood in this way by women as they gained access to the Pill, the freedom gained by contraception was also a natural process of becoming medicalized by pharmaceutical intervention and dependency. Rowbotham (1989) makes an important point to divert attention away from technological determinism: "Changes in consciousness preceded the technology which made sex possible without fear of pregnancy. Young women were beginning to challenge the assumption that motherhood was women's inevitable destiny" (p. 79). Adding constructs of choice and control over reproduction and one's body offers new ways of construing sexuality and one's everyday life.

The 1960s and 1970s were also a time when there was freedom to explore sex for pleasure, and multiple sexual partners: "For many gays coming out in the 1970s the gay world was a paradise of sexual opportunity and of sensual exploration" (Weeks, 1985, p. 48). One of the consequences of gay liberation in most Western countries was the legitimization of same-sex relationships, and the emphasis that "gay sex is just sex" (Cruikshank, 1992, p. 37), and a reinforcement of the idea that gay men wanted to choose whom, how, and where they had sexual relations, and to get rid of the surveillance of their personal lives. An early goal of the gay liberation movement was to remove the pathologization and criminalization of homosexuality, and one way to do that was to claim the term "gay" instead of "homosexual". Considerable work went into identifying the forms of surveillance and social control of gay men that different institutions (medicine, the police force, and the state) had persistently supported (Kinsman, 1996).

The development of gay communities in major cities was at first a way to get beyond the stigmatization, harassment, and gay bashing that is a part of many men's lives: "Originally, gay culture was an adaption to a bad situation, a defense. Later it became a catalyst for social change" (Cruikshank, 1992, p. 119). The gay community is usually an integral part of a gay man's life and sense of identity: "People who have been despised and rejected because of their emotional/sexual identity naturally feel great empathy or others in the same situation" (Cruikshank, 1992, p. 126). The persistent effort to not only acknowledge sexual identity but be "out" safely was a part of many gay men's lives, and would involve the development of new constructs to make some sense of one's sexual identity, to see how nonheterosexuals responded to you, and to negotiate changes in close relationships.

Some of the positive steps taken in the 1960s and 1970s to improve gay men's lives were quickly lost with the onset of AIDS in the 1980s, which also re-established the stigmatization of gays in all-too-familiar ways. This led to considerable social action by the gay liberation movement to reinforce the need to understand the disease and to gain adequate medical support for people with AIDS. One of the unintended consequences of the AIDS crisis was a reaction by gay men to make safe sex, particularly in the form of condom use, a norm among gay men. Also, to ensure that people with AIDS get the necessary support, AIDS treatment activism in several guises ensured social action to support people with AIDS. These responses of gay men to the AIDS crisis, and their attempts to protect themselves from infection, inevitably transformed the way they construed their sexual lives and identities at home, work and elsewhere.

Gay and lesbian activists and communities tended to disregard marriage as a thoroughly heteronormative institution in the 1970s, but began to make an effort to recreate same-sex weddings in new ways at the beginning of the twenty-first century. The heteronormative mainstream community has had some interesting responses to this contradiction.

Human Agency, Social Structure, and PCT

There may be some very creative and inspired individuals who monitor and take responsibility for their own construction processes, but most likely the vast majority of us rely on others for suggestions, if not the imposition, of constructs through everyday social interaction. The presence of new ideas or attitudinal expressions during periods of heightened tensions and emotions might prove to be even more appealing to some observers, let alone participants, than under other, calmer circumstances. No doubt many actions, slogans, and writings of participants and leaders of social movements in the 1960s and 1970s provided many new ways of construing sexuality. The exact content or form of such constructs is impossible to know with certainty, but we can speculate.

As a sexual minority member exposed to the turbulence of the pro-gay protests of the late 1960s, seeing oneself as proud versus ashamed, out versus closeted, or sexually liberated versus oppressed probably became obvious. Whether these were novel constructs is difficult to determine now but, even if not, the social action in the streets and elsewhere might have produced changes in the ways that sexual minorities came to construe themselves with respect to existing constructs. The actions of protesters, the repeal of existing repressive laws, and encountering less discrimination and fewer insults while walking urban streets may well have produced swings in self-perception, such as eventually coming to see oneself as free versus oppressed. It does not really matter whether the larger social action inspired new constructions or simply allowed an individual to reconstrue himself or herself as better off than in the past. The point is that social movement actions do not only attempt to promote social change; they also encourage personal change. Ideology is construction, or comprised of constructs at the very least, and the attempt to change minds is accomplished by putting constructs forward as better than other options or promoting construal in terms of one construct pole over another. We are not interested in arguing that the social trumps the personal when it comes to ideological appeals, because often the most powerful appeals include a personal element (e.g., personal story, individual pitch rather than a group presentation). Both the social and the personal, however, must be considered while trying to understand the changing of mind.

Before proceeding to any reformulation of PCT, various other social factors or aspects of the social world relevant to sexuality require some discussion. We will consider how power, the social view of bodies, and sexual commodification play parts in the construction and reconstruction of sexuality in the following three chapters.

5

Power Relations in Sexuality

Many writers from a range of disciplines have argued that all sexual relationships are first and foremost power relationships. Giddens (1992), for example, described sexuality as a social construct "operating within fields of power, not merely a set of biological promptings which either do or do not find direct release" (p. 23), and Brickell (2009) claimed that power "is intrinsic to sexuality" (p. 57). Following a series of interviews concerning sex within heterosexual relationships, Holland, Ramazanoglu, Sharpe, and Thomson (1998) came to the conclusion that both males and females collude in promoting a single standard of dominant heterosexual masculinity, the "male-in-the-head" (p. 11). Overall, the view that sexuality and power are intertwined is so common that overlooking the nature and effects of social power in sexuality would be very difficult to imagine. Understandings of power relations in different sexual contexts, complex though they may be, are central to comprehending fully various sexual expressions and sexual relationships. These understandings offer important social considerations for an expanded PCT. Not only do individuals' constructs require analysis but social factors such as oppression, privilege, social inequalities, social control, and resistance to power also demand attention. This chapter draws on theory and research from various social science disciplines on power relations in general, and sexuality in particular, to consider how power impacts sexuality and how PCT does and should accommodate social power.

Understanding the Social Nature of Power Relations

One stumbling block in discussions of power is the lack of agreement or a common understanding about how it should be defined. While it is clear that power exists in many tangible and accessible forms at several levels of society, some claim power is all-encompassing and almost intangible (Butler, 1990; Foucault, 1976/1990). Even though different perspectives offer different explanations of power, there are some common threads to consider. Weber (1947/1964), whose main interest was how decision-making occurs at a macro-sociological level, defined power as "the probability that one actor within a social relationship will be in a position to carry out his own will despite resistance, regardless of the basis on which the probability rests" (p. 152). According to Weber, the ability to gain social compliance in the face of resistance is the essence of power. While providing a clear definition of power, Weber took into consideration only those who have the power to make decisions, without considering that subordinates may also have some power that they can exert in different ways, including in forms of resistance.

Sociological perspectives often make distinctions between political power, economic power, and social power for more specific analysis of particular issues, while psychologists tend to be concerned with social power that addresses micro-level concerns. For many psychologists (e.g., Minton, 1967; Ng, 1980), power is more about the ability of an individual to change the thoughts, feelings, and/or behaviors of another individual against the desires of the second individual. Key elements of social power common to the macro- and micro-levels are the ability to change, or gain compliance with, demands involving social players, and opposition to that change. Clearly, the concern about social power is shared by both disciplines, despite their differences in focus and terminology.

In both obvious and subtle ways, power is very much a part of all social relations; unfortunately, especially in psychology, it is all too often ignored or excluded from the discussion, except in discussions about relationships involving extreme exploitation or abuse. Power, however, appears as a necessary aspect of all considerations of social interaction. Since not all social actors or entities are equal, it is necessary to consider differences between social elements in any calculation of social power in terms of social interactions. In a very real manner, social power refers to a relational characteristic between individuals or social entities (Willutzki & Duda, 1996; Wrong, 1979), despite the tendency in psychology to attribute power to a characteristic of individuals (see Minton, 1967). May (1972) provides an interesting approach based on specific characteristics or dispositions of individuals, described as "strengths". Although a person can possess physical strength because of muscular development, or a nation can possess military strength due to advanced weaponry, power is a relevant consideration only if such an attribute is presented, either directly or indirectly, when two or more players engage in a social exchange. Whatever the actual, imagined, or officially listed nature of the strengths, these players actually help to define the nature of the relationship. The individual or larger social entity with the power directs the relationship in terms of particular ends (e.g., family meals served on time but in silence; favourable terms in bilateral trade agreements).

A useful term to describe the shape and consequences of power relations on individuals' everyday lives is "hegemony", or taken-for-granted ideology. Hegemony addresses power and social inequalities and, thus, is relevant to understanding power in the social relations of sexuality. Hegemony is a term Marxists use to describe the ideology of the ruling class being universal interest in societies and imposed by the power of the ruling class to structure people's everyday lives, particularly evident in capitalist societies (Eyerman, 1981). This can mean that a seeming given in a society, such as the reservation of education for privileged males, is an ideal of the ruling class, and enforced by an imposed social structure of private education limiting educational opportunities for all but the privileged. Gramsci (1971) extended the meaning of hegemony into sociology by arguing that the ideology of the ruling classes was structured by the state not only into the public sphere but also into the daily practices of the private sphere. In this situation, without obviously using force, the ruling classes and their practices manipulate the way one thinks and acts, and actively limit and stigmatize non-hegemonic forms of thinking, often in ways largely invisible to those being manipulated. In sexuality studies, hegemony and gender have been combined into the term "hegemonic masculinity" (Connell, 1990). It refers to the assumption of male dominance over women not only at the level of policies and legislation about sexuality (e.g., if a women comes forward with charges of sexual assault, legislation often requires details women's personal sexual life as evidence, yet seldom requires the same from a man) but also at the everyday level of interpersonal sexual relations (e.g., men assuming their dominance by taking the lead in intimate relations with women). In this context, hegemonic masculinity provides an analytical tool for revealing how the often-hidden assumptions of a society's ideology become embodied so that masculinity is set above femininity, as well as how sexual practices often meet the needs of men yet actively subordinate or silence women's interests (Connell, 2005; Schippers, 2007).

Power, or power relations, can also be understood from different levels and social locations. Power in social, political and cultural contexts is central to many sociological perspectives, and some of these are worth considering in reference to PCT. Traditionally, sociology has tended to focus on institutional social structures—including the state, education, and labour force—that act as sources of authority and control in societies to create strikingly hierarchical frameworks framed primarily by social class and ethnicities. While it is meaningful from macro-analyses of power to describe societies at particular times and places (e.g., post 9/11 in Western Canada; during the Civil War in Spain), it does not provide an understanding of society or power relations at the micro-level that is readily recognizable to many people as part of their everyday lives. Instead of a psychological focus on how one individual may exert power over another's behavior based on their choice to be dominant and submissive, several areas of sociology locate the focus of power in external influences linked to social structures (e.g., family, the media, workplaces, religious institutions) that impinge on how people live their daily lives. Taking this different angle on power relations leads to different questions being raised, because it is relevant that an individual's behavior of exerting power over another is informed, intentionally or unintentionally, by not only other people but also by the social structures in the society in which they live. The individual is viewed as acting within a complex structure of power relations that can be located in quite tangible ways in a person's everyday experiences, including sexual experiences.

An assumption behind this sociological approach to power relations is that social inequalities (e.g., differences in class, gender, race and ethnicity) are part of societies, and that these inequalities, experienced in many people's daily lives, have an impact on how a person interacts within others in their social world. When social inequalities are taken as a basis for understanding power relations, the social process between individuals, communities, and institutions becomes visible and accessible for study. This is very much a part of many studies of the unequal access to opportunities and resources, like education and housing, which contributes to social inequalities within capitalist societies. To introduce this approach to understanding power relations, social inequalities linked to class, gender, race, and ethnicity are described briefly in order to demonstrate the way social processes become visible. More specific references to the relevance of power relations based on social inequalities and sexuality need to be considered, and how these insights contribute to PCT.

An analysis of social class is fundamental to understanding the social structure and everyday lives of industrialized societies. Perhaps the most rigorous analysis of class is the historical materialist analysis informed by Marxist critiques of workers' lives in capitalist economies (see Armstrong & Armstrong, 1990; Braverman, 1974; Ritzer, 1993; Thompson, 1963/1991). Social class is a social hierarchy based on access to resources, particularly income, so that people in a similar social class are in a similar economic position in the society in which they live. As a power relation, social class means that those with access to more resources have more life chances (Weber, 1947/1964) and are more likely to be economically privileged, even wealthy, during their lifetime. A person with many life chances is more likely to live in an owned home, own a car, attend schools that provide quality education, and use social networks to obtain secure permanent well-paying jobs and promotion opportunities. A person with limited life chances is more likely to be living in insecure rental housing, depend on public transit, have to struggle to gain a quality education, and be employed in low-wage, insecure work. From an analysis based on class within capitalism, the economic power, or lack of it, that is linked to class status influences everyday life experiences throughout one's life. In many societies, there is social mobility, so that social class throughout life can change, and life chances change. As an example, when a married woman becomes a single parent, she and her children (but not her husband) tend to struggle on a reduced income and shift to a less privileged class, which can change the housing, schools, income and recreational activities she and her children can access.

Gendered power relations have been studied more recently as a consequence of feminist theory, which developed from women's experiences in the women's movement in the 1960s and 1970s, and developments in gender studies. First- and second-wave feminists puzzled over the pattern in almost all societies, and particularly in capitalist societies in which they lived, of women and girls being consistently subordinate to men and boys in almost all areas of their daily lives. Unwilling to accept the essentialist argument—that the place for women and girls was inevitably a step or two behind that of men and boys—feminists investigated historical and materialist explanations, and found a wealth of support for social inequality explanations of these patterns that effectively challenged essentialist explanations of men's and women's lives (e.g., Armstrong & Armstrong, 1990; Benston, 1969; Reiter, 1991). Radical and socialist feminist research uncovered links between social structure, communities, and daily lives that explained the gendered power relations that shaped women's lives in particular. Some of the areas studied included the gender gap in pay, the undervaluing of paid and unpaid work traditionally done by women, different educational opportunities based on gender, lack of support for women as single parents, and patterns of men's violence against women.

Feminist theorists also claimed the term "patriarchy", traditionally used to describe the authority of males as heads of households. They used it to describe the power relations in many types of societies based on a system of male authority that repeatedly led to the oppression and exploitation of women through social, political, and economic institutions at all levels of these societies (Waldby, 1968). This use of the concept of patriarchy provided feminist theorists with an analytical device to distinguish how male and masculine practices play out in particular ways on a structural level—usually viewed as an integral power relation of capitalism—to influence everyday practices as part of interpersonal relations. Patriarchy has been used in tangible ways to explain policies and practices that explicitly influence the ways that men dominate and direct sexual division of labour, reproductive labour, and sexual practices to actively subordinate women (e.g., Hartmann, 1981; Smith, 1987; Waldby, 1968). These insights from feminist theory and gender studies contributed to social changes in the late twentieth and early twenty-first centuries that have reduced the social inequalities based on gender at a global level. In many countries, women now have jobs of all types and at all levels in workplaces, the sex difference in the pay gap is narrowed, media images include girls and women in active roles, caregiving work is valued as skilled for women and men, and property ownership is possible for women and men. These represent tangible changes, and support constructionist explanations over essentialist explanations of the gendered social inequalities that shape power relations.

Social inequalities based on ethnicity have been studied most effectively in terms of postcolonial and critical theoretical perspectives (e.g., Collins, 2000; Henry & Tator, 2009). Insightful studies include experiences of gaining independence in previously colonized countries, experiences of immigrant communities and minority groups in multicultural societies (e.g., Canada, Western European countries), and the effect of racialized media representations on perceptions of marginalized peoples. In these contexts, inequality is reinforced by forms of racial and ethnic discriminations, based on assumptions about skin colour and stereotypes about diverse cultural practices. For instance, in many countries, divisions based on skin colour and ethnicity continue to be maintained by the persistent use of surveillance through policy and technology and by the control and limiting of interactions by people (Nagal, 2000). The insights gained from an analysis of social inequalities also show that one of the main sources of the racialization process is institutionalized policies and practices, and not essentialist arguments about different racial stereotypes.

This brief discussion of power relations from related social inequality perspectives demonstrates how sociological analysis helps explain how unequal access to power shapes people's everyday lives at several levels, including social institutions, and also in communities, groups, and everyday lives. Common to all the examples of social inequality discussed in this chapter is the consideration of the experiences of individuals and groups as a starting point for analysis, as opposed to arrogantly interpreting other people's lives for them from above.

While this discussion has drawn out one criterion at a time to show the relevance of social inequality as a basis for analysis, in reality these criteria intersect in our lives. In a reaction to the assumption of African-American women as perpetual victims or as being heroic in their resistance to multiple oppressions, Collins (2000) argued that the intersectional domains of power allowed for conditions of oppression and resistance to occur at the same time. For instance, even though experiencing racism and poverty as a woman of colour can mean debilitating oppression, at the same time these shared oppressive conditions can spark social justice actions to change these circumstances. This refers to the way that different criteria of social inequality do not in reality occur in isolation from one another, but instead overlap, or intersect. A key feature of these different angles on social inequality is that they all take people's experiences of historical and materialist conditions as a starting point for understanding social power or power relations. The focus is from the standpoint of the experiences of subordinate or oppressed individuals, in terms of understanding how social power or power relations impact their lives and how they conform and resist the power relations in which they are embedded. To understand how power influences social relations that individuals experience daily, the ways that social inequalities reflect unequal access to and resources of power is a tangible way to conceptualize and analyze power relations and sexuality.

Sources or Bases of Power

Typically, many social scientists concerned with power consider only limited aspects of the sources of social power. French and Raven (1953), for example, presented a good psychosocial discussion of a number of power bases, but it is limited to only the use of power by authority. While authority is an important source of power conferred by society, it is far from being the only source. Wrong (1979) provided an overview of the complex nature of social power, and his work presents a good framework for considering various power bases.

"Authority" refers to formal, established, and accepted roles and relationships within a social context. According to Wrong (1979), we need to consider five important bases of power by authority: coercive, induced, legitimate, competent, and personal. Although the terms tend to differ from author to author, Wrong's five sources of authoritative power are essentially the same bases presented earlier by French and Raven (1953). Coercive authority gains compliance via the use of punishment. If you do not do as ordered by authorities, an individual (e.g., a policeman on the street) or a much larger social entity (e.g., a central government committee), something unpleasant or aversive will occur. The punishment might be a nominal fine imposed by a local court or perhaps a death sentence via state-ordered execution. Induced authority, on the other hand, bases its control on the use of payment. A pleasant result, whether a tasty snack to eat or a massive business contract from a government, is used as inducement for compliance with demands. Legitimate authority is more subtle. It is based on established norms and expectations. Compliance is the result of an unquestioning and common understanding of tradition or "the rules" (e.g., "That's just the way we do things here.") Competent authority possesses power based on specialized knowledge or skill that directs compliance (e.g., "As your physician, I direct you to take that medication."). Finally, personal authority finds power in a "personal" relationship based on love of or the charismatic nature of the authority figure. Compliance is based on the degree of the personal attachment (e.g., "As your beloved television evangelist, I command that you viewers mail in every last penny you have.")

Just as authority has multiple bases or sources of power, power employed by social entities not connected to authority is multifaceted as well. There are three further bases of power beyond authority for Wrong (1979): force, persuasion, and manipulation. Force refers to physical force, and it is clear that the application of physical force is not the only effective means by which compliance is achieved. Threats of the use of force (e.g., "Shut up or I'll punch you!", "If you do not surrender your country, our armed forces will crush your country!") are probably very effective means of gaining compliance in certain circumstances. It might also be the case that force is implied by the issue of a particular order or demand that typically is supported by a particular level of force (e.g., "That little guy wouldn't demand the money from me as a store owner if he didn't have a gun or some weapon!") Persuasion is a source of power in that prolonged discussion can bring about compliance if rational argumentation is brought to bear on a social situation. In this case, the social players know what is at stake, and understand the nature of the noncompliant action, but communicate in order to attempt to change the situation. The "silver-tongued devil" possesses power to the extent that compliance is achieved via "straight talk" about the benefits of doing or thinking what is requested. Manipulation, on the other hand, is the use of techniques to gain compliance when the outcome is not made clear to the victim, or at least the intended victim. Manipulation can take many different forms, both personal and social, and both individuals and social institutions can become "masters of manipulation" in order to gain compliance and achieve goals.

One additional power base discussed by Horley (2008) is extortion. An extortionist—again, either a single individual or a larger social entity—achieves compliance by the use of goods or information that can be used to produce compliance by the mere threat of use or possibly the brief demonstration of the capacity to do damage. In this way, it differs from both persuasion, where the weight of socially defined reasonable argument is used to gain a known outcome, and manipulation, where a number of tactics can be used to gain an outcome unknown to the intended target. Criminal extortion, more commonly known as blackmail, describes a process by which an extortionist threatens to reveal materials depicting criminal or embarrassing activities unless some payment is made to keep the material secret. Extortion can happen on a grand scale in the world of international relations (e.g., demanding cooperation in a trade deal or else certain information will be released to the media that could cripple an economy). In the realm of interpersonal relations, however, extortion can involve the threat of revealing information best left private (e.g., "You'd better be nice to me or I'll tell everyone what you did last summer."). It can also involve the threat or use of emotional blackmail (e.g., "I'll hurt myself if you end our relationship.") According to some mental health professionals concerned with theory and therapy (e.g., Laing, 1969), extortion within family relationships is quite common, and also quite difficult to address and to alter.

All criminal offenders, including sexual offenders, use power in some form during the commission of their offences. There would not, by definition, be an offence if, for example, an individual faced with a request for money immediately handed over all available cash—this would be a simple case of obliging generosity to a beggar's request rather than a grudging acquiescence to a robber's demands. Sexual offenders inevitably use at least one source of power, if not several, during the commission of an offence because, again, there would be no offence if there were true and complete consent on the part of a willing sexual partner. Many sexual offenders rely very much on authority because they are fathers, priests, teachers, and psychologists. They are able via competence, personal love, reward, or punishment to compel victims to comply with their demands. Choice of tactics to gain victim compliance is due to a number of factors including personal history/experience, social status, degree of social inequality, class and ethnicity; and this points to one problem with Wrong's (1979) analysis of power. According to Wrong, such factors are unimportant in the final analysis. If, however, a young male immigrant who is serving as a church altar boy is ordered by his priest to perform a sexual act, for example, how can social status, ethnicity, etc., not enter into an analysis of the situation? The compliance in this example is due directly to the nature of the relationship and the characteristics of the victim.

Forensic clinicians often refer to a sex offender's "victim grooming", or the process, sometimes very lengthy, of preparing an individual for sexual victimization. This process necessarily involves the use of power. Individuals selected as potential victims must be probed in terms of weak points, which include the potential victim's likelihood of succumbing to persuasive arguments, vulnerabilities with respect to authority figures, and weaknesses that might provide a basis for extortion. An obvious weak point with most children as potential victims concerns their lack of physical strength, although in a few cases an ability to obtain and to use a weapon might overcome any physical strength deficits. A single case of sexual abuse might involve a number of different sources of power.

An offender might begin with gentle persuasion (e.g., "You really want to do this, don't you?"), switch to a threat of force when a victim is isolated (e.g., "If you don't take off your clothes, I'll hurt you"), and use extortion after the incident (e.g., "If you tell anyone, I'll say that you wanted it!") Recognizing that sexual offenders employ power, however, does not answer the question of the role of power, and any consequent emotional "payoff" (e.g., elation, self-satisfaction) or sense of confidence, in the causal structure of sexual assault. Is control a primary reason for sexual assault? Is sex a primary cause? The answer may be much more complex than many might think, or hope. Personal construct theory can potentially shed light on the reasons behind sexual abuse in many forms as well as the impact that power can have on everyday sexual encounters and relationships.

Approaches to Sexuality and Power

In several areas of sexuality studies—including feminist theories, queer theory, and gender studies—it is assumed that it is necessary to understand the relevant power relations to understand sexuality. This means that much of the questioning is about the means and consequences of power in relation to sexuality; and, often, these questions are linked to issues of social inequality. To imagine how adding power relations might expand PCT, our focus here is on Brickell's (2009) work. Brickell has provided a dimensional analysis of power that considers the work of several writers in gender and sexuality studies who take power relations as a given, and question the consequences for understandings of sexualities.

Much of the discussion in this chapter has focused on theoretical approaches to power in the social sciences, with less emphasis on analytical devices for empirical studies. Earlier, Wrong's (1979) approach to distinguishing different sources of power was considered. While power bases might be important considerations in understanding power, Brickell (2009) suggested four dimensions or aspects of power with specific reference to sexuality that reflects individuals' lived experiences. These dimensions were based on a synthesis of writings and research on power and sexuality, and included definitional power, regulatory power, productive power, and unequal power, although he later (Brickell, 2012) eliminated the productive dimension in a detailed analysis of sexual relations on the internet. Brickell (2009, 2012) attempted to draw out strands of power, not mutually exclusive, as ideal types that also reflect everyday experience. His contention was that these strands offer analytical devices for studying power and sexuality at different levels.

For Brickell (2009), "definitional power" or "constitutive power" refers to the ways that power and sexuality are defined in order to set boundaries around sexuality, as a way of normalizing power in different ways. In definitional power, Brickell includes several different ways gender and sexuality researchers and writers have described power. Radical feminist writers (e.g., McIntosh, 1968; Rubin, 1984) showed that there is a hierarchy of expression of sexuality that is stereotyped from "good sex" to "tolerated sex" to "bad sex", with clear boundaries based on limits of acceptability. Rubin (1984) described "good sex" as privileged forms of monogamous heterosexual expression, "tolerated sex" as solitary and same-sex expression, and "bad sex" as stigmatized alternative forms of sexual expression and sex workers' sexual relations. Another angle on definitional power draws from queer theory, which highlights how sexuality and symbolic discourses are always set against heteronormativity at the centre, which establishes boundaries, particularly for the queer community (e.g., Rich, 1980; Seidman, 2010). The place of stigma in boundary setting continues to be emphasized in terms of identifying unacceptable sexual practices and identities, as well as becoming a means of social control of sexual boundaries in different contexts. To reinforce the definitional power that setting these boundaries requires, Brickell refers to the norms of sexually conservative societies, controlling symbol systems, and stigmatizing storytelling as means by which boundaries are maintained, all of which offer analytical devices for analysis of sexuality and power. In terms of a psychosocial perspective on power and sexuality, this covers the way that individuals describe themselves and others based on boundaries that they both experience and enforce.

Regulatory power includes the ways in which the norms and definitions linked to sexuality are enforced. According to Brickell (2009), the "agents of regulation are multiple and the effects of their interrelationships have generated a considerable contemporary and historical literature" (p. 60). These agents of regulation include the state, religion, and medicine. The state sets regulations around sexual expression, consenting and non-consenting sex, and social controls to ensure that individuals conform to practices within the boundaries set formally or informally by state policies. In most countries, the state intervenes in regulating sexual expression so that, for instance, the decriminalization and legitimization of same-sex relationships was a major breakthrough that transformed lives. Related constraints on sexuality are set by religion and implemented in a range of practices in different cultural settings. In many religions, the taboo of premarital sex, especially for women, is firmly enforced, and family members can go to great lengths to ensure this regulation is enforced. Also included in the regulatory power of sexuality is medicine and its use as a means of defining women's reproductive practices and expressions, for instance with access to contraception, and as a means of monitoring and treating same-sex relationships, for instance mental health treatment of homosexuality using aversion therapy (James, 1962). Brickell points out that these forms of institutional social control of sexuality are seldom complete and often negotiated.

Finally, power tends to be distributed in an unequal fashion, and can promote further inequality. With respect to sexual relationships and sexuality, more generally, this power dimension can have an impact in a variety of domains. Perhaps the most obvious of these inequalities are the areas identified by different aspects of feminist theory in terms of gendered power relations (e.g., Butler, 1990; Rich, 1980; Segal, 1994). One obvious example is in women's sexual relations with men, who can assume more power, which can limit a woman's expression of sexuality and leave her open to victimization via men's violence. As an offshoot of this concern, the belief that it is women's responsibility to accommodate men's desires and pleasures establishes sexual inequality in terms of the opportunity to enjoy sex. The situation of coercion in sexual practices, including degradation and stigmatization, is another more subtle form of creating inequalities, regardless of who is one's sexual partner. Brickell (2012) pointed out a number of ways in which young, white males or the "nerds" who control internet activities direct sexuality and sexual expression at sexual minorities and women on internet websites and chat rooms. Whether safe sex gets practiced or not, and who sets parameters around this issue in relationships, easily sets up an unequal sexual relationship.

To grasp the use and abuse of power, it is important to consider power dimensions and power bases not only in a general sense, but particularly concerning sexual expression and sexual relations. The regulation of sexual desires is a common phenomenon for not only sexual minorities (see Kinsman, 1991, 1996) but for any individual or group lacking the power to defend themselves against such control. Control of sexuality is often disguised and subtle (Foucault, 1976/1990), and might even be applied in a way that is so subtle that even the controller does not realize that it is being employed. The consideration and analysis of power in understanding sexuality is, therefore, difficult yet significant, and it remains to be seen if PCT can embrace this project and contribute to it.

Personal Construct Theory, Social Power, and Sexuality

Until relatively recently, power had not been afforded much prominence within PCT. Kelly (1955) had little to say about the nature of social elements, and he did not offer any discussion about the characteristics of people or larger social entities except in relative terms of the language of construction. Clearly, the relativity of tallness versus shortness of people can be considered and debated, but there is little debate over a characteristic such as height. It can, and typically is, captured using a metric or standard that defies debate, except by the grossly ignorant, the floridly psychotic, or the painfully argumentative. Hair colour, annual income, ethnicity, and a wealth of other personal characteristics are the sum total of an individual's physical and biographical existence; at the same time, population, gross domestic product, bordered land area, and similar indices are applied typically to national groupings. A variety of characteristics appears to apply to all social elements that are beyond the consideration of relativistic constructions. While we could challenge the appropriateness of any label or metric, the point is that some characteristics exist that apply to any social element. Power is one additional yet vital feature of all social elements regardless of social grouping level. As mentioned, Kelly (1955) was unconcerned with social power. Indeed, there appears to be an apparent connection, perhaps a necessary one, between class and power, but this point must be placed in parentheses for now. Actually, Kelly seemed to dismiss power as a relevant consideration, except in terms of construction, when he wrote that to "recognize that 'force' is a feature of many personal construct systems is, of course, not tantamount to embodying the notion of force in the psychology of personal constructs" (p. 240). Kelly, however, was referring to psychological attributes, or analytic units within psychology, as opposed to actual social attributes. To do otherwise would push PCT into the camp of idealism and compromise the constructivistic project that he presented so carefully.

Fortunately, power has been discussed more recently within PCT. Rowe (1994) argued from a personal construct position that power is "the ability to get other people to accept your definition of reality" (p. 29). Leitner, Begley, and Faidley (1996), following Rowe, described power as "the ability to influence another individual's construct system" (p. 323). On the surface, these similar views of power may appear adequate from a psychological perspective, but they fail to consider variations of power and power relations. In a very important respect, they miss the basic ways that power is wielded in everyday social interaction. Perhaps an occupational hazard for many psychologists, especially PCT-influenced psychologists, is mistaking thoughts rather than events as all-important. All too often in contemporary psychology, real people and processes are obscured by psychological referents and processes. Elements constitute a very basic component of the theory, and PCT needs to take elements and the nature of its different types very seriously to account for social relations adequately and become a true psychosocial theory. Specifically, there has been significant consideration of the nature of personal constructs but, with few exceptions (c.f., Horley, 1988b; Husain, 1983), very little consideration of the nature of what constructs are applied to (i.e., elements). Kelly posited a real world populated with real people, but rarely does PCT accept and consider the attributes of elements, let alone the all-too-real attributes of elemental interstices. While there is a wide variety of possible elements, the concern here is with social elements (i.e., people, social groups) exclusively.

As a relational characteristic between all social elements, power is very distinctive not only because it bridges the gulf of social grouping level (i.e., individual versus collective) but also because it appears to bridge the gap between social elements in a literal sense. Power defines the relationships among social elements. The conduct of people is very much determined by such aspects, and the determination does not just refer to the construal processes of the actors. While considerations about construct validation (see Epting et al., 1996; Leitner et al., 1996) are pertinent, they may have little to do with the nature of a social interaction. Power is a term applied to a relational characteristic that is real. If power were illusory in an ultimate sense, as Rowe (1994) implies, it would be silly to speak of powerful and powerless people, as she does. Perhaps the best that we could do is to refer to those who are persuaded and those who are persuasive. While this falls far short of acceptable, given the many sources of power, it does remind us of one aspect missing in many discussions of power—namely, the problem of voluntary acceptance of directions that are not in our own interest. Clearly, either individually or collectively, we can all be misled to see circumstances or conditions not in our best interests as being so. According to some theorists, it happens quite regularly. Holland et al. (1998), for example, argued that young heterosexual women often accept a very dominant and domineering male voice in their heads to direct their behavior, especially their sexual relationships, against their own best interests. This can certainly be seen as a form of false consciousness, or cognitive distortion involving social contradictions and the denial of class interests due to ideology from extended exposure to propaganda (Eyerman, 1981), or perhaps better still an example of existential bad faith (Sartre, 1943/1956), or lying to oneself. At times, propaganda and other sources can certainly persuade us to accept something harmful to our own interests and not resist others' attempts to get us to do their bidding.

As a relational characteristic, power can no doubt direct or determine sexual relationships or sexual encounters in profound ways. Power does, of course, need to be considered as a factor in all sexual assaults—it is very difficult to resist demands of sexual service at the point of a gun or a knife held by a large muscular man, and even direct or implied threats can be difficult to resist. A key to understanding how power plays a part, or probably a complex set of roles, in a wide range of everyday sexual encounters or relationships lies in the manner in which power is construed by both the possessor of power and by other individuals. Viewing one's social world in terms of "wolf" versus "sheep" or "predator" versus "prey"—a remarkably simple yet apparently common construction among sexual offenders, domestic abusers, and aggressive or dominant individuals (see Horley, 2008; Horley & Johnson, 2008)—might be due to a false sense of social power. But it may also be based on consensus social experience (i.e., the individual is physically strong, persuasive, a skilled extortionist, and/or has an elevated social position). Such an individual, by thinking and acting as a predator, is able to control encounters and relationships, sexual and otherwise, through the role of "boss", "head of the household", or related titles. Denial of their demands for sexual service may well be perceived as dangerous. Control of the direction and nature of any sexual encounter is probably in the hands of anyone who views himself or herself, rightly or wrongly, as an apex predator, but even very different core role constructs can produce sexually dominant actions (Horley, 1988a; Houston, 1998; Howells, 1983). There does not appear, nor should we expect there to be, a single construct or simple set of constructs to be characteristic of a sexually dominant, or passive, individual. While psychological profiles are relatively easy to generate and to use, they are rarely accurate or useful.

Lest there is any mistake that we are arguing that power is all in the head, because some constructs might capture power, a very specific example might help to clarify our position. Most of us who think seriously about the topic believe that in any patriarchal society women are taught to be submissive sexually to men. There is some direct research to confirm this view (e.g., Sanchez, Kiefer, & Ybarra, 2006), and we might even consider an extreme expression of female submission to be rape fantasies that, according to one study (Bivona & Critelli, 2009), a majority of women report having at one time or another. It may well be that women are socialized to be submissive sexually to men, that media presentations reinforce such views throughout their lives (Sanchez et al., 2006), and that women represent such views as constructs/values/beliefs at the basis of fantasy and sexual normative behavior. The backdrop of the submission and the probable constructed foundation, however, is a patriarchal society where, predominantly, men control power, and have a vested interest in ensuring that women stay submissive. The mechanisms by which men continue to control female sexuality as well as the sexual expression of sexual minorities would include media and technology, such as the internet (Brickell, 2012), but we do not understand the complete picture of such control, the very complex constructs employed by powerful men, or the constructs that they attempt to impart to those they control or hope to control. Such a study, which we should recognize as significant and pressing, remains to be done, however difficult the research may be to conduct.

6

Interpreting Sexualized Bodies

As we create our bodies, our bodies create us. Of course, such a statement carries the proviso that there are many factors, external (e.g., access to food sources, physical threats) and internal (e.g., endocrine system, genetics), that determine how the body takes form beyond intentional changes. The effect of the body, however, is not necessarily a direct effect that impacts the brain or the biochemical processes of the brain; rather, we experience the body's influence via the construct system and our active and constant interpretation of our bodies. For most of us, regularly monitoring bodily processes and morphology, whether through high-tech devices like blood pressure monitors, or relatively low-tech devices such as mirrors or weight scales, gives us some idea of how we are doing in terms of health, attractiveness, or any number of other concerns. James (1890) saw the body and the other physical objects that we surround ourselves with as components of the material self, one of several aspects of selfhood. The main point that we emphasize is that constructs are required to interpret the information that we receive from whatever source or sources that we consult, and the body supplies us with constant experiences that require interpretation and anticipation.

One purpose that our bodies can serve relates to sexuality, and the means by which bodies are sexualized as objects of desire, pain, and pleasure. With respect to sexuality, bodies are seldom passive and neutral; instead, they are integral to individuals becoming active agents in shaping and influencing their sexual lives and identities. How we understand our bodies is a critical component of our sexual identity, and the meaning of the body as canvas and symbol is exaggerated in areas such as body part fetishes, cyborgs in virtual sex, and body modifications like tattooing. In this chapter, we explore some of the ways bodies, in terms of their being inscribed and viewed in particular ways, contribute to our understandings and misunderstandings of sex and sexualization.

The main theme that links these topics is objectification. Objectification refers to the process whereby bodies are seen as objects to be manipulated, as opposed to being seen as part of a person as a subject and contributing to a sense of agency. Since objectification is a power relationship where the dominant person, group, or social structure turns an individual into a passive object rather an active subject, drawing on this concept is important for understanding how people who are oppressed, marginalized, or face discrimination see themselves and are seen by others. The advertising industry constantly objectifies seemingly detached body parts—whether it is women's reddened lips or men's muscular biceps—to sell everyday products. The person behind the body parts is invisible and irrelevant to the advertisement.

Sexualization is "the experience of being treated *as a body* (or collection of body parts) valued predominantly for its use to (or consumption by) others" (Fredrickson & Roberts, 1997, p. 174). As a specific form of objectification—sexual objectification—sexualization is crucial to understanding how individuals' bodies are understood as sexual objects and how this influences the way they understand themselves and are understood by others. Humm (1990) describes sexual objectification as "a primary process of subjugation of women, since objectification makes sexuality a material reality not simply a psychological, attitudinal or ideological one" (p. 207). Many of us may try to actively present ourselves as a sexual object to others. Frederickson and Roberts (1997) describe this as self-objectification, a process through which the observers' view or gaze is internalized. With provocative clothes, suggestive mannerisms, flirtatious gazes, and symbolic adornments, sexualization may extend objectification to a form of manipulation and control of sexuality in ways that a person does not necessarily anticipate or intend. Since we are concerned about how understanding sexualization can contribute to PCT, we will focus on the ways sexual bodies are seen as objects or canvases to be observed, who creates these embodied symbols, and for what intended audience. Some of the concerns raised in this chapter relate to how bodies are understood when they are inscribed, altered, or sexualized in different contexts. A number of questions are raised. These include: When are these changes an active process arising from feeling and being sexual? When are they used as a means to dehumanize an individual and contribute to disembodied sex? When does objectification detach the self and the fleshiness of sexuality from an individual, either by reshaping and inscribing bodies, or by using communication and robotic technology to disembody sexual experiences? Our interest in sexualized bodies includes the social context because it is critical to understand how the body, when inscribed and framed, is interpreted.

Considerable research has been conducted in psychology using objectification theory (Fredrickson & Roberts, 1997) to gain an understanding of the way women and girls have been socialized to internalize an observer's perspective as a way to perceive themselves. Research has also been conducted on the mental health issues that occur as a result of this process. From an early age, girls frequently gain positive feedback from family and friends for dressing in a provocative way that can be seen as participating in their own objectification. This is of great concern in terms of the socialization of girls, so much so that the American Psychological Association (2013) recently formed a task force to study the effects of sexualization on girls in order to intervene in this potentially harmful process, particularly given that it is taken for granted in most forms of media. Analysis of the ways objectification influences women's lives is part of feminist theory, particularly radical feminist theory, which links the male stance to women's sexual objectification. This was seen as the primary form of subjugation of women (MacKinnon, 1982), and it is also linked to women's experiences of alienation and violence. While this may have been a limited view on objectification, it was important for understanding harassment and violence against women, and the way that women appeared to participate in their own objectification by taking on the perspective on an androcentric society into which they were well socialized by the media, films, their peers, and the commodification of sexuality. The insight into the way one participates in one's oppression, including self-objectification (Fredrickson & Roberts, 1997), was subsequently developed further in masculinity studies, acknowledging that men are increasingly objectified in media presentations. This also contributes to the subjugation of men by creating an unusual awareness of the body as a sexual object in a contemporary context (APA, 2007). We would add that the process is also about acquiring a set of core role constructs that allow girls to construe themselves in a particular, detached manner as sexualized beings, bodies, and an assortment of body parts.

While there are a wide range of topics concerning sexualized bodies, we have selected five main topics that all expand on the ways inscribed bodies, whether embodied or disembodied, offer a particularly interesting window into understanding sexual and sexualized bodies. First, often ignored is the way whiteness is assumed in much of the theorizing of sexuality, yet skin colour has powerful sexual meanings. This point is evident in the racialization of gendered bodies that maps the underlying meanings of skin colour to meanings of sexuality. Second, staying with the idea of colonial history and the surface of the skin, but instead approaching skin as a canvas to create symbolic images, tattooing, piercing, and scarring in particular are considered as sexuality being literally embodied and made meaningful in both creative and oppressive ways. Third, shifting away from the fleshiness of bodies to the concerns raised by electronic technologies, the increasing interest in cyborgs draws attention to the blurred boundaries between human and machine both in enabling and limiting ways. Fourth, we will discuss how specific body parts become sexualized for some people. The sexualization of body parts and fetishes provides insights into how sexual arousal can be located in many different seemingly non-erogenous areas of the body, and can perhaps be sparked by odd experiences leading to strange connections. Finally, we conclude with a discussion of the way these examples of inscription, embodiment, and sexualization contribute to a PCT understanding of sexuality.

Racialized Bodies

If the surface of the body—the skin—is acknowledged to be sexualized, whether clothed or unclothed, then skin colour cannot be ignored in the racialization of some bodies over others. The meanings of femininities and masculinities are intimately linked to sexualities and racialization, which are too often held to the standards of whiteness as the ideal against which everyone else is measured. In many Western multicultural, racially and ethnically diverse countries, an ideology of colour blindness persists (Henry & Tator, 2009), which underestimates or ignores racialization based on skin colour by subtly reinforcing whiteness as norm. In the context of the USA and its history of colonialism and slavery, Collins (2004) provided a vivid analysis of black sexual politics that breaks through the veneer of colour blindness to expose the racialization and sexualization of black bodies. She argued that hegemonic masculinity and hegemonic femininity both set white heterosexual bodies as ideals, which marginalizes or subordinates women and men of colour. Postcolonial studies identified the ways colonization contributed to reinforcing a colour line in how bodies are understood sexually, and which bodies are most likely to be marginalized and objectified as sexual objects, or sexualized (Collins, 2004). If public perception is based on an unattainable ideal, it is certain to affect the way that bodies and sexualities are construed.

Ideals of women's beauty may include a wide range of features like size, shape, movement, hair texture and all that comprise body image, and the relevance of skin colour from tones of black to brown to white cannot be excluded. The colour of beauty can easily be ignored by the dominant white community of Western countries; and women of colour, who are rarely represented as beautiful in the media, have challenged such representation (Collins, 2004). Whether in advertising, film, or on social media, where images are the medium of communication, it is striking how skin colour is often seen as stigmatized, exoticized, demonized, and sexualized. Camille Turner used travelling performance art to challenge the beauty stereotype and the idea that Canada is represented by white bodies, and not black bodies. In her travelling performance piece, Turner, a Canadian woman of colour, convincingly and ironically adopted the character of a winner of a fictional beauty contest, Miss Canadiana, to expose the racialized stereotypes that she had experienced (see Videkanic, 2006).

A fundamental feature of racialization as a process is that it is literally a response that is marked by skin colour—the symbolic meanings that contribute to the sexualization of black- and brown-skinned individuals. The systemic process of racialization includes forms of discrimination based on the stereotyping of a person based on skin colour, which is embedded in society's social structure and affects experiences in education, work, and social control. It is also pervasive at the everyday level of social interactions, from subtle marginalization to blatant violence and victimization. The objectification and dehumanization from racialization is difficult to challenge and repeatedly painful to experience so persistently. Sexuality and sexual identity are areas of everyday life that are certainly not immune to racialization; however, the process of racialization around sexuality is so often taken for granted that it appears that the visible is at the same time made invisible yet stigmatized. Since there is a general trend of reclaiming the body in terms of sexuality, making skin colour more visible in media and in everyday interactions is important, because difference and diversity can easily be ignored.

Collins' (2000) black feminist analysis focuses on the intersection of racialization, gender, and sexuality. She investigates how black skin is interpreted when heterosexuality is normalized. As she wrote, "regardless of individual behavior, being white marks the normal category of heterosexuality. In contrast, being black signals the wild, out-of-control hypersexuality of excessive sexual appetite" (Collins, 2000, p. 129). While Collins described how both men and women of colour are sexualized, she was particularly concerned about the ways this process affects women. Black women's genitalia, especially vaginas, seem to be a point of general interest and speculation, and Collins believes that this reduces them, on one level, to sex trade workers. In a similar manner, current media and popular culture portrayals of black women as nothing but body parts (e.g., buttocks, breasts) function to commodify black bodies and body parts. If this is how women of colour see themselves represented, particularly in the media, clearly it contributes to how sexuality is construed in the racialized social contexts of their lives. Collins (1986) stresses that she is not interested in changing the way femininity for black women often includes being assertive and sassy, instead, she sees the need to value this representation over stereotypical white femininity which is based on meekness and docility.

The interrelation between sexual violence and the sexualization of men and women of colour is a disturbing indication of the persistence of stigmatization linked to racism. Black feminist theorists, who were concerned that the oppression of both women and men of colour is understood as systemic and too often is taken for granted, grappled with this issue. Hooks (1990), a feminist social theorist, was also concerned with the disturbing way men of colour were represented in American society. For Hooks, images of black men "as rapists, as dangerous menaces to society, have been sensational cultural currency for some time" (p. 61). Similarly, Collins (2000) pointed out that "rape has been one fundamental tool of sexual violence directed against African-American women" (p. 146). This refers to African-American women's history of being exploited sexually during colonization and slavery, which continues in new ways in contemporary contexts even after continued efforts at social change. Collins argued that the way sexual violence is experienced based on skin colour and gender means that "Black women, Black men, and White women experience distinctive forms of sexual violence" (p. 147).

The stigmatization of people of colour is made doubly clear when considering the experiences of gay and bisexual men of colour, where intersections of several oppressive criteria stand out. Bowleg's (2013) qualitative study on gay and bisexual men of colour described not only how their identities are formed, but also the persistence of racialization in their lives. Bowleg's study participants described how, in the predominantly white LGBT community, they are marginalized and experience racism because of their skin colour, while in the black community, they are marginalized because of their sexual identity, which is a challenge to black heterosexual masculinity. Since they are both outsiders and insiders in both spaces, Bowleg used intersectional analysis as a means to explain the complexity of the effects of different social identities in study participants' everyday lives. From a PCT perspective, this experience of being insiders and outsiders in these communities creates new constructs (e.g., my people versus not my people), and these new constructs then contribute to much more complex sexual identities for these black gay and bisexual men.

Orientalism is another version of racialization relevant to the objectification of the bodies of the "other". It was described by Said (1977) as the way the Orient (i.e., the East) has been constructed through the objectifying gaze of the Occident (i.e., the West). He was interested in the depiction of young women and men from colonized countries, often as sexual objects, in texts and paintings that were distributed primarily in the colonizer's country in the Occident, and the concept has been expanded to explain many situations framed by Orientalism in people's lives (e.g., Asian immigrants to North American countries). This was a particular representation of the Orient through the eyes of colonizers and Western society, rather than a reflection on any interest in understanding the reality of these youths' lives in colonized countries. Cummings (2003) also drew on this concept of Orientalism to describe the texts and stories that were associated with the appropriation of tattoos by sailors as early as the late 1700s. Sailors dressed and appeared different from their landlocked fellows with tattoos contributing to their sense of difference to the point that they identified as a distinctive subculture, a subculture that flourished in ports, "the physical as well as social margins of the nation and body politic" (Cummings, 2003, p. 19). The tattoos not only included exotic images of adventures in distant lands with stories to be told, they also turned the body into a canvas that likely enhanced sailors' masculinity and sexual appeal. Tattooing is a form of inscription of the body that has been developed extensively as a form of body modification in contemporary contexts.

Inscribed Bodies

What happens when the surface of the body, the skin, is inscribed such that it becomes a means of expressing one's identity or tracing one's autobiography? Instead of a focus on clothing, cosmetics, or jewellery, what if designs on the skin are used to make the body more attractive, to draw attention to the object of desire and to take advantage of one's skin as artist's canvas? Forms of body art, tattooing being the most popular, are a way for youth in many Western societies to express themselves, often in sexual ways. A woman's tattoo of a string of roses that is partially visible on her lower back in a short or cropped top can be intended not only as self-expression but also sexual suggestion to imagine where tracing the rest of the image leads the observer. Men, too, can employ this device.

A tattoo of a dragon on male biceps may be entirely visible and intentionally focus attention on strength or potency. Placement elsewhere on the male body can also be suggestive, although not very subtle in the case of penile tattoos. Considering use of skin to enhance body image can provide an opportunity to study construct formation and change.

In a contemporary context, body modification covers a wide range of practices from tattoos, piercings, branding and scarring on any area of the body, to body transformations like breast implants, hormone treatments, and reshaping of genitalia. Relevant to PCT are the body modifications that are forms of adornment—body art and markers of self-identity such as tattooing, piercing, and scarification. According to Schildkrout (2004), "tattoos, scars, brands, and piercings, when voluntarily assumed, are ways of writing one's autobiography on the surface of the body" (p. 338). Body art has been transformed over the past century from being the cultural practices of the "other" and a stigmatized practice within Western cultures to becoming almost mainstream among middle-class youth. Since tattooing, or the insertion of pigments under the skin to create permanent marks on the skin's surface, has been studied longer and from several different perspectives, more emphasis is placed on tattooed persons in this discussion. When, where, and how these inscriptions of the body are understood and interpreted as sexual or sexualized are interesting questions to ponder.

Anthropology research has shown that body art was present in a variety of forms in all cultures, although the ways tattooing in particular is interpreted has changed. An important change concerns whether or not the images are mutually understood by one's community or are individually interpreted. In reference to tattoos, Turner (1999) pointed out that in preliterate societies "because they were set within a shared society of collective meanings, the significance of the tattoo could be read unambiguously" (p. 39), and many were associated with rites of passage. As tattoo images became appropriated by colonizers, the cultural symbols became part of the body art of the exotic "other", and the images became the visual representation of Orientalism (Schildkrout, 2004). In contemporary contexts, this has changed because "body marks no longer need to indicate or to define gender in the life-cycle, and so they become optional, playful and ironic" (Turner, 1999, p. 41).

The perceiving of the skin of one's body as a space to be inscribed and a canvas for expressing identity, life experiences, group membership, and adornment is a contemporary manner of interpreting tattooing, piercing, and even scarification. Some youth in many Western countries are heavily tattooed, not necessarily due to cultural practices or traditional rites of passage, but as a voluntary process to express oneself and one's identity. Pitts (2003) described the Modern Primitive movement in body modification, primarily inscribed on white skin, as the appropriation of indigenous symbols (e.g., Celtic, Maori) so as to comprise a spiritual ritual that protects the tattooed person from the problems of the modern world. The different ways of interpreting body modification, and tattooing in particular, represent a significant switch in the meaning of tattoos that has occurred since the 1990s.

Ferreira (2014) studied heavily tattooed youth and pointed out that "young people of the present times are part of a cultural world where the sense of self is not separated from the feeling of embodiment… The body is a medium of expression, of self-experience and of self-recognition." (p. 304). Cummings (2003) added that another way of interpreting some of these practices is that tattooed Westerners acquired their body art without necessarily travelling overseas, but attempted to portray themselves as "authentically Oriental" (p. 28). At times, the body is also used as a canvas for sexual expression to enhance sexual relations.

While body art in many Western countries became popular after the 1960s (Pitts, 2003), the new body art technologies that have become more evident since the 1990s represent an increasingly positive way of understanding body modification, and they can be seen as involving a series of personal constructs. While the stigmatized stereotype has been a required mark of membership in gangs, prisons, the military, among sailors, BDSM groups, and even working-class culture, there has been a shift that legitimizes tattoos (DeMello, 1995). In many Western countries, since the 1990s, tattooing has been more visible in the mainstream, outside of a tattoo subculture, throughout celebrity societies, and even in offices in the business world, primarily claimed by men but increasingly visible with women. DeMello (1995), who traced the changes in the perception of tattoos in a North American context, concluded that what was once a counter-hegemonic and stigmatized practice has changed recently to a middle-class body art seldom challenged in mainstream culture. This represents not only a shift in visibility but also legitimization. The middle-class claimed tattoos as body art, leading to an interesting intersection of gender, sexuality and class.

DeMello's (2000) thorough study of contemporary tattoo communities, primarily in North America, also raised the issue of class when she pointed to the tension between tattooed people, social class, and tattoo symbolization. As she wrote, "I would suggest that tattoos… are a form of body praxis and that men and women, gays and straights, and working-class and middle-class people will all approach tattoos differently, based on their own social positions" (p. 140). Of interest in DeMello's analysis is a working-class view of flexible bodies linked to tattoos as symbols of affiliation versus a middle-class view reflecting body self-control with finer artwork. She pointed out that, when contemporary tattoos are carefully designed, it is as if the body is seen as a temple with tattoos as decoration. Changes in the social class of tattooed persons and the meanings of the tattoos contribute to a new set of constructs, or at least a new way of interpreting tattoos, both for the tattooed person and the onlookers or admirers. What might have been construed before as weird and repulsive is now seen as different and attractive. Actual research on body modification and body art, especially tattoos, that focus on sexuality is surprisingly limited. This seems to be an odd oversight, perhaps partially attributable to the class-based stigma that researchers associated with body modification as deviant or pathologized until recently. Whatever be the case, the few areas where sexuality has been taken into account provide some important insights into the meanings of sexual body art.

In psychological literature, and perhaps indicative of a continuation of the body modification and deviance link, there is an interesting association made between tattoos on youth as indicators of earlier, more frequent, and riskier sexual activity than in non-tattooed youth (Rivardo & Keelan, 2010; Gueguen, 2012; Frederic & Bradley, 2000). While the evidence may support this claim, it is worth questioning whether the tattoos are more an indicator of nonconformity that includes being sexually active at an earlier age, and not so directly linked to risky sexual practices. Unfortunately, the surveys used in Gueguen's (2012) study of over 2000 French university students did not ask detailed questions about the what the tattoos meant to the young respondents. Research investigating body art intention and meaning is more relevant to PCT, except that Gueguen's survey research did not clarify what sexual motivation meant to its participants, because it did not include questions about whether, for instance, sexual enhancement was a goal. Research that does reveal far more about the relevance of sexuality to tattooing and piercing generally involved more detailed interviews or ethnographic research (e.g., Atkinson, 2002), where participants are allowed to expand on what sexual interests and practices they associate with tattooing.

While it is often assumed that tattooing is for men, or reflects masculinity, even when women get tattooed, Atkinson (2002) challenged this claim. For Atkinson, researchers "have overlooked the extent to which many North American women's tattooing projects express a degree of consent to 'hegemonic masculinity' constructions of femininity" (p. 220). His study of 30 Canadian women's narratives showed that, as women got tattooed, generally with much hesitation during the initial stages, they tended to select images and placement that emphasized femininity. The tattoos were often animals, flowers, or celestial images that were placed in areas of the body that were both usually concealed and often sexualized. The visible placement of images in areas like ankles and wrists were then seen as jewellery and feminine, while heavy images with visible placement were seen as masculine. All these examples, from Atkinson's perspective, demonstrated how contemporary tattooing for women reinforces femininity and conforms to ideals created by hegemonic masculinity.

In some areas that can be considered non-mainstream body modification and body art, there appears to be a direct connection to sexual expression and enticement. Myers (1992) noted that sexual enhancement was an important reason for people to modify their bodies, "whatever the motivational category, there was typically a sexual interest lurking somewhere behind the individual's decisions to alter their bodies. (p. 288). In this study of genital piercing, Myers' participants made direct connections to the enhancement of sexual sensitivity and stimulation, both for the pierced person and their partner. According to Myers (1992), "piercing devotees believe that one's imagination and resourcefulness are the only limitations to the various sexual pleasures that can be derived from piercing." (p. 290). Similar obvious links to sexual pleasure were made by participants in Kleese's (1999) study of the Modern Primitives movement in the San Francisco area, a group that is linked to BDSM practices. Sexualization and exoticism were evident in the choice of genital and other piercings, as well as tattooing, among the body art of Modern Primitivism.

Although interpretation is limited by the few research questions asked about the sexual meanings of body art to those who get it done and to those interested in it, we would suggest that a range of constructions are likely in place here. "Edgy", "cool", and "beautiful" are all possible and common constructs applied to novel body art, and it is not difficult to see how such constructs can be seen as associated with desire, especially if the art being described is placed on the upper thigh, lower abdomen, or buttocks. As sexual attention devices, tattoos and piercings no doubt function well, but at the same time, they are not temporary additions such as "glue-on" moles or marks to draw attention to attractive facial features in days past. As permanent alterations of the body, contemporary body art has much more of a chance of altering the sexual identity of the "walking palette" than any transitory art or device. Whether the core role constructs added or altered by such body art are permanent or not, probably depend to a large extent on changing meanings, both personal and social, of the particular work of art. Terminated or even long-term but altered relationships with a significant connection to the piece of body art may produce a new perspective on the piece as well as a new view of oneself, for better or worse.

Cyborg Possibilities

Information and communication technologies have contributed in remarkable ways to what tends to be called the information age, transforming the way we communicate locally and globally in our everyday interactions, with many youth barely able to survive a day without a smartphone; basically, their personal palm-sized computer has become part of them. Changes in the way people connect with family, friends, colleagues, and strangers though different internet services and social media inevitably contributes to how sexuality is experienced and understood today and in the future. Currently, many video games (e.g., Avatar) and social media sites (e.g., SecondLife.com) offer users the option of creating an avatar identity, basically to claim a virtual identity with an idealized body of any or all sexualities to live out one's fantasies as relief from, or in addition to, everyday life in the real world. Imagining the virtual reality of identity-shifting, by experimenting with avatars, characters in gaming, and on-line sex is intriguing, because such experiences may give a person an opportunity to literally try out different identities in a virtual community before taking that step in their everyday real life. The ways that the internet and social media change everyday interactions, and give users access to different forms of sexuality, gives pause to considerations of developments and future changes in sexualities (see Chapter 10 for further discussion).

This moving between virtual and real locations can be exciting, and potentially opens up many avenues where new constructs could contribute to the way a person experiences and makes sense of their sexuality and sexual identity. Virtual and embodied experiences of gendered social relations that are facilitated by electronic and information technologies, can also be enabling and limiting, and provide intriguing insights into how individuals construe their social and sexual identities. In this section we consider the ways in which bodies are reframed and technologies are embodied in unique ways as cyborgs, and raise questions about the boundaries of bodies, machines and technologies, and everyday lives.

Cyborgs, as versions of cybernetic organisms, are a blend of animal, human and machine, whether in science fiction or in the real life of prosthetic limbs and wearable computers (Gray et al., 1995). While these mixtures of human, animal and machine are not new, the extent to which technologies are embodied in our everyday lives requires a rethinking of many topics, including sexuality (Haraway, 1985). What is novel is that instead of thinking about the lines between bodies, machines, and technologies as rigid and independent of one another, not unlike a binary analysis, current information and electronic technologies often blur those obvious boundaries. No longer do we jump to answer a ringing phone attached to a wall or put letters in a mailbox at the end of our street, instead we depend on smartphones and computers in most long-distance communication, yet it seems as close as our fingertips. This process tends to feel seamless without clear boundaries between ourselves and information technology that now shapes and controls our lives. In most Western countries, the ungainly artificial legs that would have in the past labelled and stigmatized a person as disabled or worse have been replaced by technologically enabled, specialized prosthetic limbs. Especially striking are the blades on runners' feet and a vice used as a hand to hold a stick or a bat that blends almost seamlessly into the immediate environment of a person's body (Howe, 2011).

The meaning of cyborgs to sexuality is interpreted through Donna Haraway's (1985) perspective that we are now experiencing a new technological environment that straddles machines, virtual reality, and real lives. In Haraway's (1985) article on cyborg feminism, she framed the relationship of humans to technologies using the cyborg as the core metaphor. The metaphor of the cyborg was a way for Haraway to not only challenge and breach the boundaries between the human, animal, and machine, but also to break the boundaries of gender. She imagined the cyborg as an entity that straddled the human and the other. Of interest in this project are the boundaries breached between humans and machines. She questioned what that means in terms of rethinking sexuality in the contemporary context of the information age when access to technology, specifically communication technologies, is taken for granted in many countries.

Haraway (1985) challenged the way boundaries are set up between animals, humans, and machines by suggesting that these boundaries are blurred, and have been so for a long time. In particular, she claimed that humans and technology are intimately connected, and even embodied in some situations. Instead of seeing this link between humans and technology as unusual, she took it for granted as a way to breach boundaries and imagine the consequences this could have on people's lives. While cyborgs are a concept that can expand the way sexuality as desire and pleasure can be understood, it is the questions that are raised by cyborg experiences that are more relevant to PCT. When is the experience of being a cyborg a process of objectification that is disembodied or dehumanizing or discriminatory? When does this experience enhance one's life, particularly sexuality? Some of these questions are raised again in the final chapter when we imagine sexualities in future social contexts.

The term "cyborg" has captured people's imagination in different ways to describe not only the physical and psychological experience of being part human and part machine, but also the space between boundaries, or liminal space, in different contexts. Whitney (2002) draws on cyborg feminism for a personal and political means to include liminal sexual identities, like bisexuality, that might otherwise be ignored, challenged, or discredited. She struggles with the gaps between theory and praxis in terms of bisexuality being included in queer theory abstractly, but in reality, the dualistic thinking that often defines gay and lesbian communities and queer politics can explicitly marginalize bisexuals. Because of this situation of inclusion and exclusion, the metaphor of the cyborg with its blurred boundaries is meaningful due to the liminal space in which bisexuals can find themselves.

Cyborgs are a way to describe some of the more material-based ways of changing social interactions through robotics, prosthetics, implants, and pharmaceuticals. The use of these technologies is not limited to robots to improve productivity and replace workers, to prosthetics as replacement limbs for para-athletes, implants to electronically control bodily functions, and pharmaceuticals to enhance well-being, they also contribute to changes in social interactions leading to different ways of understanding sexuality. From a PCT perspective, the addition of constructs that are related to being a kind of cyborg, in one of its many forms, far beyond the expansion of sex toys and paraphernalia, changes how sexuality is experienced and interpreted.

The use of prostheses for disabled athletes is an example of becoming cyborg. It is a striking transformation in people's lives that also attracts considerable media attention (Howe, 2011). With such dramatic changes in people's lives, all based on an ability to cope with one's cyborg body, does it change one's self-concept in ways other than athletics, including expressions of masculinity, femininity, and sexuality? A situation where this question has been raised, where the impact of cyborg bodies did raise issues of sexuality, in an empowering way, is in the lives of people with disabilities who actively create a sexual body image that embraces their enabling technology. Carlson (2013) studied how people dependent on wheelchairs see themselves, and how their cyborg identity contributes to perceptions of themselves as sexual, and of becoming a sexual person.

Her qualitative research explores how women dependent on wheelchairs attempt to transform stereotypes of disabled women, particularly as asexual and incompetent. Women participants made their wheelchairs part of their identity as they actively adorned themselves with stylish clothing, to the extent of wearing sexy high-heeled shoes without the awkwardness of actually walking on them. The study emphasizes that these cyborg women in wheelchairs were sexual, presented themselves to others as sexual, and were not easily defeated by the restrictions or stigma of their wheelchairs. These cyborg women blurred boundaries between themselves and their enabling technologies allowing them freedom to be sexual and act sexually.

Possibilities for cyborgs appear limited only by scientists' and designers' imaginations. While this kind of topic often gets lost in technical details at the expense of the humans behind the machines and electronics, we argue that seeing these technologies as part of a social relation that involves people in very tangible ways is essential. In many situations, this also involves the addition of constructs that become a part of the way people understand themselves sexually or contribute to their sexual practices.

Sexualized Body Parts

It is probably true that whenever and wherever people have donned clothing, that at least some have used clothes to draw attention to certain body parts or areas for sexual purposes (Flugel, 1930). The use of clothing to accent body parts sexually might be interesting, but what is truly fascinating is that body parts sometimes become the focus, sometimes the sole focus, of sexual attention and desire. While much of the professional concern with regard to sexual fascination with particular body parts is about the pathology and treatment of such sexual attention, we prefer to see such desires as an oddity rather than illness, one that surely requires an explanation but rarely treatment. We believe that PCT can shed some light on sexual obsessions with particular body parts.

When considering body part obsessions, it is important to attempt to limit the nature of the inquiry. We are not concerned here with related notions such as erogenic, erotogenic, or erogenous zones. As Freud

(1905/1975) argued within his emerging psychoanalytic framework, erogenic zones are body parts or areas where libidinal energy concentrated to produce pleasurable sensations during stimulation, but the energy shifted throughout development to fix finally on the genitals, assuming successful progression through the developmental stages. Ellis (1906/1920) expanded on this idea, adopting the term "erogenous zone", to refer to any area of the body capable of arousing erotic excitement such as "the palm of the hand, the nape of the neck" (p. 143). Recent research (Cordeau et al., 2014) has found that, not too surprisingly, that areas like the clitoris and nipples in adult females are especially sensitive to touch. Rather than delve into the hows and whys of such notions, we would rather consider the nature of what has been termed "body part fetishes".

The construct or notion of a sexual fetish, borrowed from a European term for idols or "charms" used to represent a god or spirit carried by non-European non-Christians, has become a broad term for any body part or object that produces a very distinct sexual response. In a very real sense, the fetish item or non-genital body part is the source of sexual arousal for the individual. When referencing body parts, the term partialism has been used frequently, at least until recently (see APA, 2013), when the most recent version of the *DSM* avoided its use in an attempt to transform "sexual kink" from disorder to variation, despite still being considered a paraphilia or "love disorder". Sexual arousal caused by non-genital body parts appears to be the most common fetish grouping, accounting for more than 30% of fetishes (Scorolli et al., 2007), although the internet-based survey conducted by Scorolli and colleagues included body markings (e.g., tattoos, piercings) along with body parts or areas of the human body. The important question that remains is: How can a non-genital body part like a foot or an ear-lobe produce extreme and complete sexual arousal?

Explanatory accounts of sexual fetishes involving body parts have been few and far between, or at least rather incomplete, to date. Binet (1887), who was perhaps the first to use the term "fetish" to describe this form of "perversion sexuelle" (p. 144), offered one explanation. For Binet, fetishes were the result of an association of ideas. The small and elegant foot or hand of an attractive woman might, for the right man, become connected with ideas like beauty and lust and thereby produce a strong sexual response. Binet was not very clear on why or for whom the body part can become sexualized, but at least he attempted to account for such a fetish desire. Ellis (1906/1920), too, relied on the association of ideas to explain foot fetishes, and he provided more detail than Binet. According to Ellis, ideas related to body fetishes can occur through "seemingly accidental associations or shocks early in life" (p. 28). He described an example of a boy who stumbled across the town beauty combing her long and beautiful hair and developed a fetish for hair that lasted his entire adult life. The exact nature of why this moment produced such a reaction in this particular boy was not explained—might we not all have hair or foot fetishes if associations between body parts and sexual attractiveness was so simple?—but, again, at least we were provided with a brave and reasonable explanatory attempt.

More recent and detailed accounts have been provided. Freud (1905/1975) offered an explanation for a male client's body part fetish, rather fortuitously, a nose. Noses can become fetish parts as the result of the sexual substitution of a nose for a mother's penis, a belief of all males but typically discarded with time, a belief that Freud contended his client refused to abandon. Also offered as an explanation of an adult male client's foot fetish—it was due to his attempt to look up his mother's skirt, but her feet were in his line of sight of her genitalia. Such attempts to account for particular body part fetishes might win Freud top marks for imagination, but a failure in terms of irresistibility or convincingness. Rachman (1966) succeeded in using classical conditioning to produce a sexual response to a previously neutral stimulus (viz., a pair of women's boots) among a small group of male research participants. Unfortunately, subsequent attempts to replicate this study, including a sustained effort by one of us (JH), have proved less successful—perhaps the use of abstract shapes (i.e., triangles) as a conditioned stimulus is far too ambitious or remote from the sexual experience of young, heterosexual males. It appears that, while there may be a learning component to fetish acquisition among those few mostly adolescent males who do acquire an extreme sexual interest in body parts, classical and operant conditioning alone cannot account for fetishes. Learning associations of constructs, however, might provide a more elegant and compelling account of fetish acquisition.

It may seem far too diplomatic, but Binet, Freud, and Rachman may all have made a contribution to interpreting body fetish. One problem with all their understandings, however, appears to be the limited, individual psychological perspective that each adopts. Viewing sexual fetish in a broader cultural and social context seems necessary. As Dant (1996) pointed out, both Freud and Marx began to discuss the notion of fetishism at about the same time and, although each had a particular and very different use for the term, each made a contribution to expanding the notion. For Marx, fetishism occurs within a capitalist economy where there is a tendency towards commodification and the division of things, both literally and figuratively, into constituent and saleable parts. Bodies, even in a sexual manner, are considered in terms of important aspects (e.g., "get a piece of ass"), and this may account for an increase in body part fetishes in the West over the past couple of centuries, if indeed there has been one which is difficult to determine. There does, however, seem to be some suggestion and limited evidence of cultural differences in terms of body part fetish (Scorolli et al., 2007) as would be expected given different socio-economic conditions. In a general sense, this points to a social limitation on personal constructs as we have maintained, if only by implication.

The more personal experiential aspects of body part fetish emergence are difficult to pinpoint, but they may well have much to do with interactions between development and idiosyncratic encounters that take on a sexual import due to conditions conducive to learning. As Binet (1887) suggested, the association of particular ideas, like hair and erotic beauty, might occur during a particular encounter. Associationism or associationistic psychology, with a long and storied history (see Warren, 1921), has always focused on the connection between ideas and the principles by which ideas become associated within the mind. It is not a long leap, however, to see constructs as the foundational aspects of beliefs (Horley, 1991), as forming the real mental connections. Abstracted elements or things like hair or feet are perceived to have certain characteristics, and after a particularly eventful encounter with hair, perhaps leaving one breathlessly hoping for some way of making sense of the profound impact that the hair had (i.e., present construct system falls short), a new set of associated constructs are no doubt the result. These novel or repurposed constructs may dictate a new and exciting way of regarding hair in general, but more likely a particular pattern of hair according to the original "exciting" hair based on the perceived erotic characteristics (e.g., length, colour, shape) becomes the object of sensual and sexual obsession. Although the effect may be instantaneous, a number of exposures along with the creation of relevant fantasies, perhaps accompanied by masturbation, are likely necessary before a truly obsessive sexual fetish is cemented in place, and here is where the learning conditions and the role of learning principles are relevant. Again, the specific constructs involved are difficult to determine, and no one is likely to insist that the same set will be present for all individuals with a similar body part obsession, but all will be viewed as relevant to the individual hair fetishist's interpretation of arousing and non-arousing coiffures.

Body parts as a component of sexuality can be viewed in many more ways than just in terms of fetishes, and Ringrose and colleagues (e.g., Ringrose & Harvey, 2015; Ringrose, Harvey, Gill, & Livingstone, 2013) have examined the meanings and consequences of sexting with a focus on female teens. They pointed out that internet digital technology means that images of bodies and body parts are exchangeable and can turn into differentially valued commodities that circulate on virtual social networks. As noted by Ringrose and Harvey (2015), sexting, or the sending of nude photos, often of specific body parts, via the internet to phones or computers, seems to be a modern social problem or even a "postfeminist moral panic" (p. 205) where teenage girls are viewed as both exploited victims of male oppressors and uncontrolled agents of self-sexualization. Among their many findings from various qualitative research projects, they demonstrated that postings of exposed female breasts, whether alone or in a full-body shot, tended to mean for both female and male viewers that the female was "slutty", and the larger the breasts the greater the degree of "sluttiness". Teenaged males, on the other hand, did not seem to be held to the same standards and could increase their reputation and desirability by posting nude body part photos of themselves or even those of teenaged girls. Ringrose and Harvey (2015) concluded that teenaged girls as opposed to teenaged boys were at a disadvantage in the display and performance of active sexuality on internet-based social media.

Certainly the concern with body parts and sexualization can be seen as being part of a larger issue. Fredrickson and Roberts (1997) have argued that females are socialized to accept an observer's perspective, typically a white male perspective, of their bodies as their own view of their physical self. This internalization process is long and subtle, but it has very marked and negative effects on women's health and well-being. One aspect of this process, presented by Fredrickson and Roberts (1997) as objectification theory, is that girls, and eventually women, come to see themselves as collections of body parts that are evaluated in terms of their sexual appeal to others, mostly by white, middle-class men. While the sexual fascination and fixation of certain individuals with body part fetishes seems to go well beyond such an explanation, this explanation may well set the stage for the subsequent development of body part fetishes for a small minority of individuals, who appear to be mostly men. We would note here, too, that objectification theory is compatible to some extent with PCT, especially an expanded psychosocial PCT, insofar as Fredrickson and Roberts refer to selfhood as constructed.

7

Sexual Commodification: Pornography, Prostitution, and Personal Constructs

Sexual desire is a personal, if not extremely intimate, aspect of most individuals' lives. At the same time, it is an increasingly public part of everyday lives in the form of advertising and other components of global capitalism. In spite of periodic moral outrage and limited restrictive legislation, the sex industry continues to generate massive annual profits internationally. With the assistance of information technologies, this expansion continues with even fewer restrictions. Commercial sex is by no means unique to capitalist economies, but it takes on a particular form as a commodity with the massive reach of global capitalism. The market is not critical of what is bought, sold, and traded, as long as it generates a profit. The process of sexual commodification involves turning sexuality, in all its forms, from reproduction to bodies to sex acts, into objects of economic desire for exchange in the marketplace. While sex as a commodity can be used to sell pleasant and benign objects like crimson lipstick through pictures of naked or near-naked bodies, the trouble with the commodification of sexuality is that sexuality can become detached from people's experiences, intentionally exploitative, and downright harmful.

In this chapter we discuss only two aspects of sexual commodification: pornography and sex work. These two topics might appear to be the two most obvious and most discussed, but Weitzer (2009) has noted that pornography is often ignored in social science investigations, although this lack of concern may be shifting given increasing research on the topic over the past several years. In our examination, we aim to question how and when the commodification of sexuality is exploitative and oppressive, and when is it more positive. The debate on the pros and cons of erotica and pornography, and the question of which is which, exemplifies the way that exploitative pornography dominates the market in so many areas. In comparison, erotica has become even difficult to recognize and has almost become lost in the market. Our concern is the less visible effects of porn and erotica—the potential impact on the construction processes of participants and consumers. We also address some aspects of the sex trade business, but our focus is on the constructs of workers and clients.

Pornography and PCT

Media of any type are sources of construction. Many parents who have set their toddler in front of a television set have returned later to discover that the youngster has acquired strange, novel behaviors and perhaps undesirable language. No doubt, too, they have acquired new and possibly brilliant ways of viewing the world. Another medium, expanding over the past two decades largely due to the expansion of the internet, is sexually explicit or sexually focused movies. Often labelled "pornography", this medium is not just a source of low-cost or no-cost excitement and arousal, but it is an important source of sexual construction. Before discussing the possible impact of sexually explicit movies and related materials, a brief consideration of an important distinction appears required. Sexually explicit materials can be divided into two separate yet somewhat overlapping types—erotica and pornography—and we believe that such a distinction has merits. As Steinem (1980) argued, not only can erotica and pornography be separated, but they should be separated, in that violence has neither an acceptable nor a required relationship with sex. A major problem with the use of an emotionally-laden term such as pornography is that it means many different things to many different people, and such a state of affairs is especially problematic when conducting and interpreting research on the effect of materials described as pornographic. Some effort to define such a term seems obligatory here beyond a weak response such as "I know it when I see it" (Andrews, 2012, p. 457). Unfortunately, very few writers define their terms or attempt to make any sense of difficult notions such as pornography. We will present a very brief examination here.

Erotica Versus Pornography: Defining Our Terms

Typically, within social science research on pornography, especially within psychology, few distinctions are made between pornography and erotica. Whether this is due to the view that separating sexually explicit material renders "scientific operational definitions difficult to construct" (Malamuth & Billings, 1986, p. 84), or whether the research reflects an implicit religious or moral position that all depictions of nudity and sexuality are "evil" or "wrong", it seems to be a mistake (Steinem, 1980). By grouping together a broad range of depictions, the effects of explicit yet consenting and "gentle" sexual encounters can be confounded with the impact of aggressive, non-consenting sexuality. In other words, the effects of each are "washed out" by an understanding of all sexual depictions as equal. Definitions of pornography that are too broad may explain why research into its effects tends to be highly inconsistent. Some reviewers have concluded that there are clear negative effects on children and youth (Flood, 2009); others have concluded that "it is time to discard the hypothesis that pornography contributes to increased sexual assault" (Ferguson & Hartley, 2009, p. 323); while still others perhaps wisely have described the research to date as resulting in "more questions than answers" (Fisher & Barak, 1991, p. 65). Obviously, such a result can be avoided by scrupulously defining the particular form of stimuli presented to research participants, such as "aggressive erotic films" (Donnerstein & Berkowitz, 1981), but this approach still leaves little room for clear distinctions that might produce more useful research, and it colors an entire category of potentially positive sexual depictions as somewhat tainted or morally suspect. While we might be able to agree with Malamuth and Billings (1986) that there will always be some overlap between pornography and erotica, such agreement does not override efforts to distinguish and to use the two terms as somewhat distinct.

The question "What is pornography?" has been tackled by many thinkers and theorists, perhaps none as systematic and legalistic as Rea (2001). After providing a detailed discussion on several categories of definitions, including pornography as bad art and as sexual material offensive to community standards, and rejecting all as inadequate, Rea (2001) offered a provisional definition of pornography as material intended to be sexually arousing that is indeed sexually arousing. Such a succinct definition with a limited concern (i.e., sexual arousal) might appear to be an easy solution to definitional woes, but this definition, like many other attempts, makes no attempt to separate pornography from other related notions such as erotica. It also seems to ignore some other important considerations in the typical or common use of the term. What, for example, is not capable of causing sexual arousal? Some catalogues with pictures of models in undergarments can no doubt produce arousal. If we accept that "clothed porn"—where there is no nudity—is a sub-genre of pornography (Andrews, 2012), though it may be better described as "clothed erotica", it appears that pornography refers to everything and nothing at the same time. Some limits on our concern appear essential—less legality and more nuance is required if we are to address issues related to the impact of sexually explicit material.

Erotica, when it has been separated from pornography, has also been defined very succinctly. It has, for example, been described as any "sexually explicit material that presents nonviolent, non-degrading, and consensual sexual activity" (Fisher & Barak, 1991, p. 66). While Fisher and Barak acknowledge that such a definition is far from perfect, it does seem to capture important features of erotica. This definition contrasts erotica nicely with other material, especially today, that seems to typically have themes such as abuse, aggression, and degradation. Erotica as the material related to erotic love or sensuality seems to have a number of features that can distinguish it from pornography or the writings about or by prostitutes. In reference to love, erotica does, or can, relate to sensuality or sexuality that involves mutual pleasure. Many depictions of sexuality—gay, straight, and otherwise—show encounters where all participants experience physical delight, if not orgasm. Pornography, on the other hand, as the domain of prostitution, is about one-way pleasure (i.e., he who pays the piper calls the tune). Frequently, the tune is unpleasant for the provider of the service. As Dines (2010) has argued, pornography depicts women as "porn stars", the receptacles or servicers of men, especially within the "gonzo porn" of recent years. The men in turn degrade, humiliate, and harm the women, in part because they are seen as "whores" who actually desire or deserve rough treatment and abuse. There is certainly no concern with the pleasure of a woman involved in an encounter where she is being penetrated roughly by three men at the same time. While gonzo porn is more a style or form of film-making, which involves hand-held cameras and many close-up shots (see Tibbals, 2014), much of the heterosexual content in recent gonzo efforts presents women as more passive participants and objects of the action. They are often presented as insatiable sluts, wanting more and more of whatever use and abuse the male participants are interested in. Based on a strong foundation mutuality, erotica seems to depict or to involve consent. All participants agree, not just at the start of the proceedings but throughout, to all aspects of the sexual acts. Pornography, again with gonzo porn at the forefront, often shows women or men in positions of helplessness and with an inability to decline some or all of what is inflicted on them. They may not be in a situation where the term "rape" would definitely apply, but they appear to be suffering and desiring the end of the experience. Erotica, then, appears to be more about mutual pleasure, whereas pornography is about personal male pleasure, at least when straight porn is concerned. Mainstream contemporary gay and lesbian versions of pornography seem to represent or present less aggressive sexual depictions, despite each having more violent sub-genres, although objectification of the body and body parts are common.

A number of writers (e.g., Dines, 2010; Fredrickson & Roberts, 1997) have written about pornography and the objectification of women. Female porn stars are not so much complete, successful women as they are a collection of breasts (often oversized), vaginas (often infantilized), and buttocks (often exaggerated). Gay porn, likewise, seems to objectify certain participants, typically more passive or effeminate ones, which of course could be seen as reflecting the trend of female objectification, but may represent a more complex issue. Representing women or men as receptacles of other individuals' bodily fluids and the brunt of their aggression and abuse does nothing to humanize the sexual act, rather, it dehumanizes it. Erotica, conversely, portrays individuals as active, interested agents in sexual acts where sexuality is depicted as positive, pleasurable, and life affirming.

The internet. in particular, appears to be the media domain of pornography. Barron and Kimmel (2000) examined the sexually violent content of magazines, videos, and internet video postings, which they acknowledged represented three historic eras of media presentation, with internet material representing the most recent. Not surprisingly, internet content surpassed significantly both magazine and video content in terms of graphic depictions of sexual violence, with most of the violence by men directed at women, although magazine and video content has become increasingly violent over the past two decades. For Barron and Kimmel, the increasing violence directed at women in internet porn may say more about men's relationships with other men than with women. They argued that a homosocial explanation of the violence, where men try to compete with other men in terms of being—or posting content featuring— bigger and harder protagonists, is an interesting account that requires further evidence and consideration. Whatever the outcome of further study, any increase in violence in internet pornography cannot bode well for male–female relations in general, when the term "rape culture" is being used frequently not just to describe American college campuses, but many nations around the world (Boswell & Spade, 1996), a warning sounded much earlier by a variety of feminist thinkers and writers (e.g., Brownmiller, 1975; Steinem, 1980).

Effects of Erotica

As mentioned, it is very difficult to find research that separates erotica from pornography, but fortunately, some recent studies have made an attempt to study the impact of sexually explicit, nonviolent material on individuals and the sexual relationships of couples. One study by Staley and Prause (2013) examined the effects of erotic movie exposure on the sexual behavior and self–partner evaluations of 48 heterosexual couples. The couples, who were shown a set of movies, including one erotic film, as part of a study on "emotional movies", reported more positive evaluations of personal sexual behaviors and increased positive and negative emotions while viewing the erotic films. The researchers did not find that partner presence or absence during the film viewing affected these conclusions. Staley and Prause concluded that exposure to erotica is complex, involving both positive and negative reactions, and they argued that personal history (e.g., prior sexual abuse) may help to account for a mixture of feelings, although it is worth noting that their American participants reported higher levels of religiosity than the national average, and "value conflict" may have had some effect on the reactions of these particular individuals. At any rate, overall exposure to erotic movies appeared to have had a positive impact on these study participants and not all of the negative effects, including the ones anticipated by the researchers (e.g., devaluing of the attractiveness of one's partner after viewing attractive actors having sex), were reported.

Certainly therapists who specialize in sexual dysfunction have been able to use erotica as an adjunct to psychotherapy or couples therapy. Gambescia and Weeks (2007), for example, discussed the use of various homework devices, including erotic materials, to help improve sexual relationships among couples experiencing problems. Winter (1988), too, in a very good introduction to sex therapy from a PCT perspective, described the use of a number of homework devices to maximize male clients' anticipation of a successful, pleasurable sexual encounter. For Winter, fantasy and other sensual techniques can, and were used successfully to promote "sex positive" construct subsystems. Indeed, these appear to be the benefits of erotic material: depictions of sex as "natural" and "mutually pleasurable" produce an anticipation of anxiety-free sexual experiences, thus permitting fuller and longer erections and more satisfying orgasms for both men and women. A broader view of erotica, unencumbered by prescriptions and prejudices such as "sinful", would show the material to be a plentiful source of potential sexual constructs. As noted by Attwood (2002) in her review of qualitative studies on the function of pornographic and other sexually explicit material, pornography and erotica function as sources of identity construction among other purposes. Identity construction, in the language of PCT, is the exposure to, and the adoption of, relevant sexual core constructs.

Unlike horror stories about children surfing the internet in search of stories or videos involving fuzzy bunnies and finding instead ultra-violent rape scenes, erotica is likely what most children are exposed to, whether in the form of naked bodies in magazines like *Playboy*, nude calendars, or titillating scenes in movies. What they take away from such experiences is open to debate. Far from being the destroyer of young minds, it is likely that sexual depictions are either ignored because the information is just too novel to consider—perhaps described as "gross"—or children come to understand bodies and what they are capable of without any extreme anxiety or trauma. If they do learn anything new, it is not necessarily in the form of behavioral acquisition as it is in the form of construct acquisition. Most psychologists now accept that one important learning mechanism is social learning, and this is credited to the tireless work of Albert Bandura over several decades. As Bandura (1986) argued, the observation and acquisition of new behaviors only proceeds through the filter of cognitive processes, and we would argue that the cognitive processes involve construct acquisition, rejection, modulation, and overall systemic change. Exposure to a nude pin-up might result in new constructs like curvy, muscled, or hairy, which may be accompanied by further questions about the curves of women's breasts, the nature of adult muscles, or the hair surrounding adult genitalia. While the picture may well be remembered as it was presented, it may be remembered very differently depending on existing constructs, and the recollection will likely change over time as construct subsystems ebb and flow. Old constructs are not only replaced, but may acquire new or slightly different meanings over time from experience, and sexual constructs are certainly no different. No doubt children and youth acquire new and revised sexual constructs from stories narrated by peers, but they probably rely as much on erotic material for a sense of body image and sexual information (see Smith, Moyer-Gusé, & Donnerstein, 2004).

The kinds of messages, or sexual constructs, conveyed by erotic material cannot be condemned except by the most ardent anti-sensualist or sexual repressor. True, most erotica is little concerned with issues such as safe sex—condom use is probably not construed by many as "hot" or "sexy" with breaks in the action to slip on a condom probably interpreted as irritating by most viewers—but the gist of action in most erotic media presents loving and caring couples or groups participating in activities pleasurable to everyone involved. The messages in the form of constructs presented by the depictions run a gamut from pleasant, interesting, and exciting to athletic, mind-blowing, and orgiastic. Erotica can be seen legitimately as "sex education", or a source of new ideas and activities, at least for those interested in new ideas or sexual possibilities. In an interesting study of responses to sexual material in China, Wang and Davidson (2006) found that Chinese women, especially in rural areas, often viewed sexual material as educational and a source of new ideas, although some of the ideas could be interpreted as risky and demeaning. Again, however, separating erotica and pornography might identify threats to the viewer, both physical and emotional.

If nothing else, erotica appears to offer almost everyone a guilt-free understanding and acceptance of their own sexuality, if of course they choose to recognize it and make it a part of their selfhood (Bogaert, 2012). Guilt, as mentioned, has a very specific meaning within PCT—it refers to a perceived dislodging of "core role structures" (Kelly, 1955, p. 502), or an inner experience of discomfort due to action that invalidates a core role construct (e.g., not being a "good wife" by fantasizing about sex with a celebrity). Explicit dissociation of consenting and mutually pleasurable, to say nothing of novel and exciting, sexual depictions from violent, aggressive, and power-explicit depictions, whether involving same-sex or opposite-sex material, may not guarantee that viewers of erotica avoid feelings involving guilt, but it would make such an unpleasant experiences less likely. Indeed, for individuals with same-sex or queer desires, access to certain erotica might provide some benefits beyond arousal; it may address the guilt experienced through internalized prejudices against sexual minorities and may even enhance self-esteem (see Moradi, van den Berg, & Epting, 2009).

Pornography and Personal Constructs

Even after distinguishing erotica from hard-core, violent, gonzo porn, it remains difficult to determine the impact of the material on those consumers exposed to it habitually. Certainly, a number of researchers have pointed to the increase in aggression, especially sexual aggression, among young males exposed to depictions of sexual violence (e.g., Demare, Briere, & Lips, 1988). Other researchers have pointed to the impact of depictions of sexual aggression on sexual offending at least among "those so inclined" (see Seto, Maric, & Barbaree, 2001). As mentioned, however, some investigators (e.g., Ferguson & Hartley, 2009) concluded that violent pornography has no effect of on sex assault proclivities.

Certainly a prudent approach at this point would be to recognize potential problems, especially subtle ones, with pornography exposure. Smith et al. (2004), among others, have pointed to viewers' possible desensitization to violence due to repeated exposure to violent pornography. In an interesting examination of women's self-objectification related to male partners' pornography consumption, Tylka and Van Diest (2015) found that previous partners' pornography use showed an inverse relationship to self-esteem and body appreciation and a positive relationship to relationship anxiety, although such results might be found with erotica consumption as well. A large survey (Braithwaite, Coulson, Keddington, & Fincham, 2015) of American college students' sexual attitudes and behaviors, including pornography use, found that pornography viewing was associated with riskier sexual behaviors and more likelihood of "hooking up" or engaging in casual sexual encounters. A meta-analysis of pornography effects on consumers was conducted by Allen, D'Alessio, and Brezgel (1995). Analyzing the effect sizes from 30 separate studies, including from much of what we have defined as erotica, they found that nudity alone reduced subsequent aggressive behavior, consumption of material depicting nonviolent sexual activity increased aggressive behavior, and media depictions of violent sexual activity generated more aggression than nonviolent sexual activity.

Some of this research may reflect changes in the underlying constructs of consumers of pornography. Braithwaite et al. (2015), for example, interpreted their results as pointing to shifts in sexual scripts (Gagnon & Simon, 1973) due to pornography which, unfortunately, they failed to define for readers and for study participants. While sexual script shift may be one outcome of increased use of pornography, a more direct finding of this research is that there appears to be an increased acceptance of casual sexual encounters, at least among American college students. Given many of the themes of contemporary "adult" movies (e.g., woman home alone has sex with a pizza delivery teen, a television cable installer, and a pool cleaner, usually all of them together), it is hardly surprising to find greater acceptance of a hook-up culture, especially when combined with various other factors (e.g., news media portrayal of hook-ups as novel and "cool"). There is no doubt that brain changes occur in response to new events, adding new connections and even shifting function on occasion. And included in the input that can change brain structure is pornography, especially regular exposure (Doidge, 2007). What is more interesting and important for us are shifts in underlying constructions or, to use a computer metaphor again, the changing software rather than hardware. It is speculation on our part as to hypothesize on what might be happening in the construct systems of regular consumers of pornography, but we will present a brief examination of the changes that may occur. Before continuing, we would warn, once more, there is neither a single set of constructs nor a manner of construing that is common to all people or all members of a particular group. Without a doubt, pornography consumers represent a very diverse group, and the messages that they take from pornography are probably extremely varied. That said, we might find some common themes among users.

Several years ago, a number of young men who had become very regular internet porn consumers began to notice that they were experiencing erectile dysfunction when faced with live partners in actual sexual situations (Wilson, 2014). This condition became known as Porn-Induced Erectile Dysfunction (PIED), and it became tied to neuroscience and an underlying brain function or dysfunction related to overstimulation by internet porn was discovered. At about the same time, a treatment, sexual reboot therapy, appeared. It proposed to "reboot" a user's brain to a "pre-porn" state (Wilson, 2014). Not surprisingly, some neuroscientists, psychiatrists, and psychologists responded that porn cannot cause erectile dysfunction and that PIED is a pseudo-condition (see Prause & Pfaus, 2015). Such a problem may be a matter of perception or belief (i.e., "all in the head"), but this does not make it any less real. In fact, the power of a belief or the placebo effect is very much an important and an actual cause of much psychological distress, as well as the basis for relief from such distress (see Chapter 9).

Rather than delve into the problems of both sides of this emerging debate, we note that both sides seem to be talking about apples and oranges, insofar as researchers like Prause and Pfaus (2015) employ brief film clips of "consenting" genital-genital contact (i.e., pleasant, sensual, "soft-core" or erotic presentations) while the men reporting PIED tend to be exposed to "hard-core" or gonzo internet clips or full-length films (Wilson, 2014). We are not surprised to find that most men exposed to consenting sex films in a lab report that an increase in the number of hours spent viewing this material was related to sexual responses experienced more strongly and a "stronger desire for sex with a partner" (Prause & Pfaus, 2015, p. 90). It would seem that the debate may be less about the impact of erotica on brains, than about violent pornography on impressionable minds, or the constructs that comprise the basic building blocks of the mind. Constant exposure to violent porn accompanied by regular masturbation to orgasm from as early as 11 years of age would no doubt influence an individual's sexual fantasies, which may include aggression and various acts that most real-life partners would not likely tolerate (Wilson, 2014). The underlying constructs that these youths and young men have come to embrace include those related to toughness, roughness, performance, and domination of partners rather than softness, sensuality, mutuality, and negotiation. It is not hard to imagine that real-life encounters no longer, nor ever did, compare favourably to passive observation of internet porn productions. The idea of rebooting, despite the difficult comparison of the brain or mind to a machine or computer, is understandable in that a return to a pre-porn set of constructs might be possible for some porn consumers by avoiding porn and "purging" themselves of new and troubling constructions, followed by the slow and steady re-introduction of sexual encounters into the individual's life with real participants who would not tolerate abuse or rough treatment. While it appears that the exact process of rebooting is rather variable, the entire process seems to take a few months rather than a few days or a few years (Wilson, 2014).

Marston and Lewis (2014) conducted a qualitative study of heterosexual anal sex among English youth of 16–18 years of age. They found some interesting results in terms of individuals' reasons for increased anal sex in the United Kingdom. While neither young male participants nor young female participants reported real pleasure from anal intercourse, there seemed to be a consensus among the males at least that they "wanted to copy what they saw in pornography" (Marston & Lewis, 2014, p. 3). The study authors believed that pornography was only a partial reason for men "pushing" for anal sex, often ignoring the objections of their partners, and they cited competition for increased sexual experience among men as a likely contributing reason for promoting anal sex. Such a factor, however, might be related to pornography consumption in that they are watching male porn actors doing it and recognizing it as a possibility for themselves and interpreting it as a mark of accomplishment. Both young men and women agreed that "tightness" was a desired sensation, although only one woman among the several dozen in the study admitted that she had experienced extreme pleasure and an orgasm during anal intercourse. In this one study we can see that a sexual practice that may be seen as somewhat risky in terms of injury to both parties, and described as not particularly pleasurable by either partner, is still pursued because of constructions by at least one partner such as "tight" (versus loose?), "experienced" (versus inexperienced?), "cool" (versus old-fashioned?), "manly" (versus feminine?), and even "aggressive" (versus passive?).

Although the specific impact of contemporary, internet-based pornography on consumers' constructs, particularly those of young and impressionable individuals, it seems fair to understand the impact as potentially troublesome. Of course some may shrug the material off, others may partake of it with few long-lasting effects, but others- often seen as "the vulnerable" or "high-risk" population, whatever such terms really mean- may take away messages that will not serve them or others well in the future. It is not mere speculation to anticipate more male constructions of women in general as objects, sexual vessels, whores, sexually insatiable, passive, and desiring pain if violent and degrading sexual images continue to be uploaded and viewed on the internet. The outcomes are likely going to be unpleasant for both women and men, with the relations between the two souring quickly. While same-sex porn may not be in the same camp as heterosexual porn at present, it may well proceed down the same path leading to similar outcomes. It is possible, too, that the outcomes may prove more deadly than they have to date. The emergence of "snuff porn", or films that end with the murder of an "actor-victim", often involving a female victim who at some point is sexually assaulted (see Keith, 2001), is a particularly troubling development. Although many accounts of such snuff films may belong to the category of "urban myth" (Hagan, 2010), there are enough credible accounts of movies produced to satisfy a very small group of individuals who find the rape–murder of another human being extremely sexual and exciting. Violence and death can indeed become linked to sexual desire via experiences involving particular constructions (Horley, 2008). This does not bode well for the likelihood that all current consumers of extremely violent porn will come to the realization that the progression of violence may be leading them down a slippery cognitive-affective slope; indeed, the slope or progression seems to have been predicted by one early psychological theory, adaptation level theory (Helson, 1964), that explains the increase in stimulation level in people as frequent adjustments or "ramping up" of extreme, perverse sexual stimulation. We can only hope that such a possibility is taken seriously enough to prevent any further declines where power and money lead to the production of material so ultimately devastating to human life, and not just the lives of individuals but all human life.

Sex Trade Workers and Their Clients

Sex trade workers occupy a number of different roles and deliver various products in the world of commercial sex (see Weitzer, 2009, for an overview and review). The daily routine of sex trade workers can vary in risk from the relative safety of internet sex workers, to the relative privilege and moderate risk to call girls, to the high risk to streetwalkers, all involved in selling their bodies for sexual purposes. Terms such as "sex trade workers" or "sex labour" reflects feminist and labour studies' interests in identifying the wide range of workers who sell sex-based labour. While the stereotype of sex trade workers refers primarily women, it includes everyone in a variety of legal and illegal contexts. From exotic dancers and lap dancers, to call girls and prostitutes, the power relations that sex workers have with clients vary from playing the dominatrix, to some control of the sexual service, to utter degradation and dehumanizing practices. Understanding sex trade workers from the workers' perspective was very much on the agenda for second wave feminist groups who tended to see sex work as oppressive and based on the exploitation of women. In contrast, there was also an interest in not only framing sex trade workers as active, but as willing participants in the sex trade, empowered by their ability to claim their body as a sexual space that is being shared for money.

Concern for prostitution is growing as the industry grows internationally. As Bernstein (2001) concluded in her empirical examination of the meanings of sex for sale, the increasing purchase of sex is driven by "the shift from a relational to a recreational model of sexual intimacy" (p. 411) among other factors. If, for no other reason, the growth in an area that has been recognized generally over the past two centuries as ranking as one of the most serious social problems justifies increased research on the sex trade and sex trade workers.

Much of the work in this area has examined the lives of female sex trade workers, and some interesting empirical work has been conducted with this group. Saunders (2005), for example, found that many of the female sex workers that she interviewed had developed a workplace identity, very different from their "true selves", and viewed their sex work as an acting job. They create, according to Saunders, a "manufactured identity" in order to cope with potentially dangerous clients and also to distance their true selves from who they are required to be for their clients at work. Kong (2006), in a detailed examination of Chinese sex workers, found much the same and concluded that Hong Kong prostitutes "negotiate an identity of the 'prostitute' that is sensitive and flexible to different institutional areas that seems to jeopardise the neat binaries of Madonna/whore, good girl/bad girl" (p. 409). Much earlier, Heyl (1977) reported on the process of training, or the professional socialization, of female prostitutes in brothels. The madam, or female house manager, must train new workers not only in house rules and the physical techniques required to service clients, but impart specialized knowledge of types of clients (e.g., "kinky tricks") as well as more general knowledge about the business and the appropriate terminology (e.g., the difference between "whores" and "hustlers"). All of the prostitutes' socialization involves exposure to familiar and unfamiliar terms—all of which can be seen as personal constructs—along with learning the acceptable use and meanings of particular labels.

Following in-depth interviews with nearly six dozen female prostitutes working in a variety of settings, Jackson, Bennett, and Sowinski (2007) found that their respondents reported significant stressors in their lives beyond the fear of harm on the job. Many of their concerns revolved around stigma, and the fear of being discovered by friends and acquaintances in the "straight" world. Tomura (2009), too, investigated the experience of stigma, particularly "internalized stigma" and shame, among female sex workers, and found that one respondent supported her image as good versus bad by referring to the amount of "emotional effort" that she put into her work.

Phoenix (2000), in a fascinating study involving three dozen female sex workers, inquired into the identities of women who walk urban streets around three issues (viz., men, money, and violence) in order to examine the changing meanings of the issues and how they coped with them. The women that she interviewed were able to cope with what many would see as nightmarish by making sense of the people and events, ironing out contradictions, and developing a coherent narrative of their working lives. These resilient women showed that, despite constant victimization and their direct experience with extreme violence and inhumanity, they were able to use their limited agency to make informed choices that kept them alive and well. With the proper form of community assistance, female sex workers appear able to exit the profession. Oselin (2009) described an urban, 18-month "quasi-total" institutional programme for female sex workers wanting to leave the streets. Throughout the three-stage programme, participants are encouraged to change their lifestyles and patterns of thought, thereby experiencing an identity transformation. Oselin tracked some programme clients who did appear to change both their language and behavior throughout the course of the regimented and strict programme, although there was no follow-up to see if they succeeded in maintaining a non-deviant identity.

Among the relatively limited number of studies on male sex trade workers, Smith (2012) pointed out that, while there is much overlap between male and female sex workers, there are differences. One of her respondents, for example, noted that as a "top" (i.e., more active sex participant), a male sex worker could maintain his self-image as a man versus one providing "bottom" services. Male sex trade workers seem to experience as much, if not more, social stigma and alienation as women, and one report (Smith, Grov, & Seal, 2007) discussed a community agency that supported male sex workers with services that included "stigma management". This report emphasized that stigma is much farther reaching than negative social comments or exclusion, and includes negative self-descriptors such as "dirty" and experiencing "moral conflict" about the work.

Along a somewhat similar vein, some research has examined male actors in the porn industry. Escoffier (2003b), for example, studied straight men who work in gay porn films through the lens of sexual scripts theory. He found that the men, who are described by some gay porn directors as preferable to gay actors because they tend not to be as "insecure" and "sensitive" (p. 549), adopt a persona with a porn film pseudonym that allows them to perform well with actors they are not attracted to. He described this sex-for-money transaction as reflecting "situational sexuality" (p. 531). Escoffier also noted that straight actors in gay porn "frequently have used their work in gay pornography to launch lucrative careers as escorts" (p. 539) servicing mostly male clients. While it may seem implausible that straight men would be able to become aroused and have sex with other men in films, the PCT fragmentation corollary, pointing to the possibility if not the probability of maintaining logically incompatible construct subsystems, can help to explain such a phenomenon—these men have simply adopted a new subsystem of constructs that, while on the job, permits them to become aroused and perform as they are required.

Clients of sex workers, often referred to as "Johns" generally because they are men and anonymous "John Does", tend to slip beneath the radar of most authorities that police the sex trade as well as social science researchers. While female sex workers garner the most attention from police and prosecutors, male clients are often overlooked or, in more recent times, ordered to attend "John Schools", or psycho-educational programmes lasting a few weeks in order to address their "bad habits" of paying for sex. Rarely are clients referred to as sexual offenders, even nuisance ones, despite what their activities cost communities in terms of familial breakdown and healthcare outcomes (Horley, 2008). Fortunately, some social scientists have investigated clients, at least male clients, of sex workers in the hopes of finding why they are interested in paying for sex.

Jordan (1997), in a well conducted and presented qualitative study of male clients in New Zealand, found a range of motives and experiences that kept some men returning to sex workers, while others found alternatives to paid sex. Among the reasons discussed by the men in this study, the men's constructs are very readily identified. More than one interviewee referred to a lack of commitment, no emotional attachment, or the "professional" nature of the sexual encounters. Though some of the men were aged 60 years or over, with no experience of marriage or long-term sexual relationships, there seemed to be little or no awareness of the cost to them, aside from the financial cost, of continuing their "successful" relations with paid sex workers. Some did acknowledge that loneliness and negative emotions were alleviated by good encounters with sex workers, but they did not recognize, or at least acknowledge, any personal non-financial cost such as seeing sex as separate from intimacy. In a more recent and much larger study, Monto and Julka (2009) reported similar results, and they concluded that the purchase of sex had potential negative psychosocial outcomes for clients, sex workers, and "gender relations" in general.

Some johns may have moved their activities off the streets these days, or perhaps never did troll the streets looking to buy sex, but modern technology has provided a new opportunity for buying sex. The internet has become a favourite place for "virtual johns" (Blevins & Holt, 2009) to cruise and to hang-out. While the language employed by these individuals is very different and complex compared to street terminology, in part to avoid detection by law enforcement on the internet, the intent of these individuals has not changed (Blevins & Holt, 2009).

At least to our knowledge, there has never been an explicit PCT study of prostitution, but there very well could be. Certainly the idea that both sex workers and their clients—indeed, police officers who arrest each on occasion—employ constructs in order to create a sense of personal identity, however odd or deviant, as well as to provide meaning to their sexual activities, however risky, is compelling. PCT permits an analysis of law-breakers and law-enforcers that puts both on the same footing in the sense that we are all able to create a coherent sense of self from what might, from an outsider's perspective, seem like incoherence and chaos. Even the very idea of viewing the body as comprised of saleable sexual parts, given a capitalistic context, is rendered intelligible by invoking PCT—we can interpret genitalia as objects with a particular value just as we can see them as integral components of a whole, inseparable person.

8

Sexual Offenders

Sexually anomalous behavior, sometimes referred to colloquially as perversion, tends to baffle and to outrage many people. We need to question, however, common understandings of normality. Given the wide range of sexual both exhibited and tolerated now, at least within many Western countries, it is very difficult to pinpoint any generally agreed upon sexual acts that can be described as generally abnormal aside from a few illegal ones. Until relatively recently in much of the Western world, same-sex relationships were regarded not just as abnormal but, depending on the nature of the sexual acts and the jurisdiction, illegal. Such a state of affairs still exists in some nations. Engaging in anything other than heterosexual relationships or heterosexual encounters can result in a death sentence, whether state conducted or simply state encouraged.

Clearly, all non-normative sexual desires and , although abnormal in the sense that they are not held or practiced by a majority, cannot be viewed as extreme or unacceptable. As James (1899) stated so well, a "first thing to learn in intercourse with others is non-interference with their own peculiar ways of being happy, provided those ways do not assume to interfere by violence with ours" (pp. 49–50). James, of course, was referring to social intercourse rather than sexual intercourse, but his sentiments seem transferable. For our purposes, extreme sexual desires are those which involve pain, suffering, and long-term harm as potential outcomes of a sexual interaction. A key consideration appears to be full and informed consent to sexual involvement. All prepubescent individuals are incapable of providing fully informed consent, because they are unlikely to understand completely what they are consenting to. In addition, adults who commit sexual acts without obtaining the fully informed consent of the other person or persons, whether or not touching is involved, are sexual extremists. Such acts are illegal in most jurisdictions and such actors are considered sexual offenders.

Although not well understood, sexual offenders are often regarded as "lowest of the low" in specific settings (e.g., prisons) and society as a whole. It is perhaps because their sexual transgressions strike many as both repugnant and incomprehensible that sex offenders are most often regarded as "them" versus "us", those who do not commit sexual assaults. Such an interpretation, however, seems insufficient and, in a way, unacceptable. While it may serve to protect "the unaffected" from the prospect of becoming so truly repulsive and dangerous, such a construction simply isolates those who commit sexually offensive acts, delivering harsh conditions or even lethal punishments where understanding and assistance are the most effective means to protect everyone. Some ways to assist sex offenders are presented in the following chapter but, first, we need to describe a personal construct understanding of harmful sexual desires and. We will argue here that, however harmful and bizarre, the precursors to any anomalous sexual expression appear to be identical to those of any so-called normal. This is not to excuse the actions of those who commit sexual offences; rather we hope to make their actions more comprehensible through the lens of PCT.

Sexual Offenders and PCT: General Considerations

While research in PCT proper has been limited to date, enough research in the field of sexual offense has been conducted to allow us to search relatively disparate areas, including sociology and beyond the narrow boundaries of forensic mental health research, to examine various findings that seem to point to the relevance and value of PCT. Sometimes, the connection between the topic and PCT is not all that apparent. Fantasy, for example, appears to play an important role in deviant sexual behavior, if not all sexual behavior, and we believe that it is an aspect of a personal construct perspective.

Marshall (1973) showed that an attempt to control and alter the deviant sexual fantasies of five child molesters was effective in reducing penile responses to child stimuli as well as inappropriate sexual behavior outside the treatment setting. Therefore, Marshall and Barbaree (1988) have included alteration of deviant fantasies as a key component in a treatment programme for child molesters. Abel and Blanchard (1974), too, demonstrated the centrality of deviant fantasy in sex offender treatment. In reviews of the sex offender treatment literature, Lanyon (1986) and Quinsey (1986) concluded that an account of sexual fantasy is essential for any adequate explanation of child molestation, and an examination of the sexual fantasy is an important component of any effective treatment programme. We would argue that there is a clear connection between fantasy and construction. Fantasies have been described as "try-outs" or "experimental planning" (MacCulloch, Snowden, Wood, & Mills, 1983). As cognitive rehearsals, fantasies serve as a safe yet effective means of anticipating the outcomes of potential construct-based behavioral experiments, and the lack of enactment in many cases probably illustrates the safety of "just mulling it over"—we often do not follow through on fantasy, even recurring or obsessive fantasies, but fantasy appears built on constructs and allows for potential acts should conditions arise or change.

A number of studies and theories (e.g., Marshall & Barbaree, 1990; Quinsey, 1986) have emphasized the lack of social skill displayed by sex offenders, particularly those who molest children. This is undoubtedly the case if we view social skill narrowly as a set of behaviors (e.g., displaying respect, appropriate self-disclosure, politeness) that produce long-term, intimate relationships. Even the brandishing of power, in whatever form, often demonstrates or requires a degree of social skill. Many sexual offenders, far from being pathetic and ineffectual losers, are very skilful in avoiding detection and in the use of various forms of power. Some sexual extremists, especially those working as priests or therapists, are able to read people quickly and flawlessly. In effect, they are able to assess others' construct systems in an instant and exploit what they interpret. Based on their insights, they employ careful manipulation, persuasive arguments, and various forms of authoritative power in order to gain their victims' compliance. These are not crass, knife-waving goons or buffoons, but extremely clever individuals who, knowing what they want, have the skills to achieve it. In some cases, they are able to conceal their deeds involving many victims for many years. The point here is not to applaud the efforts of people who use and abuse others by employing subtle tactics, but we need to keep in mind that those who abuse others sexually have abilities and, in many cases, many redeeming features. Their skills, unfortunately, are obscured by their malevolence.

Recognizing the skills of sex offenders is important for a number of reasons. First, clinicians and counsellors need to build on existing strengths rather than pick away at personal deficits. Viewing someone who has abused others sexually as lacking all positive attributes is not a realistic perspective, and not likely to produce quick or even positive movement in therapy. Perhaps more importantly, vilifying sexual offenders and creating extreme caricatures of them will only make a real abuser more difficult to spot. In fact, most individuals who offend sexually are not dishevelled, dwarfish men in dirty trench-coats who lurk in bushes and live in temporary shelters. Rather, they are more likely to be well-dressed and respectable middle-class men who live in the suburban house next-door. We tend to be shocked by news stories about the successful family doctor who abused children in his surgery for years, or the venerated parish priest who abused many teenage girls or alter boys in the church hall, but we should not be surprised at all; this is indeed the norm. No doubt our collective tendency to search for sexual deviants in a filthy or unfashionable costume contributes to the ability of many abusers to fly below the community radar, which is often not effective because it is pointed in the wrong direction. Another consequence of what could be termed as the "extreme deviant" stereotype of sexual abusers is that eccentric individuals in the community are the ones often initially identified quickly as suspects in sexual assault cases. The man or woman, often a social isolate or a vagrant, is often detained by the authorities.

Too often, the usual suspects, the misfits or oddballs, are convicted of horrendous sexual assaults or sex murders with little or no evidence (Karp & Rosner, 1991). To put an end to such outrageous injustice, it is not enough to point fingers at the police and demand better police training and more competent investigations, because the police operate with the same stereotypes as the rest of us. We all need to amend our assumed stereotypes regarding those responsible for sexual assaults.

It appears that sexual assault is not a simple result of the abuse of power; in fact, there does not appear to be a simple or singular answer as to why some individuals commit sexual assaults. Sexual assault appears, first and foremost, concerned with self-validation, although it does involve much more. If non-abusive sexual relationships, or even brief sexual encounters, are very complex in terms of what they mean for the participants, abusive ones are likely just as complex. While power might be a tool used by abusers, and perhaps an extremely attractive one for some offenders, it appears to be a means to an end, and the end is not a simple or singular one.

Constructing an Abnormal Identity

Personal construct perspectives can help explain the vast varieties of human sexual interests and expressions, including extreme ones. As mentioned in Chapter 2, pain can be pleasurable when it reinforces or validates a view of oneself as deserving or wanting pain. People are agents—active interpreters and anticipators of the world around them—and even if every other person alive would construe certain types of sexual activities as unpleasant, if not downright horrible and despicable, all sexual acts can provide some validation for the particular constructs held by an individual. A long-term view of oneself as unworthy or unacceptable in some fashion may well provide a backdrop for the idea that continual pain and humiliation as quite acceptable if not pleasurable. It may also be that pain is perceived as pleasure as part of a generally overall positive view of oneself, if for example, if one understands oneself as sexually liberated. The pleasure, here, is obtained by the commission of an act that reinforces the core role construct of being sexually free.

Whatever the construct is—flawed, unworthy, domineering, liberated, a master manipulator—a successful assault can provide a "warm glow" through confirmation of the construct or set of constructs. The resultant self-knowledge or the affirmation of current self-understanding is inherently pleasant or satisfying even if the construct involved is one that might have a generally "negative" understanding. This position, presented initially by Horley (2000a, 2000b, 2000c), requires further elaboration and exploration.

Power, Control, and Violence

According to Brownmiller (1975), Darke (1990), and other writers, sexual aggression in all of its forms deals with issues of power and control and not issues related to sexual gratification. Brownmiller's important book, *Against Our Will*, a critique of patriarchy from a radical feminist perspective, presented such a case against rape across time and culture. Through an examination of the various ways that men have committed sexual assault, Brownmiller concluded that sexual assault is a means by which men oppress women. Sexual assault, whether an individual man attacking one woman, or a conquering army employing rape systematically to denigrate thousands of women, is simply one means by which men attain and maintain social dominance. There certainly appears to be support for this position; for example, a sizable minority, if not the majority of men who assault women sexually, are unable to achieve penile penetration and use other means (e.g., hands, gun barrels) to commit the offense. The issue, however, does not appear quite so clear-cut, and questions need to be raised. If sex is irrelevant or unimportant, why do so many assaults have a clear, central sexual component? Would not a sexual component, however effective at adding humiliation and degradation to an assault, impede the use of force or more direct means of domination? Does not the sexual component leave the attacker at risk or more vulnerable than, say, a physical beating would?

Unquestionably, power can be viewed as a construct without diminishing its status as a relational component. This is akin to viewing any person, a "social element" in the language of PCT, as a construct (e.g.,

"Like mother–not like mother") which does not compromise his or her ontological status as a real person. Powerful–powerless, predator–prey, wolf–sheep, master–slave, and boss–bitch are just a few of the power-relevant construct pairs that forensic clients employ on a regular basis. Generally, offenders view themselves on the more aggressive or dominant pole of the construct. As one client of mine (JH) once remarked, "Who in his right mind would want to be weak prey like sheep? This is a dog eat dog world, right?" Sex offenders often see themselves as all-powerful and in charge of their destinies although there are times when the opposite appears true initially. Many, if not most, sexual offenders are aware of an inherent vulnerability, a force within them that they are powerless in the face of, and they attempt to compensate for this powerlessness.

Frequently, sex offenders describe themselves as sex addicts. They crave sex constantly on their own terms. If they are unable to gain satisfaction from a partner, and few can for long periods, they will turn to a prostitute or an unwilling man, woman, child, or, in a few cases, animal. Some are not very particular sexually, while others are very particular about the characteristics of their victims. This addiction metaphor has been expanded by some in the treatment field, and specialized therapy groups now exist for sex addicts. Although the focus of many of these groups are so-called "nymphomaniacs" and "Don Juans", or sexually-compulsive individuals, some groups and clinicians encourage more serious sexual abusers to join. Setting aside concerns about the nature of the treatment, the conceptualization of deviant sexual behavior as addiction is troublesome. As Peele (1995) and others have pointed out, the "treatment industry" has expanded the notion of addiction to include all forms of troublesome or habitually maladaptive behavior and have based it on a notion—addiction—that emphasizes weakness on the part of the sufferer. An addict has no willpower, there is no possibility of him or her resisting the addictive substance or activity, at least not without the constant involvement of a therapist or a therapeutic group. Peele (1995) argued that, at least in the USA, such a development has advanced to a point that most US citizens have at least one addiction that dominates and controls them. Due to this diagnosis or conceptualization, billions of dollars are invested annually in an industry that only feeds a sense of powerlessness. This may be less true for sex offenders, in part because there are few therapists interested in working with them on a full-time basis, but offenders who do get involved in addiction-centered groups do report a certain increase in comfort. They feel relieved of any shame that they experienced as a result of their sex assaults because, after all, they were helpless to resist in the face of their addiction. Offenders who adopt an addiction view of their extreme sexual acts often become zealots, and generally attempt to convince fellow prison inmates—or anyone who will listen—about the benefits of joining one addiction group, or a specific addiction therapist, or another.

Most sexual offenders, perhaps without participating in a formal movement, come to recognize that they have an innate, congenital, or deep-seated problem that they find impossible to resist. No doubt many are convinced of such a "condition" or "disorder" by clinicians, perhaps forensic clinicians, who, in the process of an assessment session, discuss a particular diagnosis. Others likely acquire the perspective from popular books, the media, friends, or family members. Whatever the source of understanding, it can often overwhelm them on first consideration. Many of the harsh and repulsive self-labels employed by some repeat sex offenders, such as predator versus prey, seem to come after a period of hopelessness and resignation to "fate". Constructs become, in a sense, a way of taking back control of one's self and life in that the individual, rather than being weak and helpless regarding his sexual compulsion, claims it as his own. He truly becomes a serious, long-term threat by accepting the various means by which he sees himself as "in charge" and dominant, the powerful one in the relationship with potential victims. He has truly accepted his role of sex offender or sexual predator at this point. Even the most vicious and sadistic sex killers have admitted to me (JH) that they really did not know what to make of themselves after their first assault. They were uncomfortable about the attacks that they were planning, and the memory of the first victim, often not murdered or even badly injured physically, haunted them. At the same time, there was something compelling or deeply satisfying about the assault. It was only over time and usually after more violent experiences that they gained the sense that these offences against others were indeed quite acceptable. They were doing what they were compelled to do; they were actualizing their true selves. The violence, at this point, had become an integral part of how they defined themselves. It had become, or was soon to become, truly a way of life (Winter, 2003b).

May (1972) talks about the interplay between power and powerlessness as well. He sees a large portion of life as being dedicated to the conflict between powerfulness and powerlessness. While too much power may corrupt, too little power is equally if not more corrupting from May's perspective. More often than not, when we consider sexual offenders and their victims, we think of the victims as being powerless and being left even more powerless by their victimization (Berliner, 1991). Offenders, however, can feel powerless while stalking or assaulting victims. In a sense, the victims have power over the offenders, although only in a rather indirect and, ultimately, unsatisfactory manner. The powerlessness of the offender may be due to the previous victimization that he himself has endured. Even a horrible childhood memory can be repeated if the earlier experience has left its mark psychologically, not just in terms of physical and emotional pain and turmoil, but in the seed that was planted in the abused individual's own self-identity. Obviously, not all victims of sexual abuse go on to abuse others, but those who do so may trace an altered sense of self to their own victimization. An assault during childhood or adolescence, when self-identity is malleable and open to change, can make the victim think that not only are they somewhat responsible, but may actually have enjoyed the abuse. Perverted, sick, screwed-up, strange, conflicted, and confused are terms that sex offenders apply to their own victimization if they had experienced abuse earlier in life. They begin, as a function of their own experiences, to question who they must have been to allow such an experience to occur. Remarkably, some of the most confused individuals were the ones least injured physically by the abuse. Because there was a positive aspect to the assault (e.g., attention from a valued adult, emotional support), they wondered about themselves and began to construe themselves as "different" or "twisted".

Often, the most extreme of the extreme, the 'less than 1%", who engage in the most lethal and sadistic acts, achieve no sexual arousal to violent sexual stimuli, as might be expected; instead, they are excited by strictly violent imagery. During penile plethysmographic testing, they often respond solely to stories or visual depictions of attacks on victims that involve maiming, torture, extreme violence, and often death. Their sexual responses, and ultimately orgasmic responses—if allowed to proceed— are related only to grotesque violence and death, where harm and lethality are the triggers for arousal. Given such a pattern, it is easy to see how a common assault might escalate into a session of extreme torture, and possibly death, because each blow, cut, scream, or stream of blood will only provoke more arousal. The exact route to such an extreme condition is far from certain, but one feature that appears common to some, perhaps many extreme sadists is long-term, ritualized, public brutalization (Horley, 2008). Most often, these men—there may be such women, but they are likely even rarer than men—have been beaten or sexually assaulted in front of family members over years as part of a regular ritual, and it is not difficult to imagine the impact this had on a construct system, especially sexual constructs, that such abuse might lead to. To construe oneself as a victim of extreme abuse, it is possible that moving beyond it may be best accomplished by switching from victim to victimizer, but only for those who have experienced a situation where they began to identify with their tormenter, such as a father or father-figure. No doubt, not all victims of extreme violence adopt a later view of themselves as a perpetrator or a vicious extremist, but the conditions of some young lives may lend themselves to an exchange of sex and violence. The entire question of prior abuse producing future abusers is a controversial and thorny one, and certainly we would not argue that it is necessarily the case that anyone who suffers sexual abuse will continue to abuse others. There may be some circumstances such as repeated and extreme abuse that occurs in certain forms, however, where the chances do increase. If any experience that confirms existing core construction is inherently satisfying, there is no reason to believe that the constructs that are validated or reinforced will be normatively positive; therefore, we can and should expect that at least some individuals who have extremely abuse, traumatic early life experiences will develop a world view, a personal construct system, that demands extremely abusive acts on their part.

Specific Forms of Sexual Abuse

Sexual Interest in Prepubescent Individuals

The term "paedophilia" is often applied to adults who engage in sexual relationships or have sexual desires for prepubescent individuals that they have never acted upon. The term seems problematic for a number of reasons. First, as a medical term coined by Krafft-Ebing (1886/ 1935), it refers to the "brotherly love of youths" or the love of children. In fact, an overwhelming sexual desire for children is the focus of the so-called disorder, and Krafft-Ebing's original diagnostic label, paedophilia erotica, is perhaps a better term despite the internal contradiction (viz., "philias" means brotherly love versus "eros" which means erotic love). The term points to no known disease entity although it was considered by Krafft-Ebing to be one possible expression of distortion in the normal sexual instinct, an understanding that almost no clinicians would embrace today. A serious problem with the term is its frequent application to all adults who have sex with or who lust after children. The majority of individuals, probably two-thirds to three-quarters, who do have sex with prepubescent individuals, however, show no significant sexual responses to children—they should be seen, as they sometimes are, more as situational offenders, engaging in child sex due to situational factors (e.g., negative emotional experiences, disinhibition from alcohol) rather than constitutional factors. The diagnostic label appears to be a confused use of Latin to confer medical status on a problem that is not in our view due to medical issues. Since the term seems to be a broad summary of behavior, whether actual or verbal (i.e., having molested children or stating a sexual desire for children), it is perhaps best to refer to those who have sex with children or those who have desires for children, as child molesters, child sex abusers, or some related term however inadequate, thereby avoiding pseudo-medical diagnostic language and confusion.

Abel, Becker, and Cunningham-Rathner (1984) have investigated the role that certain beliefs and attitudes play in adults' continued sexual involvement with children. They have focused in particular on seven types of beliefs about children and sex that they term "cognitive distortions." These distorted beliefs include: if children fail to resist advances, they must want sex; sexual activity with children is an appropriate means to increase the sexual knowledge of the child; if children fail to report sexual activity, they must condone it; in the future, sex between adults and children will be acceptable if not encouraged; if one fondles rather than penetrates, sex with children is acceptable; any children who ask questions about sex really desire it; and one can develop a close relationship with a child through sexual contact. According to Abel et al., the commonality among all of these "wrong" views (i.e., inappropriate insofar as children cannot consent meaningfully to sexual interaction) is that child molesters make no attempt to validate them against the experience of others. A number of writers confirm that child molesters do report these and similar sexual attitudes and beliefs about children. Stermac and Segal (1990), for example, reported that child molesters think that children benefit as a result of adult sexual contact. They also perceive greater complicity on the child's part, and less responsibility on the adult's part than do non-molesters. Hayashino et al. (1995) used a shortened version of the Abel et al. Cognition Scale to show that extra-familial molesters, compared to non-offenders and even incest offenders, report more distorted cognitions. However, there appears to be some limitations to the full or modified Cognition Scale. Horley and Quinsey (1995) failed to find any hypothesized differences using Abel's Cognition Scale because of high top end loading. Because of the transparency of the items, all expressed very negatively but scored in the reverse, incarcerated molesters in particular may be reluctant to report distortions. This concern and others (see Ward, Hudson, Johnston, & Marshall, 1997) led Bumby (1996) to develop a 38-item MOLEST Scale. This assessment of cognitive distortions in child molesters is similar to the Cognition Scale, but items appear to be much more "neutral" in tone (e.g., "Some children can act very seductively.") and may avoid some of the problems encountered by those using the Cognition Scale. Preliminary psychometric reports of the internal and test–retest reliabilities of the MOLEST Scale, as well as its convergent and discriminative validities, are encouraging (Bumby, 1996), but it is premature to endorse this scale without reservation. Collings (1997), too, has developed a 15-item scale to examine child sexual abuse myths, or really distorted beliefs or cognitions. Again, initial psychometric data for his CSA scale are quite adequate, but further efforts are demanded.

Although studies on the attribution processes per se of child molesters are few in number, some sociological and social–psychological investigations have examined offenders' beliefs and social cognition. McCaghy (1967, 1968) showed that the amount of coercion used in the sexual activity with children predicted the offender's level of denial and his attempts to maintain an identity as "sexually normal". Interestingly, he also found that, although incarceration and probation had no significant impact on motivational change, the number of psychotherapeutic sessions did affect the report of personal motives. After 11 individual or 21 group sessions (McCaghy, 1967), or roughly 20 sessions of unspecified therapy (McCaghy, 1968), child molesters tended to accept more personal responsibility for their actions, as opposed to blaming an alcohol or drug problem. They also tended to provide many "psychodynamic" explanations for their behavior, not surprisingly given the psychoanalytic orientation of most of their therapists, past and present. McCaghy (1968) warned, however, that the label "child molester" should be avoided, lest offenders come to accept such a deviant role as an integral part of their identities. Taylor (1972) had judges sort motivational accounts into categories on a scale from "likely to be true" to "unlikely to be true". He found that the sexual offenders themselves invoked "mental breakdown" as a reason for their behavior, much more often than "social skill deficit" explanations. Judges, however, rated "social skill deficit" reasons as more credible than "mental breakdown" reasons. These patterns of attribution, characterized by the minimization and denial of deviance, appear consistent with clinical findings concerning offenders' use of denial and minimization (Barbaree, 1989).

Ward, Hudson, and France (1994) had incarcerated child molesters complete an attribution scale at three points in time while describing and explaining their most recent sexual offense. They found that sexual needs were reported by far the most often, followed by intimacy needs, especially during their recall of the lapse (stage two) just prior to their sexual assault. Along similar lines, Ward, Loudon, Hudson, and Marshall (1995) examined molesters' accounts of the chain of thoughts and feelings that accompanied their most recent offenses. The resulting qualitative data led them to propose a nine stage process for child molesters' offense chains that emphasized distorted beliefs. Earlier, Ward, Hudson, and Marshall (1994) found that child molesters who reported a lapse viewed the causes of their deviant behavior as more uncontrollable than molesters without a lapse.

Child molesters' attitudes have been examined by some investigators. The technique of choice has been the semantic differential technique, first presented by Osgood, Suci, and Tannenbaum (1957). Marks and Sartorius (1967) argued that sexual attitude is an important component in the assessment and treatment of sexual deviation, and they presented a "sexualized" version of the semantic differential. Their technique included not only bipolar adjectives that Osgood et al. would classify as general evaluative (e.g., kind vs. cruel, good vs. bad), but they also included sexual evaluative adjectives as well (e.g., seductive vs. repulsive, erotic vs. frigid). Factor analysis of the assessment device showed that there was some distinction between the general and sexual evaluative scales, although the two factors were similar. While testing the clinical utility of the technique, which working with eight clients who revealed a variety of sexual deviations, they found that attitude change paralleled clinical change. They concluded, therefore, that their version of the semantic differential provided "useful indicators of clinical progress" (p. 448). For a concise clinical tool, they recommended an abbreviated version of their technique with three sexual evaluative (viz., sexy vs. sexless, seductive vs. repulsive, and erotic vs. frigid) and three general evaluative scales (viz., kind vs. cruel, good vs. bad, and pleasant vs. unpleasant). Quinsey, Bergersen, and Steinman (1976) used this brief sexual semantic differential as part of their test battery in a study of change in child molesters over the course of an aversion therapy programme. Together with significant pre-treatment versus post-treatment changes in penile plethysmographic responses and skin conductance responses, Quinsey et al. found that the general evaluative and sexual evaluative scales were highly correlated and that both showed the expected correlation of increased ratings for adults and decreased ratings for children, in line with both penile circumference and skin conductance results. Thus, the semantic differential appears to be a useful paper and pencil measure of attitudes that are relevant to the treatment of child molestation. One warning sounded later by Quinsey (1977, 1986), however, concerned the transparency of any devices that include only sexually relevant dimensions. The ability of respondents, many of whom are highly motivated to dissemble, to appear as they wish to be seen should not be overlooked.

Another study of the semantic differential when used with child molesters was provided by Frisbie and colleagues (Frisbie, Vanasek, & Dingman, 1967; Dingman, Frisbie, & Vanasek, 1968). They described the general technique as "relatively ambiguous" and "non-threatening" (Frisbie et al., 1967, p. 700). They argued further that it, and similar psychological assessment techniques, are important "because an adult male's selection of a child as a sexual object seems to be related to his perceptions of the self, his role in a given social structure, and his recognition and/or acceptance of ethical values and social expectations" (p. 699). Their research involved examining incarcerated and released child molesters' views of themselves and their ideal selves. One bipolar adjective pair, "happy vs. sad", was found to distinguish incarcerated from community molesters, with community molesters reporting greater resemblance between their actual versus ideal selves on this dimension than incarcerated offenders. This finding in part led to the conclusion that released offenders were "better integrated" than incarcerated offenders, but Frisbie et al. correctly noted that this could be a reflection of their different situations rather than personality differences. A one year follow-up with 79 of the released molesters (Dingman et al., 1968) showed that the respondents' views of both their real and ideal selves declined. This finding was described in terms of erosion of morale, and it was related to concerns about impending recidivism.

Borrowing from Marks and Sartorius (1967), Frisbie et al., and others, Horley and Quinsey (1994) developed a semantic differential to examine child molesters' attitudes or thoughts about themselves and other individuals. Child molesters, relative to matched comparisons who have not molested children, described themselves as submissive and sexually unattractive, while they described women as oppressive and unattractive. Examining the child molester group alone revealed some intra-group differences using Kelly's (1955) role construct repertory grid (rep grid). The responses of the molesters who had exclusively victimized girls included significantly more external appearance constructs, while offenders against young boys used more emotional and self-sufficiency terms to describe people. Molesters who had killed their young victims described men and boys as cruel but sexy. Untreated molesters reported more social anxiety than treated offenders (Horley & Quinsey, 1995). A subsequent study (Horley, Quinsey, & Jones, 1997), using a revised semantic differential, confirmed that molesters described themselves as less positive sexually than did non-molesters. Women were seen by molesters more negatively in terms of sexual descriptors than by non-molesters, although, somewhat paradoxically, molesters described women as more trusting and mature than those who did not abuse children. Molesters also reported a more positive view of women on the Attitudes Toward Women Scale (Nelson, 1988) than comparison participants. Molesters and non-molesters also differed in terms of their responses to the Criminal Sentiments Scale (Andrews & Wormith, 1990), with child molesters reporting more favourable views on the police, courts, and the legal process than comparison participants. A similar finding was revealed in ratings of authority figures: child molesters described authorities as kinder and less repulsive, deceitful, and unpleasant than comparisons. Marshall et al. (2003) found that this semantic differential did not differentiate between child molesters, non-sex offenders, and community-based non-offenders with respect to their views on women and children. It is important to note, however, that Marshall et al. modified our original semantic differential for their research and did not use the Horley et al. (1997) modified scale.

A modest but potentially significant study by Howells (1979) examined the thoughts of child molesters and offenders without sexual offenses concerning people in their social environments in terms of personal constructs. Howells compared the personal constructs of 10 "mentally disordered", heterosexual child molesters and 10 non-sex offenders using versions of the rep grid. The constructs elicited from Howells' respondents were sorted according to an amended version of Landfield's (1971) categorization scheme, and analyses revealed certain key differences between offender groups. Perhaps most importantly, child molesters used more "egoistic" constructs, such as "domineering vs. passive" and "dominant vs. submissive", than non-molesters. Children were described generally as passive and submissive. There was also a suggestion that molesters were concerned with small body parts such as small genitalia. When the results of both offender groups were combined, and constructs elicited using male and female elements were compared, it was reported that women were construed in terms of sexual and physical appearance while men were interpreted in terms of status and organization.

Wilson and Cox (1983a, 1983b) provided some indirect support for Howells' (1979) egoism finding. In a study of the personalities of 77 members of a British child molester organization, Wilson and Cox (1983a) found that child molesters frequently described themselves as shy and attracted to children because of the children's naive innocence.

They concluded that dominance was a key to understanding a man's choice of a child as a sexual partner. A conceptual replication of Howells' work was attempted by Horley (1988a), who compared the personal constructs of 10 "mentally disordered", mixed (heterosexual and homosexual) child molesters and 10 "mentally disordered" non-sex offenders. Analyses confirmed the previous findings concerning the tendency of the combined groups to think of women, compared to men, in terms of sexual and physical appearance, but the egoistic construct difference between groups was not found. Neither did there seem to be a preoccupation with small body size among child sexual abusers. The failure to replicate the between group egoism finding may be due to differences between the two studies (e.g., heterosexual versus mixed molesters, prison comparison versus mental health comparison), but it is also possible that the original egoism finding is attributable to statistical artefact.

Marshall and colleagues (e.g., Marshall & Mazzucco, 1995) have pointed to a related concern with the self-perception and self-esteem of child molesters. Low self-esteem does appear to be a consequence of the actions of child molesters in terms of the impact on their victims (Freshwater, Leach, & Aldridge, 2001), but Marshall and colleagues have argued that low self-esteem leads adult males to seek sexual relationships with children. Certainly, some child molesters report negative feelings about themselves, and this may help to explain their offending (Ward, Hudson, & France, 1994). Ward, McCormack, and Hudson (1997) also reported low self-esteem among molesters, although one study by Marshall et al. (2003) did not find that child molesters' self-esteem differed significantly from comparisons. Horley et al. (1997) suggested that the situation may be more complex, in that child molesters may perceive themselves as inadequate sexually, or not very physically attractive, but they are not low in self-esteem generally. At least two studies with incarcerated molesters appear to support this view (Horley & Quinsey, 1994; Horley et al., 1997). This issue has yet to be settled.

A valuable study by Johnston, Hudson, and Ward (1997) examined the "sexual thoughts" (i.e., words relevant to children and sexual activity) of incarcerated child molesters, in particular, their ability to suppress unwanted or inappropriate thoughts. They concluded that there is both "some hope and some notes of caution" (p. 303) after showing that sexual thoughts could be suppressed, but more so by situational offenders than obsessed molesters. They also concluded that thought suppression techniques alone are insufficient for changing child molesters' inappropriate behavior.

The empirical literature concerning the cognition of child molesters has been expanding, especially over the past two decades. At this point, very little of substance can be concluded safely. Certainly, fantasy, particularly deviant sexual fantasy, appears to be an important factor in producing and maintaining child molestation. Altering the deviant fantasy is an important target in many treatment programmes designed for child molesters. Cognitive distortions, as described by Abel, Bumby, and others, do appear to be factors, but whether they are causes, effects, or correlations of molestation is unknown. Whether certain types of distorted beliefs about sexuality are more "serious" (i.e., are more likely to sexually offensive behavior) than others remains unanswered as well. The adequacy of some of the techniques we use to assess beliefs, attitudes, values, distorted cognitions, or personal constructs are certainly open to question too. Doubts have been raised about the usefulness of the Cognition Scale, but more work needs to be done on alternatives (e.g., MOLEST Scale, CSA scale). The semantic differential and the rep grid are two methods, as opposed to specific scales, that have been used in a variety of studies but, because they represent general methodological approaches, specific content needs to be identified. To do this, more informed "hunches" or clinical insights are needed. The lack of overarching theory or general theoretical insights, however, is a limitation here.

The question of child molesters' thoughts about themselves, particularly concerning self-worth and self-esteem, is very much that—a question. Child molesters may see themselves as undesirable or less than adequate individuals, as Marshall and Mazzucco (1995) would argue, but molesters may only perceive and report a lack of attractiveness or sexual adequacy, and even this might be truer for molesters with male victims rather than female victims. It may also be true only for certain incarcerated offenders. Whatever be the case, negative self-image may provide the basis for the relatively consistent behavioral finding that many child molesters display or report shyness or difficulty in social interaction

(Quinsey, 1986; Salter, 1988). The importance of assessing and altering thoughts about inadequacy or lack of social or sexual efficacy is indicated. At this point, it seems clear that most, if not all, child molesters hold some distorted cognitions or beliefs about adult–child sex or what constitute appropriate relationships with children. The problem is that this appears to be the case almost by definition. The specific types of distortion, or the degrees of risk associated with various distorted views, are unknown. The different types of distorted cognition exhibited by different types of offenders (e.g., male versus female victim, amount of force or sadistic behavior in assault) demand examination. Assessment development in this area appears important whether one is interested specifically in distorted cognitions, beliefs, values, or fantasies. The use of the Cognition Scale, particularly with incarcerated offenders, seems limited by its narrow focus and construction. The MOLEST Scale or CSA Scale may prove better, but again they may be too narrow in design.

Social cognitive research into child molesters' attributional processes has found, not surprisingly, that molesters tend to have difficulty accounting for their sexually deviant behavior. Many ascribe their offenses to alcohol abuse. Their deviance disavowal is understandable as an attempt to appear more normal sexually than how they in fact behave. More detailed studies examining differences among molesters need to be done. Such work may reveal, for example, that practicing heterosexual males who molest young boys need to engage in more "mental gymnastics". As a result of this, they experience more anxiety while explaining themselves, because they have more perceived deviance to disavow or to account for. Assessing causal attributions of sexually inappropriate behavior is helpful in programming, and it serves as a specific therapeutic target in treatment.

The situation of child abusers may be even more complicated. As mentioned, they seem to experience or at least report more social anxiety and a fear of being around others, compared to non-molesters. This finding was confirmed in a recent meta-analysis conducted by Nunes, McPhail, and Babchishin (2012). Whether the social fear is the result of understanding oneself as a deviant and dangerous around children, and perhaps resulting in a deeper sense of one's own identity as deviant, or whether the fear is due simply to a fear of being recognized as a deviant, not just by past victims, but by members of the public who may have followed media reports of court proceedings, remains to be determined. Whatever be the case, the circumstances that surround child sexual abusers is difficult, and it is far from clear how someone who gets involved in inappropriate sexual relationships with children can extract themselves psychologically, socially, or legally. The hole for them can only get deeper when mental health and legal professionals label them "paedophiles" and describe the condition as a sexual orientation (Seto, 2012).

Sexual Aggression Directed Against Adults

Sexual aggression against adults, often simply referred to as rape, may be considered a heinous offense by the public and many legal jurisdictions, but surprisingly relatively little work has been conducted in the social sciences on rapists. The paucity of research done on men who assault adults sexually may reflect or be reflected by the lack of interest on the part of mental health clinicians in rape—the American Psychiatric Association and their diagnostic manual (APA, 1952, 2013) seems to be a good example of how little to no attention is granted to those who assault others sexually, especially given how much attention is focused on such "disorders" as Gender Identity Disorder (see APA, 2013). Certainly some interesting and useful empirical research relevant to rapists' constructions of themselves and their victims has been presented. Men who assault women have been found to have views supportive of "rape myths" (e.g., women desire rape), and this may increase their likelihood of using force during a sexual encounter (Stermac, Segal, & Gillis, 1990). Stermac et al. also discussed the role of a sense of hostility towards women that many men who assault adult females report.

Shorts (1985) described one case of a rapist who came to view himself as more like men who assault women over the course of therapy, not a surprising finding given that many forms of therapy emphasize the importance of having sexual offenders recognize their "true selves" and their harmful proclivities despite the likelihood that this may have a negative impact on long-term change. In addition, Shorts' rapist maintained a psychological distance from women in terms of his present and ideal self both before and after therapy. This finding may reflect Malamuth's

(1984) view of "hostile masculinity", or a very patronizing and aggressive machismo on the part of some men who rape women. One problem in attempting to study rapists' constructs, however, is the tendency to view all offenders as sharing similar constructions. On the same lines, Rada (1978) argued that rapists suffer from what he termed the "Madonna-Prostitute Complex", or a tendency to think in extreme terms of women as either extremely pure, and not to be touched, or extremely impure, and to be touched whenever desired. Carnahan (1987) investigated this hypothesis using a form of rep grid with incarcerated rapists. He could find no overall support, although he did find that rapists viewed rape victims as 'less pure' than did incarcerated property offenders. Carnahan's sample included only rapists who had been sentenced to only two years of confinement or less, and it is possible that a group of more serious or repeat offenders might show more extreme construal patterns. Again, the problem with the limited work on rapists to date, however, is the tendency to view all rapists as having common constructions. In fact, Prentky and Knight (1991) have demonstrated that there are many different subtypes of rapists with different "motives" defining each. Some first time violent offenders, especially assaultive individuals, may act to validate essentially invalid predictions (Houston, 1998). Many repeat violent offenders, however, act in accordance with self-relevant constructs and views of others that involve aggressive or violent labels (Needs, 1988). Gang violence, in particular, may be the "cement" by which individuals establish a group identity for themselves. Specific forms of violent offense have been examined by a number of investigators. Howells (1983) administered repertory grids to a number of violent offenders deemed to be 'mentally disordered'. He found that repeat offenders, compared to first offenders, saw themselves in a more positive light despite, or perhaps because of, their lengthy criminal histories. Needs (1988), too, found that a repeatedly violent offender saw himself in a positive manner (for example, 'wild' as opposed to 'soft'). Landfield (1971), however, found evidence that some violent offenders do not construe violence positively. One violent individual saw many people as violent and unhappy, including himself, and lashed out impulsively against the perceived offenses of others. This individual was a severe alcoholic, however, which may have had a significant impact on his construal of self and others. A case of an arsonist (Landfield, 1971) was similarly intriguing in that the arsonist had a very tight construct system with themes of religion and morality, and generally saw herself as a good and God-fearing person, but may well have shifted to the 'bad, Devilish' view when unable to keep to her very high standards. The arsonist examined by Fransella and Adams (1966), too, was a very religious individual. Horley and Quinsey (1995) found differences between child molesters who kill victims compared with those who do not, in that child killers viewed men as more cruel and stronger than those who did not kill. One problem with these and other studies of violent offenders is that they involve very different expressions of violence. If we accept that specific types of sexual offenders vary significantly from each other, then violent offenders cannot be considered a single group. For further research, the specific nature of the violence, such as assault of homicide, needs to be taken into account.

Other Sexual Offenders

There are a variety of other forms of sexual deviation, commonly classed as "nuisance" offenses because of a lack of physical contact or at least less physical trauma inflicted on victims. In general, partly because they are viewed as less severe offenses, we know little about the offenders in general—they tend to not be incarcerated for long periods when discovered and adjudicated, and they tend not to step forward on their own for treatment—and very little work from a PCT perspective has been done.

Men who gain sexual gratification from exhibiting their genitalia are usually referred to as exhibitionists (APA, 2013). Strangely, they are seldom studied in spite of very high offense rates (Mohr, Turner, & Jerry, 1964). As Mohr, Turner, and Jerry noted, the shocked reactions of the victims of such offenders tend to be the reason for the unsolicited exposure, but the obvious question left unanswered concerns why victims react with shock or fear. Landfield and Epting (1987) reported on a single exhibitionist who, when completing psychological assessments, had difficulty naming any acquaintances, especially women. Whether this is a common circumstance for these individuals, and whether it is a precursor or effect of the problem, is unknown. One partially successful treatment presented by Horley (1995) involved a repeat exhibitionist who viewed himself as a "pervert", and his repeated offenses were seen in part as a black mark against his family as a whole. To argue that such a personal construction like "pervert" is at the basis of all exhibitionism is too simple and easy, but it may help to explain the continued behavior in the face of escalating punishment and "pain". The "shocked" or "surprised" reactions of victims might, at least in some cases, be more non-verbal revulsion and disgust that validates the actor's identity as a pervert or disgusting person. Much more research with these offenders is required.

Those individuals who observe others without their knowledge, usually while they are disrobing or engaging in sexual activity, for sexual gratification purposes, or voyeurs (APA, 2013), are especially difficult to study (i.e., rarely incarcerated or hospitalized). Often, such individuals are not nor never have been specialists (Horley, 2008). They may have some other form of offensive sexual behavior, either exhibitionism or obscene telephone calling, and this pattern has been reported elsewhere (Abel, Becker, & Cunningham-Rathner, 1984). One limited insight into this pattern of perversion is that these men who view themselves as "normal", by noting that anyone who consumes "adult" media or who attends "exotic" shows is voyeuristic, admit to timidity when approaching potential sexual partners. However, it is unclear whether this is the result of a desire for "intimidating" partners or a perceived social deficiency.

A number of more exotic forms of sexual deviance also exist, at least according to the APA (2013). Frotteurism, or the public rubbing against non-consenting partners for sexual gratification, have been examined, albeit infrequently and rarely from a PCT perspective. Horley (2001) argued that there is no need for a separate diagnostic category for frotteurism, because testing of these individuals reveals that they appear to be timid, potential rapists. Necrophilia, or sexual attraction to death and the dead, has become the focus of some recent books and films, generally reflecting more voyeuristic and sales intent than any real insight, with the possible exception of the 1996 Canadian movie *Kissed*. The desire for dead bodies may actually be a desire for total sexual control (i.e., corpses do not object to any sexual acts), especially given that there appear to be many, relatively speaking, limited or quasi-necrophiles who seek out live partners willing to pretend to be dead (e.g., ice-cold baths, no movement, sex in a coffin) during a sexual encounter. Other categories of sexual deviance, such as gerontophilia (i.e., sexual attraction to elderly adults), appear silly, offensive, or both—no doubt they speak loudly about the personal constructs of some mental health professionals rather than their potential clients.

A Recommendation

Whether we are talking about "minor" or "major" sexual offenders based on the nature of their anomalous behavior, it is very easy to see the activity and the actors as so repugnant and puzzling that we take an easy approach and name it as genetic or at least rooted so deeply in biological factors as to be unchangeable. Similarly, it is easy to adopt language that is not malleable or avoids corrigibility, such as referring to offenders as having a sexual orientation towards children (see Seto, 2012). We can rely on assumptions rather than theory and an established research base, but it will be to our own detriment, to say nothing of the detriment of everyone we so label. Those who have committed sexual offenses may possess such an established set of constructs supportive of the abuse, and may have committed abusive acts for so long, that they are unable to alter their perspective and their harmful ways. For all intents and purposes they are incorrigible and possibly very dangerous offenders and should be treated as such. Many offenders, however, have only experimented with constructs that, while indicative of suspect decision-making and disregard for others, do not suggest a malevolent and incorrigible nature. While it may not be an easy task, we need to be able to separate the dangerous long-term offenders from the single-mistake or short-term offenders and offer them some hope of change. Condemning all who commit sexual offenses to a life of incarceration, social isolation, or worse (e.g., torture, execution) is inexcusably simplistic, wasteful, and unjust. By providing them with an inescapable explanation for their offenses (e.g., born preprogrammed to abuse women), in effect, we are handicapping any who may wish to understand and to change their lives. It is very easy to accept a "scientific" explanation, especially if Darwin and evolutionary theories are trotted out, and much more difficult to understand abnormal sexual identities or construct systems that lead one down a path of sexual abuse.

Unfortunately, such explanations and theories abound, and far too many offenders accept, quite understandably, the theories and the consequences offered by well-meaning professionals. Professionals within criminal justice systems—judges, lawyers, forensic clinicians, and probation-parole officers, to say nothing of police officers—often make pronouncements that are, in effect, condemning offenders to a life sentence if not a death sentence. Forensic theorists need to be very careful before suggesting that "we know" that sexual offenders are "born that way" and there is little hope of change. We suspect that the vast majority are relying on what they may have come across most recently, touting the viability of the latest bio-evolutionary theory of sexual offending, and we would not accuse most of callously and cynically supporting their own positions by creating a demand for their services by creating born criminals, or clients who believe that they are unable to change their offending behavior. We need to offer hope for change, and a good basis for moving forward is a theory such as PCT that accounts for both, stability and change, and also offers some help for achieving personal improvement.

We probably should face the charge that we are offering false hope to sexual offenders through a theory like PCT. First of all, it is only a theory and we may be wrong, although at this point we do not believe this to be the case. All theories need to gain research support, and at this time, there is little support for any theory of sexual offending. It is very easy to conclude that nothing works in attempting to alter criminal behavior (see Martinson, 1974), but we have been engaged in forensic treatment for relatively little time, and have really lacked both the imagination and the resources, to rule out effective treatment for sexual offenders. Given that some promising treatment possibilities seem to be appearing now(see Marshall, 2006, for a more optimistic view of sex offender treatment), we should at least reserve judgement about being able to assist offenders to change significantly, if not be somewhat optimistic that efficacious treatment options are just around the corner. We will present a few clinical assessment and treatment techniques that have proven to be useful tools for a limited number of sexual offenders to date. They may be shown to be very effective in the future but, if not, they appear to be better alternatives than what we often do today—reuse the same old, tired strategies and expect different results.

9

Changing Sexual Interests, Identities, and Behaviours

One obvious implication of a theory of human sexuality based on choice is that if something can be chosen it can also be rejected at a later time. The acceptance of a channelized choice, however, means that the rejection of an adopted and employed construct does not mean that the entire system reverts to its state immediately prior to the adoption of the construct. Constructs come and constructs go; they also evolve with system change. As construct system change occurs, there is a very good chance that self-identity, including a sense of the self as a sexual being, is modified. While this may be true for a PCT-based theory of sexual desire, changing sexual desires let alone sexual identity is easier said than done. We may want to alter our desires and sexual engagements but, aside from a sudden and massive alteration in our current system, any change is likely to be slow, difficult, and perhaps more likely to move backward than forward, especially if we attempt it on our own. While epiphanies can and do occur, they are very rare, and long and slow change is more common and often involves help and support, whether through professional or informal helping networks. Though some therapists may believe in the efficacy of their theories and techniques, the change that can occur through formal helping networks and professionals must be seen as slow, gradual, and incremental change.

Just to be clear, we are not talking here about changing the sexual identities and practices of any sexual minority group members, unless those individuals engage in sexual relationships with prepubescent individuals or gain sexual compliance via physical force or threats. The focus of this chapter will be on assisting or promoting change among those who engage in the extreme and harmful sexual practices described in the previous chapter. While we will emphasize the PCT-based possibilities of work with sexual aggressors, in part due to work with both incarcerated and non-incarcerated sexual offenders over 30 years by one of us (JH), we are using the term "change" in a broad sense. We stand well clear of any reference to or connection with such approaches to sexual change as conversion therapy or reparation therapy, a class of treatments popular from the 1960s to the 1980s that intended to mould gay individuals into straight ones (Drescher, 1998). Change is not to be equated with conversion (c.f., Stein, 1999) and the concept of conversion should probably be avoided entirely. Setting aside obvious problematic issues such as the choice of such terminology, conversion or reparation therapies are based on learning principles (e.g., Skinnerian operant learning), social–psychological principles (e.g., value identification and change), psychoanalysis, or some combination of these different approaches. All seem to offer a relatively "quick fix" (i.e., weeks or months to complete change) for gay, lesbian, or other sexual minority clients. Overall, conversion–reparation strategies appear to be rather ineffective at "converting" sexual minorities to a majority position (see reviews by Blackwell, 2008; Haldeman, 2004), and some clients who engage in such therapies appear to be at risk of some harm (Shidlo & Schroeder, 2002). Spitzer (2003), to be fair, did argue that many "highly motivated" gays and lesbians appeared to have come around to a heterosexual orientation, at least to some extent, but he retracted this conclusion after a few years of further reflection (Spitzer, 2012). We will also avoid a number of areas of sexual therapy that are more reputable or acceptable than the conversion of sexual minorities, such as sexual dysfunction and addressing issues (e.g., low self-esteem, social anxiety) that may be related to having a sexual minority identity. We can only refer interested readers to some limited work done in personal construct counselling and psychotherapy (e. g., Moradi, van den Berg, & Epting, 2009; Winter, 1992a), since each of these topics likely deserves book-length treatment.

We plan to examine sample strategies that are consistent with PCT, and certainly not all the psychotherapies or treatment techniques available, simply a few representative and interesting examples that we are relatively familiar with through direct implementation and development. For a more complete set of possibilities, see Epting (1984) or Winter (1992a). Before presenting formal techniques for change, however, a brief description of clinical assessment within PCT appears necessary. Clearly, any reader who is not a psychologist, or just not interested in sexual change, can proceed directly to the final chapter without missing a serious aspect of the theory since our concern here is primarily clinical practice. However, we encourage you to continue with this chapter because this is where we link theory to technique to change—an essential component of applying PCT in any discipline.

For those non-psychologists who are interested in the study of sexual change, there is some important material to be gained by following detailed and complex descriptions of clinical assessments within PCT. This discussion on PCT assessment techniques clearly links theory to data collection and vice versa—an important point often emphasized in social sciences research. This is obvious in studies that involve symbolic interactionism drawing on ethnographic studies and in-depth interviews for data collection. Since symbolic interactionism explains what symbols stand for in individuals' everyday lives, any study framed by this theory requires detailed and rich data on how individuals make meaning in their everyday actions in complex ways. From a non-psychological perspective, the techniques used for clinical assessment in PCT are not simply quantitative but qualitative as well. Qualitative techniques permit the eliciting of rich personal details, a focus on meaning from the client's or participant's perspective, and contribute to change in the individual's life. It appears to us that many of the clinical assessment tools described in this section can be adapted very easily to research studies on sexuality in non-clinical settings to yield textured and ecologically relevant information.

Clinical Assessment in PCT

When it comes to clinical assessment, generally speaking, PCT would have all clinicians avoid all hard–and–fast diagnostic labels. Kelly proposed a novel and useful approach to clinical assessment. He suggested using "transitive diagnosis... {to avoid any} nosological pigeonhole" (Kelly, 1955, p. 775). A transitive diagnosis is a dynamic statement of the important issues at hand in therapy in order to help a client identify "bridges between the client's present and his future" (p. 775). A diagnosis that changes constantly, as the client changes, avoids the trap of being preemptive by trying to place an active, struggling client into a box formed by a traditional nosological category, and the box may turn out to be more of a Procrustean bed for the individual. An egalitarian theory that avoids distinctions between "we as psychotherapists" and "them as patients", is perhaps a good starting point to limit the harmful effects of labelling since it would accept that patients or clients have at least as much agency as the professionals who provide them assistance. PCT avoids the problematic notion of personality traits altogether, never mind the really thorny issue of negative or dysfunctional traits. Some personal constructs can, without a doubt, lead to trouble and a failure to anticipate the future effectively, but such constructs can be purged or altered by any individual, with or without assistance, although the consequences to the system as a whole may be serious. The midlife change of "psychopaths", for example, may be due to the realization that, after years of hitting one's head against a wall or the bars of a jail cell, something needs to change because what is passing for life is looking pretty grim. Insight, epiphany, maturation, or whatever term is more acceptable can apply to those who are nasty just as much as to those who are not.

The repertory test (rep test) is a broad-ranging assessment approach to elicit and examine a very small sample or segment of an individual's vast array, his or her repertoire, of personal constructs (Kelly, 1955). The rep test comes in a variety of formats, including card sorts (e.g., Badesha & Horley, 2000) and a verbally administered group format (Kelly, 1955), but the most popular format by far is the repertory grid technique (rep grid). The rep grid (see Fransella, Bell, & Bannister, 2004) is the rep test in matrix form. The rep grid has played an integral role as both a research instrument and a clinical tool in the development of PCT. Indeed, some form of repertory grid procedure has been used in over 90 % of published empirical research in PCT (Neimeyer, Baker, & Neimeyer, 1990). This methodology also has been employed widely by researchers outside the field of personal construct psychology (Adams-Webber, 1989).

The rep grid is essentially a complex sorting task in which a list of elements is categorized dichotomously in terms of each of a set of bipolar dimensions. An assessor can elicit a sample of personal constructs from each respondent individually, supply the same standard or normative set of dimensions to all test-takers alike, or use an individual–normative combination. The data elicited from each respondent is entered into a separate two-dimensional matrix or grid in which there is a column for every element and a row for every construct. Each box made out of a row–column intersection in this grid contains a symbol (e.g., a binary digit) indicating which pole of a given construct was applied to a particular element. Many forms of rep grids in current use, unlike Kelly's original procedure, require rating elements on n-point scales where n is greater than 2. For example, 1 might represent the assignment of an element to the left-hand pole of a construct, and n its assignment to the right-hand pole. Scalars within the range 2 –> n - 1 can be used to represent intermediate response alternatives. To permit a natural midpoint, n is usually a small odd number, such as 3, 5, or 7. As demonstrated by Gaines and Shaw (1980), each pole of a given construct can be viewed as representing a predicate that designates a set, with or without distinct logical boundaries, and every rating indicates a particular element's degree of membership in that set.

All constructs, as mentioned in Chapter 2, are bipolar or have a binary format. Every construct pair represents a single dichotomous distinction. Repertory grid research utilizes this assumption sometimes without paying sufficient attention to the contrast pole that is often assumed rather than elicited. Kelly (1955) himself devised several different ways in which personal constructs can be elicited. His "difference method" is the most commonly used among these approaches. In this method, respondents are presented with sets of three elements, or triads, and are asked to indicate how two elements are alike in some important way in which they differ from the third (e.g., "My father and I are both weak while my sister is strong.") There is no strict requirement that the contrasts are genuinely bipolar. Mair (1967) observed that:

> the contrasts between poles of constructs often differ considerably from those that seem to be dictated by the logic of public language...studies seem

to demonstrate enough variety in pole contrasts to encourage more attention to this problem in psychological measurement generally and grid measurement in particular (p. 226).

As Fransella and Bannister (1977) noted, "we may assume that charitable to you means the same as charitable to me. But for you the opposite pole might be intolerant and for me hold strong opinions" (p. 105). Mair (1967) found sufficient variety when respondents were asked to supply contrast poles to provided constructs to recommend that greater attention should be paid to contrast constructs, especially since there is a small but consistent effect of overlapping endorsements of "opposite" constructs when construing the same elements. He cautioned against our making inferences about construct relationships, particularly the implicit contrast pole, and suggested that people often use amalgamations of ideas rather than single verbal labels to describe others.

Epting, Suchman, and Nickeson (1971) found that the "opposite method" (i.e., giving the opposite of the construct) elicited significantly more genuinely bipolar constructs; however, it also generated significantly less differentiated personal constructs, a finding subsequently replicated by Hagans et al. (2000) and Neimeyer et al. (2002). Hagans et al. (2000) suggested that there are two distinct ways in which the difference and the opposite methods might influence the kinds of constructs that are elicited. First, instructions that require an individual to provide the opposite of a given pole might elicit a more extreme contrast. For example, asking an individual to specify the opposite of "friendly" might elicit "hostile", rather than a less extreme response such as "aloof". In short, the opposite method creates a demand characteristic for contrast poles with a stronger valence. Second, the opposite method also allows for the possibility that the contrast pole may not apply to any element in the grid. In contrast, the difference method requires that at least one element in the triad is assigned to the contrast pole because it is elicited on the basis of that element's difference from the first two. The opposite method does not impose this specific constraint.

Hagans et al. (2000) pointed out that "differences between the opposite and difference methods of construct elicitation carry direct implications for measures of construct system structure" (p. 158). Elicitation instructions that require the distribution of ratings across both poles of constructs, as in the difference method, can increase differentiation between constructs. Techniques that limit this distribution, or even allow all the elements to be allotted to the same pole of a construct, can reduce overall construct differentiation. A pair of experiments by Hagans et al. (2000) showed that the opposite method elicited more extreme and negative contrast poles. They also observed that the negativity of the contrast poles inversely correlated with the degree of differentiation between constructs (i.e., constructs with more extreme and negative contrast poles were less differentiated). Moreover, when the influence of negativity per se was adjusted for, there was no effect in terms of differentiation. These results support the hypothesis that the opposite method leads to the elicitation of more extreme contrasts that are then applied to a narrower range of elements. In short, differences in the complexity, negativity, and bipolarity of personal construct systems are related to variations in the method of construct elicitation.

Relatively little PCT research has been done on evaluating rep grid methodology in terms of its reliability and validity despite calls for more attention from some investigators (e.g., Chambers, 1985). An important study by Bavelas, Chan, and Guthrie (1976) that examined the reliability and validity of a variety of repertory grid indices produced some challenging results. They found, as did Adams-Webber (1970a), a satisfactory level of agreement among different repertory grid measures assessing the same formal index (e.g., cognitive complexity, identification, construct constellatoriness), but they also found other indices unreliable over short-time intervals such as one, two, and three weeks. They argued that this lack of reliability at the structural level implied a lack of reliability at the content level as well, although this has not been found to be the case by other investigators (e.g., Horley, 1996; Horley & Quinsey, 1995; Sperlinger, 1976). Both Sperlinger (1976) and Horley (1996) reported moderate reliability in terms of content, albeit within limited samples. Other explanations for Bavelas et al.'s findings are possible; for example, they themselves suggested that, first, not all the figures on the grid were within the range of convenience of all the constructs, leading to some random responding, and second, the size of the grid (19 × 19) possibly produced random responding due to fatigue and impermeability. The questions raised by this study have been passed over too often in rep grid research. Some early research into grid methodology, while stressing its flexibility, tended to discount the importance of reliability. For example, Bannister and Mair (1968) took the position that, "since there is no such thing as the grid, there can be no such thing as the reliability of the grid" (p. 156). It follows that questions concerning reliability and validity can be applieddirectly to the particular composite indices and methods of analysis employed, rather than to the repertory grid technique as a general measurement format.

In recent years, there has been a tremendous proliferation of new forms of the rep grid. Despite early warnings by Bonarius (1965) and others, clinicians have forged ahead and have developed novel and complex grid measures, often without much regard for reliability. Hagans, Neimeyer, and Goodholm (2000) noted that "variations in grid methods affect not only the structure of the construct system, but also the nature of the constructs elicited" (p. 170). If the rep grid is to be used in PCT research in the future, it requires a conscientious effort to investigate its strengths and limitations both in terms of structure and content. There does exist, however, some fairly convincing evidence that, whatever be its limitations, the repertory grid technique can be used to produce highly reliable measurements–strong support for its construct validity in terms of the central assumptions of PCT.

The degree of differentiation between the self and others is a good example of grid consistency. This factor can be defined in grid terms simply as the extent to which people assign themselves and others to the same pole of a set of dichotomous constructs (e.g., good vs. bad). It has been referred to in the relevant literature by a variety of different names, including "identification" (Jones, 1961) and "assimilative projection" (Bieri, 1955). Reported estimates of the temporal or test–retest reliability of this composite index have ranged from 0.86 to 0.95 (Benjafield & Adams-Webber, 1975, Feixas, Molinder, Montes, Marie, & Neimeyer, 1992, Jones, 1961, Pedersen, 1958, Sperlinger, 1976). There is also evidence that some of its component substructures, for instance, the degree of differentiation between mother and self, are highly reliable (Pedersen, 1958). Indeed, self-differentiation may be one of the most stable rep grid indices (Winter, 1992a). Moreover, the correlations observed between this particular measure and several other formal indices in the rep grid structure tend to be higher than their own test–retest correlations. These include the overall degree of statistical association between constructs, the average distance between figures, the number of significant linkages between constructs, and the explanatory power of the first factor (see Adams-Webber, 1979, 1989). Thus, self-differentiation is not only both consistent and stable as a grid measure, it also helps explain much of the systematic variations in other aspects of the rep grid structure. It is possible that this index represents an important factor in the organization of personal construct systems.

With respect to self–other differentiation in PCT research, Bannister and Agnew (1977), among other investigators, have hypothesized that, as children mature and gain new interpersonal experiences, they should gradually differentiate between themselves and others to a greater degree. On the basis of this hypothesis, it is possible to predict that the extent to which children and adolescents distinguish between themselves and others on bipolar constructs will gradually increase throughout childhood and adolescence. In support of this hypothesis, Carr and Townes (1975) reported systematic increases in differentiation between the self and others during late adolescence and early adulthood.

Strachan and Jones (1982) hypothesized that the degree to which adolescents differentiate themselves specifically from their parents also increases with age. As Winter (1992a) pointed out, a "particular aspect of identification with parents which has received some research attention is the extent to which an individual's identification with the parent of the same sex as himself or herself is greater than that with the opposite-sex parent" (p. 134). An early study by Giles and Rychlak (1965) indicated that students tend to characterize themselves as more similar to the parent of the same gender than to the parent of the opposite gender, although the results of Ryle and Lunghi (1972) suggest that this may hold true only for women. In their guidelines for interpreting rep grid data, Landfield and Epting (1987) recommended that we "observe whether mother is differentiated from father" (p. 132). Adams-Webber and Neff (1996) found a significant correlation between the age of children and adolescents (from 8 to 18 years) and the degree to which they differentiated themselves from parents of their own and opposite gender. Moreover, the extent of differentiation between the parents correlated with the degree of differentiation between the self and each parent. Across all 11 age groups, both boys and girls differentiated themselves to a greater degree from parents of the opposite gender than from parents of the same gender. Although girls and boys differentiated themselves from their mothers to about the same extent, girls differentiated themselves from their fathers significantly more than boys did. It also has been found consistently that, when people evaluate themselves negatively on any bipolar construct, either elicited or supplied, they evaluate approximately 50% of other persons negatively on that particular construct (Adams-Webber, 1989; Adams-Webber & Davidson, 1979; Adams-Webber & Rodney, 1983; Benjafield & Adams-Webber, 1975). Thus, "positive–negative asymmetry", which seems so ubiquitous in social cognition (see Warr, 1971), appears specific to constructs in terms of which self is assigned to positive poles. Depressed psychiatric patients, compared to various other groups, not only assign both themselves and others to the negative poles of more constructs, but they also characterize others as less similar to themselves (Space & Cromwell, 1980; Space et al., 1983). Space and Cromwell (1980) refer to this latter result as an unexpected finding, on the basis of which they suggest that "low identification with others should be included along with other features of depression" (p. 156). When Adams-Webber and Rodney (1983) instructed undergraduates to role-play a negative mood, acting out imagined experiences that involve intense disappointment, there was a significant decrease in the proportion of similar–to–self evaluations. When the same participants enacted euphoric moods associated with imagined successes (in counter-balanced order), the proportion of similar–to–self judgments increased significantly. In a replication of this study by Lefebvre et al. (1986), the relative frequency of similar–to–self evaluations also decreased during the enactment of a 'negative' mood and increased during the enactment of a 'positive' mood.

Kelly (1955) provided more than one technique for assessing personality, although the wide use of the rep grid has overshadowed this fact. Self-characterization was suggested (Kelly, 1955) as an assessment technique consistent with the PCT's credulous approach, where the client is directly asked about himself or herself. Self-characterization, similarly, is a technique where the client is asked to provide a third-person sketch of

9 Changing Sexual Interests, Identities, and Behaviours   203

himself or herself. Through an autobiographical yet somewhat distant description, the individual may provide important information about his or her salient personal constructs and characteristic manner of anticipating events. The self-characterization technique appears to have been used infrequently and typically in a clinical context (see Landfield & Epting, 1987; Winter, 1992a). It remains, however, a technique that can yield interesting data for personality investigators because of its appealing "open" format and ability to provide access to core constructs (Horley, 2005a, 2005b). Horley and Johnson (2008) have discussed a treatment group for domestic abusers where self-characterization provided not only an approach to construct assessment, but the framework for initial group discussions as members described their current selves.

Another interesting modification of the standard repertory grid was introduced by Ryle and Lunghi (1970). Instead of using figures as elements, they used relationships between people (e.g., John to Mary, Mary to John). Their dyad grid helps measure of a person's perception of interpersonal relationships. Ryle and Lunghi favoured a repertory grid method because data is collected directly from the respondent so that the therapist's own theoretical constructs cannot bias it, and because the particular aims of therapy can be defined in grid terms and measured afterward. The dyad grid is analyzed in terms of two principal components (Slater, 1969) which can be diagrammed as orthogonal axes. Elements can be displayed on the diagram to illustrate the way in which relationships are construed (e.g., if the dyad lines for two elements are parallel, a similarity of reciprocal roles is suggested). The grid elucidates the way the respondent perceives a range of dyadic relationships such as self–mother, self–spouse, and mother–father. The dyad grid was recommended for investigating certain therapy clients who had disturbed relationships. It has also been as the standard grid to assess the therapist's understanding of his or her client (Ryle & Lunghi, 1971). Ryle and Breen (1972) used the dyad grid to measure empathy in adjusted and maladjusted couples.

The grid technique has been expanded for exploring more specialized interests. Hinkle (1965) was interested in the implicative network of constructs in understanding the explanatory power of individual constructs. He wanted to examine the superordinate and subordinate relationships among constructs. In order to reveal this hierarchical structure, he devised the implication grid or imp grid. The imp grid involves a fairly elaborate means of deriving a construct hierarchy by a process called laddering. A person is asked why a particular pole of a construct is preferred, and as a new construct is generated in explanation, the question is repeated until no further dimensions are given. The implications of these constructs are then derived by having the person imagine himself or herself changing poles on a construct and then stating what other changes would occur as a result of the initial change. The imp grid is one of the few grid modifications built upon a sound theoretical basis, and it has been adapted by other investigators (e.g., Honikman, 1973). Honikman noted that gaining experience in a particular domain of activity fosters the development of implications among constructs that are specifically applied to events in that domain, and the more implications a particular construct carries throughout an individual's system, the greater its subjective importance and immediate accessibility. Additionally, there is a lower likelihood that the individual will change a self-evaluation on the basis of the construct.

Other attempts have been made to derive specialized techniques for particular groups. The attempt of Horley and colleagues (e.g., Horley & Quinsey, 1994, 1995; Horley, Quinsey, & Jones, 1997) to develop a technique to examine child molesters' thoughts about themselves and others based on the Osgood et al. (1957) semantic differential appears consistent with PCT assessment. Although the particular technique developed originally has been modified, and may require further modification (see Marshall, Marshall, Sachdev, & Kruger, 2003) to be very useful, the semantic differential technique, like the rep grid, is a methodological approach that could be used to develop further forms for specific sex offender assessments. It has certain clear advantages (e.g., flexibility, less transparency) over some existing techniques in use for assessing offenders' constructs and cognitions (see previous chapter for examples). A somewhat related technique, the IAT, was recently adapted for use with child molesters by a number of researchers (e.g., Gray, Brown, MacCulloch, Smith, & Snowden, 2005; Nunes, Firestone, & Baldwin, 2007). The IAT is an indirect technique, administered via computer, that calculates the response latency between various bipolar terms (e.g., pleasant-unpleasant) and target terms (e.g., child, adult). Gray et al. (2005) showed that men convicted of sexual offences against children revealed less response latency between children and sex than adults and sex, while Nunes et al. (2007) found a relationship between molesters' responses to children and attraction. Both concluded that the IAT is a useful technique to assess child molesters' thoughts about children and adults, and the approach could be used easily with other sexual offenders (e.g., men who assault adults, those who exhibit genitalia in public) as well.

Brief Review of the PCT Treatment Literature

Before attempting to explain how PCT-related psychotherapeutic techniques and approaches can be used to alter and to improve sexual responses and behavior, a brief overview and review of personal construct clinical perspectives appears necessary. PCT has been elaborated within the clinical context in terms of various forms of psychotherapy, with the rep grid and other PCT techniques used as adjuncts to clinical work. Most notable among the various books on psychotherapy and clinical work are Epting (1984), Landfield and Epting (1987), Landfield (1971), Winter (1992a), and Winter and Viney (2005).

Landfield (1971) based his work on the therapeutic uses of PCT and elaborated on grid techniques that can be used in assessing both the content and structure of personal constructs. Landfield (1970, 1971) recommended assessing both, because content indicates an individual's preoccupation while structure indicates how an individual's constructs are related. In his system, content can be differentiated into 22 categories representing a variety of meaning implications (e.g., social interaction, forcefulness, emotional arousal). Organization is measured in terms of the number of FIC or separate dimensions used by the subject. A low FIC score means that the constructs are highly integrated and organized, while a high FIC score indicates that constructs are used independently of one another. Landfield (1970) found that clients who terminate therapy prematurely are less congruent with the therapist in terms of the content of their construct systems than are clients who do not end therapy. He added that some client–therapist incongruency in conceptual structures is related to improvements in long-term cases.

Landfield's approach to construct content analysis has been employed by a number of investigators concerned with grid content reliability (e.g., Horley, 1996) and the nature of construct content among client groups (e.g., Horley & Quinsey, 1995). Harter, Erbes, and Hart (2004) used Landfield's system to examine the construct content of women who report childhood sexual abuse. In an interesting study where the content of women who reported abuse was compared to young women who did not report abuse, Harter and colleagues found that women reporting abuse used fewer constructs concerning emotion and freedom from care, while using more constructs of a factual nature. Such findings can certainly inform efforts to treat survivors of child sexual abuse (see Erbes & Harter, 2005).

Using self-ideal–self-discrepancy as the criterion to measure success in psychotherapy, Varble and Landfield (1969) found that the discrepancy decreased significantly from pre-therapy to post-therapy. The rep test enables measurement of the self-concept and ideal self-concept in terms meaningful to the individual by placing a patient's elicited dimensions on cards which are rank ordered from most to least important in understanding people, with the lowest and highest ranks defined as peripheral and core constructs respectively. Varble and Landfield found some support for Kelly's assertion that peripheral constructs change more quickly and easily than core constructs. Independent judges assessed improvement in the patients and the unimproved patients were found to have greater discrepancy scores. Changes in the present self were more frequent than changes in the ideal self.

Landfield (1975) offered a personal construct interpretation of suicidal behavior. Suicide is seen within the framework of personal anticipation as failure to encompass or interpret relative social events. When a person's organization fails to minimize conflict, it constricts its focus until suicide may occur. The rep grid provides a measure of this constriction in two ways. The content may be constricted if the constructs are highly concrete, and the total number of ratings on the grid measures constriction in terms of constructs. The FIC score measures disorganization. If the person's construct system is disorganized and constricted, the resulting failure to predict can result in dread of a total breakdown of any structure for comprehending life. Landfield found that a group of students who had failed in serious suicide attempts had significantly higher constriction scores than comparable students who were undergoing therapy but who were not suicidal. Grids were available for a number of the most suicidal individuals in the sample before the attempt took place, thereby avoiding the usual problem in related research (i.e., data are collected only after the fact, rendering the state of mind of the potential suicide unknown).

Ryle and his colleagues have analyzed rep grids in order to study therapeutic groups. Ryle and Lunghi (1969) recommended the use of the rep grid to provide an objective measure of variables of interest to the therapist. The therapist can examine the dispersion of significant people within a client's construct system and the aims of treatment can be translated into a prediction of change in construct relationships. Such a strategy can provide a subtle means of evaluating psychiatric treatment although it can also prove tricky and time-consuming. Ryle and Lunghi (1970) modified the grid using relationships as elements, creating what they termed a "dyad grid", because they felt the rep grid method provided a means of collecting data directly from the patient without the bias of a therapist's own theoretical constructs. In addition, the aims of therapy could be defined in grid terms and measured afterward. The dyad grid is analyzed in terms of two principle components using Slater's INGRID programme (Slater, 1969) which can be diagrammed as orthogonal axes. Elements can be displayed on the diagram to illustrate the way in which relationships are construed when the client's hopes and therapist's aims are relatively independent. Symptom loss and dynamic change, as indicated by the grid, were highly correlated.

The grid is often extended beyond the single client to a group situation. Watson (1970b) used group members as grid elements, with constructs provided by the therapists. The constructs were thought to be important in understanding group activities (e.g., comparative constructs, "like me"; or emotional constructs, "angry"). Each member was rated on a scale from 0–100 on each construct. These grids were used to provide hypotheses about the group, indicate therapeutic change, and reveal individual construct relationships. Watson (1972) found measurable changes during treatment, particularly among the patients, as opposed to the therapists, when the grids were completed at two- or three-month intervals.

An empathy score was derived from the relationship between the subject prediction of ranking and the actual ranking by every other subject. As might be expected, and certainly as one would hope, the therapist who was ranked highest on understanding, by the clients and by himself, had the highest grid score on empathy. There was a high correlation between grid empathy and rated empathy. The amount of overlap between own and others' constructs, and shared experience, correlated highly with empathy, although patients high on understanding were able to distance themselves from their own views in order to predict the view of others.

Rep grids have also been used as indicators of change in different therapy situations such as forensic settings. Shorts (1985) employed a rep grid as a measure of change in personality, and more specifically, construing in individual therapy with a rapist. The alteration of this hospitalized client's self and other views was interpreted by Shorts as evidence of the sensitivity and utility of the rep grid in therapeutic settings. Houston and Adshead (1993) also employed a rep grid as a measure of change for a small group of child molesters who participated in a community-based treatment group. Although a pilot project, Houston and Adshead found that changes in grid results mirrored qualitative measures of change provided by the group leaders. They recommended that grids be used more often by therapists interested in more sensitive and less transparent change indices.

Research into the efficacy of PCT-based psychotherapy for offenders has been relatively limited, and like the situation in personal construct psychotherapy, more generally (see Winter, 2003a), often based on case studies. Some of the forensic case studies reported in the clinical literature to date are difficult to interpret in terms of therapeutic result. Skene's (1971) report of the treatment using FRT on a "homosexual" is a good case in point. From Skene's description of the client, it is impossible to know whether the teenager being treated was sexually aggressive with young males at least five years his junior and therefore "hebephilic" to use current, psychiatric terminology, or was simply engaged in consenting sexual relationships with similar aged peers. Shorts's (1985) report of PCT psychotherapy with an adult male who assaulted adult females is rather unclear as to the result of therapy, insofar as identifying with rapists at the termination of treatment is not necessarily the mark of success that many clinicians would accept. Case studies and single case experiments do suggest that various PCT-based treatments, especially FRT, can and have been used with some efficacy with arsonists (Fransella & Adams, 1966; Landfield, 1971), exhibitionists (Horley, 1995; Landfield & Epting, 1987), complex sexual anomalies (e.g., Horley, 2005b), and mentally disordered offenders (Houston, 2003).

While there are few formal and systematic evaluations of psychotherapeutic programmes, there is reason to believe that this situation is changing. Among the more formal evaluations of PCT-based offender therapies, Cummins (2003) described a programme that he offers for those with anger problems. Cummins reported that on the basis of qualitative indices, such as client feedback, that he had gathered post treatment, the therapy was a success in terms of personal insight gained from participation in his group therapy. Horley and Johnson (2008) collected some limited data on a treatment group for domestic abusers. They found that the self-esteem of male abusers, as measured by a self-ideal discrepancy, increased over the course of a 12-week programme, although the significance of such a finding on future abusive behavior is debatable.

Rowe (1971) examined the accuracy of a psychiatrist's understanding of his client's constructs, where the rep grid served to measure the extent of misunderstanding between therapist and client. A patient generated eight bipolar constructs and was provided with an additional seven. These were used to construe 20 significant figures. The psychiatrist was given the same 20 elements and constructs with which to make predictive sorts. While Rowe's psychiatrist showed a fair degree of insight into the patient's construct system, he made some systematic errors as well. A similar study (Watson, 1970b) was extended over a nine-month period during which a therapist and client completed four identical grids. The results were very similar to those of Rowe in that the therapist had a reasonable understanding of the patient on the whole, but relatively little understanding of the client's use of several constructs.

Fransella and Joyston-Bechal (1971) examined a therapy group using the grid in order to study changes in the patterning of ideas and to identify group processes in both the patients and therapists. Caplan, Rohde, Shapiro, and Watson (1975) correlated clients' grids with behavioral indices, such as participation during group sessions and processes occurring during therapy. They found that individual participation and the level and type of verbal activity within the group as a whole affected the ratings on the grid. They noted that the grid can present difficulty in analysis because it is difficult to distinguish unreliable measurements from valid indications of change. Shapiro, Caplan, Rohde, and Watson (1975) suggested combining information from other sources, such as the personal questionnaires and verbal behavior, to assist in interpreting results. Fielding (1975) used the rep grid in combination with the Symptom Check List Rating Scale to measure the outcome of group therapy.

A study of marital success and construct congruence within couples found no relationship between the number of shared constructs and marital adjustment (Weigel, Weigel, & Richardson, 1973). However, the dimensions used were forty supplied constructs rather than personal constructs. The researchers concluded that marital success may relate more to one's ability to predict the partner's construct system than to shared constructs.

Fransella (1968) used the rep grid to look at the self-concepts of stutterers. She found that people who stutter do not conceptualize themselves as stutterers; instead, they see stutterers in the same sort of way speech experts and laymen do. On a grid with photographs as elements and with supplied constructs, there was no significant correlation between the construct "like me in character" and "stutterer". Fransella proposed that therapy should endeavour to help the stutterer accept stuttering as part of his or her true self, and then help the patient build up a system of constructs that relate to seeing himself or herself as a person who speaks normally. The dichotomy between self and behavior found with stutterers also appears in the grids of alcoholics. Orford (1974) used the rep grid to study the construing of alcoholics. He examined early dropouts from an alcoholism halfway house in terms of cognitive complexity and simplicity in construing other people. Orford's measures of simplicity involved unipolarity of free descriptions and grid redundancy. He found some support for the hypothesis that individuals with relatively simple constructions of others tend to leave treatment sooner than more complex individuals.

Overall, while formal evaluations of the efficacy of PCT-related psychotherapeutic techniques are relatively few and the question of overall impact remains open, there is some evidence of efficacy (Holland et al., 2007). Viney, Metcalfe, and Winter (2005) concluded that there appears to be "encouraging evidence of the effectiveness of personal construct psychotherapy" (p. 363) following their review of PCT literature. Included here would be work done with individuals exhibiting harmful sexual extremes that has been, in general, effective (Horley, 2005b).

PCT-Based Psychotherapy with Sexual Offenders

Fixed-Role Therapy

Introduced by Kelly (1955) and elaborated by Bonarius (1970), Epting (1984), and Winter (1992a) among others, FRT tends to be used in individual therapy although it has been attempted in a small group settings (Beail & Parker, 1991). FRT is a dramaturgical approach to psychotherapy, based loosely on some of the early writings of Moreno (1934/1960), an interesting innovator in many areas of psychology (Horley & Strickland, 1984) who proposed two forms of psychotherapy—psychodrama and sociodrama—based on formal role-playing. According to Kelly (1955), anyone can restructure his or her construct system by considering and enacting new roles. This is a position that appears consistent with a number of thinkers (e.g., Goffman, 1959) who emphasize the performative nature of behavior. Even Butler (1990, 2004), by emphasizing the performative aspects of gender-based behavior, appears to endorse such a perspective. In FRT, a client is asked to adopt a "new personality"—the fixed sketch of a character at odds in particular dimensions from his or her current troubled self. The emphasis is placed on a thematic shift rather than the correction of minor personal problems. By acting out a new and more functional role, important changes in the client should be manifested over time, although Epting, Gemignani, and Cross (2003) suggested that the point of FRT is to demonstrate that personal change is possible. Developing an acceptable personality sketch is the task of the therapist only after an assessment of the client, which includes an in-depth understanding of the nature of the person that the client would like to become. The sketch, rarely if ever representing an ideal individual, is presented to the client with "the full protection of 'make believe'" (Kelly, 1955, p. 373), which means that the client is asked to engage in a creative endeavour rather than an attempt to become what he or she should be or what the therapist desires. The client is encouraged, via discussion around character development and role-playing, to see the world through the eyes of the new character. In contrast to Kelly (1955), who suggested that FRT could be viewed as a form of short-term or brief therapy with some extension for more difficult cases, it might be best viewed as a much more extended project when it involves certain client groups and certain types of problems (Horley, 2008). Kelly, it must be accepted, worked primarily with university students showing relatively minor adjustment problems.

Interestingly, FRT has been used with sexual offenders for a considerable period of time. In one of the first reports, Skene (1973) discussed the treatment of a "case of homosexuality" using FRT, although it is unclear whether Skene's male client was attracted to pubescent or prepubescent males. Skene reported the successful "reorientation" of the client following some months of FRT, despite providing few details of the process of the therapy. Various forensic therapists (e.g., Horley, 2003b, 2008; Houston, 1998) have argued that FRT should be used in more forensic treatment settings, especially involving complex and difficult cases. Horley (2005a, 2005b) demonstrated the effectiveness of FRT in a single case experiment involving an individual with a number of sexually problematic interests. Clients with multiple and harmful sexual extremes, which appear fairly common (Adams & McAnulty, 1993), are very appropriate candidates, especially given that they are not considered ideal candidates by many therapists. Unravelling and treating the various sexual difficulties of some individuals presents a daunting task, especially when such individuals often demand wholesale change yet offer few personal insights. The ability to help a client address various problems at once, as opposed to dealing with each separately then combining the outcomes to examine possible interactions, is important. Dramaturgical approaches like FRT may not suit all clients, but many forensic clients have used confidence games or role-playing in order to dupe others and they may well accept a role-playing challenge in therapy. A therapist can actually employ FRT to focus on building existing personal strengths rather concentrate on overcoming personal weaknesses (see Roesch, 1988).

In the context of sex therapy, FRT might be employed effectively to address a number of psychogenic problems. Role-playing, specifically role reversal therapy, has been used to effect marital outcomes (De Silva, 1987). Rewriting a personal script as "more of a sexual adventurer", or in some cases as "less of a sexual adventurer", might open up new and sexually productive ways of construing one's self. It is also likely that survivors of child sexual abuse, who suffer from a fear of sexual contact or touch as an adult (see Easton et al., 2011), may benefit from FRT as a less intrusive approach to finding alternative constructions of their childhood experiences and their current construct sequelae. So-called dysfunctions can be addressed in a number of different ways with FRT, all with the protection of "make believe" and in a non-threatening manner.

Cognitive Restructuring

One very common form of individual psychotherapy is cognitive restructuring. The popularity of the treatment may be due in part to the breadth of such a term, since it can refer to any treatment that targets thought in any fashion from rationalist forms of psychotherapy focusing on "right versus wrong" ideas or beliefs (e.g., Ellis, 1962), to constructivistic forms of therapy where concerns about meaning, beliefs, and values leave aside any judgments about right versus wrong (Horley, 2008). This form of individual psychotherapy is appropriate for situations where FRT or enactment therapies are difficult to use, or when clients object to enactment-based approaches since, for example, it may be seen as too superficial or concerned with the very "acting" that led to their present difficulties. Cognitive restructuring can be an elaborative technique as described by Winter (1992a). A client is invited to identify and to explore his own construct system by way of "talking about yourself, your past, and how you think about things". This process inevitably involves addressing a client's inconsistencies, construct system fragments or subsystems, and personal concerns with the intent of allowing him or her to resolve inconsistencies and to elaborate his or her personal meaning. Sometimes, seemingly minor insights and changes are significant when it comes to addressing sexually dangerous bebaviors. Reconstruing one's self as "thoughtful" versus "thoughtless" or "in control" versus "out of control" when one is a habitual rapist is far from trivial in terms of possible outcomes that involveothers.

Challenging accounts or understandings of one's life and actions are part of the process of cognitive restructuring but, because this is not a rationalistic therapy, there is no "name–calling" or "finger–pointing" with respect to a client's account of events. Indeed, much of the work of a constructivist is spent examining and, in many cases, attempting to disabuse the client of negative labels or "names" that others, especially therapists, have placed on him (e.g., homosexual paedophile, psychopath, paranoid schizophrenic). The use of guilt, at least in PCT terms, and even displacement from "negative" core roles (e.g., slut, pervert), can be an important tool to get an individual to reconstrue himself or herself in relation to others sexually. What is vital is that clients express themselves and are given hope for change. Allowing individuals to talk about themselves and respecting their views, according to Kelly's (1955) credulous approach (Chin Keung, 1988; Winter & Watson, 1999), does not demand that the listener accept everything presented at face value—indeed, constant interpretation on the part of the listener–therapist is required, but it does place the emphasis on active listening rather than active responding (c.f., Ellis, 1962).

Although they may not have used a term like cognitive restructuring, perhaps due to its frequent use in rationalistic cognitive therapy, Erbes and Harter (2005) presented an approach to working with female survivors of child sexual abuse that can be seen as a constructivistic version of cognitive restructuring. Their approach to psychotherapy, that "privileges the client's experience" (p. 189) by allowing them to describe events and feelings without interruption or questioning, emphasizes a therapeutic setting where the therapist and client co-create a sense of acceptance and personal validation. Progress is seen in terms of the client's new meanings that permit her to face affect and the experience in order to reconstrue them and come to a healthier, more resilient sense of present identity.

Barker's (2011) rather innovative approach to sex therapy based on existential theory and therapy is very compatible with a personal construct perspective on cognitive restructuring. Allowing an individual to express their concerns, fears, meanings, and interpretations permits Barker to offer a therapeutic perspective on the "truths of life" (e.g., we all die, we must create our own life meaning) that can assist in overcoming sexual difficulties and obstacles in sexual relationships. From a more explicit PCT position, Winter (1988, 2005) described cases where a personal construct approach appeared effective in addressing psychogenic impotence and other sexual issues for particular clients. The treatment was primarily concerned with the exploration of core constructs, as well as clients' views of ongoing relationships. Winter (2005) has argued that, despite little research on efficacy, PCT be used more often by sex therapists because of its holistic approach and technical eclecticism. No doubt, PCT therapists can easily include some of Barker's techniques and insights, at least if the existential aspects and relevance of PCT are acknowledged (Holland, 1970).

Personal Projects Therapy

Some psychotherapy clients, and not just sex offenders, live "too much in their heads" and need to focus on concrete changes in order to address psychosocial difficulties. Altering one's social ecology is one way to proceed in a relatively concrete manner. Little (1987) argued convincingly that purposive activity should be the focus of many areas within psychology, and he introduced a new unit of analysis, the personal project, consonant with this argument. The personal project is an interrelated sequence of actions intended to attain or to maintain a state of affairs foreseen by an individual, as limited as "brushing my teeth" or as grand as "finding a cure for cancer", with the level of phraseology likely betraying something significant about the person engaged in the activity (Little, 1983). The examination of personal projects involves an ecologically valid assessment that accounts for social and physical environmental contexts of activity (Little, 1983, 1987). According to Little (2014), mounting and conducting certain kinds of projects in a sustainable fashion can increase overall life quality.

Personal projects have been elicited and examined using a number of techniques, but most notably the PPM has been used (see Little, 1983; Palys & Little, 1983). PPM is a matrix or grid technique that can be seen as one manifestation of Kelly's rep grid (Horley, 1988a, 1988b) and, like the rep grid, it is based on Kelly's credulous approach to assessment (Little & Grant, 2006). In contrast to Palys and Little (1983), Horley (1988a, 1988b) argued that the set of analytic dimensions used by PPM respondents to examine their own personal projects are not fundamentally different from Kelly's personal constructs. If personal constructs can be understood in terms of values and beliefs (Horley, 1991, 2012), so too can project dimensions, albeit with some care when provided dimensions or constructs are used. Thus, according to Horley (1987, 1988a, 1988b), the choice of analytic units like personal constructs and personal projects are not an "either-or" situation, rather more of a "both-and" possibility. Constructs and projects appear to fit together, although it has to be admitted that personality traits and projects can be employed together too (Little, 2006).

Analyses of personal projects have been relatively silent on the improvement of lives via change in project construction or pursuit. Horley (2008) discussed his use of personal project therapy in his work with criminal offenders, especially sex offenders, with some mixed results. The major concerns that surround the formulation, staging, and completion of everyday activities related to sexual change might centre round a number of issues.

One obvious issue with personal projects involves the construal of projects. If activities are viewed as highly desirable yet completely unattainable or extremely unpleasant, there should be little expectation of success. One avenue of intervention could focus on the reinterpretation of particular activities, where, for example, "troublesome" is recast as "character-building challenge" or "too time-consuming" is seen as "worth struggling for". This approach would be clearly constructivistic, but other modes or types of intervention are also possible.

Many valuable projects appear to be set in the wrong places and, as a result, have no or limited chances of successful completion. A project like "stop groping young boys" set in an athletic centre in a school may not prove very successful in the long term. Moving a project, or the person with the project, to a more conducive place might help in conducting and, ultimately, completing the activity. The practices of some probation and parole officers, especially highly effective ones who engage clients and are concerned with their everyday lives, focus on this approach. They discover what activities the client is engaged in, from job searches to avoiding criminal involvement, and suggest places where such activities might be best conducted. It might also be the case that associates, or a pool of potential project assistants, are the source of project problems. No social support is a problem, but many offenders suffer from exposure to the wrong kind of support. "Finding a legal job" is a project doomed to failure if conducted around associates who sell cocaine or shoplift for a living. Again, good probation and parole workers unquestionably offer advice on this matter, not only in terms of avoiding criminal associates, but in terms of seeking others who can provide real help with particular projects. People and places, without a question, populate the real world of projects. Discovering the most conducive people and places to facilitate activities is not always easy, particularly for released offenders who have few available resources, including information about help in a particular community. Often, long-term incarcerates have no one, including family members, to turn to for help with even the most basic projects. Personal projects therapy has been used to effect change with a limited number of sexual offenders (see Horley, 2008), and it could be adapted for use in some sex therapy. Some examples of sexual dysfunction may be attributable to sexual projects enacted in the wrong type of places (e.g., bedrooms with paper-thin walls in multi-family apartments or houses) where another setting might provide more success (e.g., a tent in a secluded wood).

Group Approaches for Altering Sexual Constructs

Although the literature on group psychotherapy with sexual offenders is far from extensive, it does appear to be among the earliest treatment approaches employed with sexual offenders (see Cabeen & Coleman, 1961). Group therapy for sex offenders has been advocated for a number of reasons, including acceptance by a peer group and the "reassurance" that results from "discussion of secret feelings and actions without fear of punishment" (Cabeen & Coleman, 1961, p. 125). Lothstein and LaFleur Bach (2002) added other considerations, such as the ability of a group setting to allow participants to deal with "developmental arrests, and gender and masculinity conflicts while attaining genuine intimacy" (p. 503). Unfortunately, group therapy appears to be the choice of overworked therapists in settings, such as prisons, with very limited therapeutic resources because of its perceived efficiency (Horley, 2008). A variety of different forms of group therapy have been developed and employed by PCT therapists (see Winter, 1992a, 1992b), including those who work with sexual offenders (e.g., Houston & Adshead, 1993), although few, if any, would be seen as efficient.

Problem Identification

Developed as an initial step to aid sexual offenders interested in some help with psychological problems, problem identification was designed to provide a supportive environment for sexual offenders to discuss their lives, personal difficulties, and construct systems in order to receive feedback from therapist(s) and peers (Horley, 2008). Problem identification groups conducted in prison settings are process oriented groups planned as a first step rather than an end in itself. Groups operate as a closed therapy group as opposed to an open group (i.e., no new members are admitted after the first week's meeting) in order to promote group cohesion and trust among participants. Clients, usually six to eight per group, are allowed to speak without fear of attack (i.e., there is no "hot seat", insults, physical contact), although questioning and challenge is encouraged. Each group member is permitted over two weeks (or eight hours of group time) to tell his life story in whatever manner is deemed appropriate. Some participants relied on rambling accounts of recent, significant events, while others—including one who produced a 400 plus page autobiography—presented a detailed and coherent account of their entire life to date. Each participant is left to decide the focus of his or her own story.

The group composition that seems to work best is a homogenous one with respect to offence and personal background. In fact, more homogeneity is perhaps best (e.g., all middle-aged, middle-class, white males with offences involving prepubescent male victims). One pitfall with this homogeneity concerns the creation of "alliances" or collections of individuals who relate so well that they band together to support each other. While this is a real danger insofar as allies can and do validate mutually deviant perspectives, it can be countered by challenges to all potential allies at the first sign of such a formation. In extreme cases of unbreakable alliances, members of the alliance can be moved to the following group or removed from the group entirely (see Horley, 2008, for more details).

A problem with any form of group psychotherapy with sex offenders, especially in a correctional institution, is the fear of physical retribution by virtue of being identified as a sex offender. This is minimized by the generic and relatively benign title of the group, but the issue of confidentiality is important in any group such as this. The main intent of the group is to allow individuals to examine and to "troubleshoot", usually in very preliminary ways, their construct systems. As such, this group functions as an elaborative forum in a PCT sense. A very comfortable environment is required (e.g., couches, dim lighting). Dropouts from this group—to date, usually less than 25%—seem to result from an individual's inability to feel secure with other participants or therapists.

Once again, this group format has yet to be evaluated in a formal, systematic manner. The main short-term benefits of this group approach to treatment appear to include a sense of not being alone. A number of participants have remarked that, until they had become involved in the group, they felt as if they alone had their particular sexually anomalous behavior (see Horley, 2008). Along with a sense of not being alone, the group seemed to foster a sense of hope concerning the ability to change. They witnessed some minor changes in other participants, and some reported noticing changes in their own thoughts and feelings as well. Participants often expressed an appreciation for being able to talk about their experiences and to have their personal stories heard and appreciated by others. Many participants in problem identification groups proceed to further therapy groups or to individual psychotherapy.

Relapse Prevention

Relapse prevention is a popular form of therapy, typically in group format, borrowed from the field of alcohol addiction treatment and used by various therapists, including those who work with sex offenders (see Laws, 1989). It is described as a cognitive behavioral approach to helping clients recognize how and why problem behaviors occur and how to avoid repetition. The language or jargon of relapse prevention is extensive, and the aspects of different programmes do vary, but we will present my variation of relapse prevention without jargon. Relapse prevention groups that I (JH) have operated for incarcerated sexual offenders involve biweekly meetings over a 12 week period. Usually, a single therapist or group leader works with between 6 and 10 participants. Because the format tends to be didactic with open discussion, it will certainly accommodate more participants, although 20 is probably the upper limit. Most individuals become involved in this group just prior to release, and it might be viewed best as an opportunity to consolidate gains made throughout prior aspects of rehabilitation during incarceration (Horley, 2008).

A number of topics, typically one per session, are presented to the group for discussion. One issue for consideration concerns the notion of offence chains, or the chains of events that precede a sexual offence. Each participant is encouraged to think back on his last sexual offence and identify each event that led up to the offence. By doing so, insight into the particular sequence of events that can produce an offence is promoted. Although sometimes a separate discussion, the idea of a high-risk situation is often introduced here, and participants attempt to identify for themselves the types of situations that might lead to re-offence. The notion of a "red-flag", or a warning point or event, is introduced so that the participants, by identifying their personal flags for the future, can be aware of cues that serve to warn them about the likely unacceptable series of events to follow. In a sense, this is an empowering exercise insofar as there is personal understanding and acceptance that everyone has choices to make at various times that have clear consequences.

Another concern of this form of relapse group is the nature of negative emotion. This usually follows offence chaining because most participants can identify at least one negative emotional link in the chain of events that led to their latest offence. The nature of negative affect in general, common negative feelings experienced by individual participants, and adaptive ways of coping with negative affect are some of the issues discussed. Ways of coping appropriately often leads into a discussion of natural helping networks. This issue always involves some advice on the development of social support and also on how to provide effective help to those in need. An awareness of mutuality, sometimes a revelation for group participants, is important because some may avoid asking for help because they think that a debt has been created since they have t nothing to give in return.

One issue that can be included concerns victim impact and the development of empathy. This usually involves a videotaped interview with a victim of sexual assault talking about the personal impact of the attack and certainly not face-to-face encounters with actual victims, let alone a client's personal victims. Group participants are then requested to compose a letter of apology over the next two or three days in the privacy of their cells to their last victims explaining how they now feel, but focusing on the likely feelings of the victim himself or herself. Empathy training is not the focus here because, as argued by Horley (2008), it is viewed less as a simple social skill to be acquired readily through trial-and-error and reinforcement, and more as a highly complex personal ability that is the result of significant early childhood experiences involving the accurate reading and experiencingof others' affectiveexperiences. Any adult who has never been able to be concerned about others' feelings might be able to acquire true empathy, but not without significant and prolonged effort. This does not mean, however, that they are condemned to a lifetime of committing sexual assaults, because many non-empathic people never commit sexual assaults.

The emphasis of this form of relapse prevention is neither on behavior per se nor on didactic information to prevent re-offence. Learning content tends to be unimportant. The discussions about thoughts and feelings, explorations of the self, and understanding how particular events can produce specific, important personal reactions are a central theme throughout the group meetings. This form of group therapy permits participants to explore how their own constructions of the world can lead directly to inappropriate actions in a setting where they can receive prompting and support. Participants' changing views of people and the world can then lead to new behavioral experiments, both within prison walls and in the broader community on release. All too often, relapse prevention becomes a lecture or even harangue about the obvious cues that offenders are unable or unwilling to recognize in order to avoid negative behaviors. Lecturing and berating offenders, whether in a group or individually, is not therapeutic and is unlikely to lead to personal change. A group focused on relapse prevention needs to proceed with respect for the construal processes of all individuals.

While the previous examples of PCT-based formal therapies may provide some help to those attempting to change their inappropriate sexual behaviors, the intensive and extensive rehabilitation programme designed to help sex trade workers leave the streets behind (Oselin, 2009) may be a much better overarching setting for such treatment techniques. As described by Oselin, the process of identity change is both long and difficult, especially when years or decades have been spent with a previous though undesirable identity. Despite a lack of evaluative data at present, assisting individuals through the process with various change options seems like the best formal approach to success for those wishing to change deviant sexual identities. No doubt the costs are high, but the cost for individuals and society of not offering such programmes are far too high in the long run.

Less Formal Approaches to Change

Obviously, no one has to engage in formal psychotherapy in order for personal construction relevant to sexual identity to alter slightly or to change dramatically. For most of us, comfortable and relatively successful with an existing sexual identity, change is unlikely or minor and over a long period of time. If we do experience upheaval or some type of profound insight (see Chapter 2), we can re-examine our current sexual beliefs, desires, and overall identity and attempt to make what we believe to be the necessary changes in response to our new situation, but serious or dramatic change is uncommon unless certain factors or resources are available. A brief consideration of some of these factors seems necessary.

9 Changing Sexual Interests, Identities, and Behaviours 223

Culture is among the less formal means through which sexual construct change can be attained. If Halperin (2010) is correct, as he appears to us to be, becoming gay is not just about a set of sexual desires but becoming socialized into gay culture. Parenthetically, we would suggest that "a gay culture" is more accurate since there appear to be many different gay cultures, or subcultures, around the world at present, although it may be that the spread of Western culture globally in the near future will mean that there may become a single, global gay culture. For Halperin, becoming gay involves the acceptance of at least some of a particular set of styles and cultural content through an exposure to appropriate models and experiences. What is fundamental to becoming gay, however, is an underlying set of beliefs, attitudes, and values that embody the gay experience and, more importantly, allow one to interpret future experience through gay eyes. Such goggles are, for us, a complex set of personal constructs that allow an individual to recognize and to interpret one's own identity as well as that of others as gay, straight, or something different. It is not that an exposure to gay culture alone can create a gay individual, any more than an exposure to straight culture invariably creates straight individuals; however, exposure to the culture can help convince a person and those around them that they are indeed gay, straight, or something completely different. While Halperin is silent about the source of the sexual desires that begin to get one wondering about one's personal sexual identity, we see these desires as defined and produced by earlier experiences and the acceptance of a particular set and pattern of constructs that are then cemented into place by further validation acquired through experiences in particular cultural contexts. Needless to add, we are not just referring to experiences that lead to gay or lesbian identities but also straight and other identities. Even sexual subcultural identities such as BDSM require exposure to the particular subculture and its practices (Faccio, Casini, & Cipolletta, 2014). Experienceswithin a cultural context matter to everyone in terms of sexual identity.

Models influence many, if not most, of our lives. Heroes and popular cultural icons; even spiritual icons and leaders act as exemplars of the good life or the life well lived, and this influence can extend into sexual spheres. Celebrity figures, whether or not one lives in a celebrity-dominated culture or not, can provide sexual influence if not direction. When a well-known and respected female pop singer croons about kissing a girl and liking it, same-sex sexual relationships or sexual encounters are not only de-stigmatized, but are also probably made to seem more attractive to some fans. Closer to home, quite literally, are role models who may not be among the rich and famous, but are well respected local or personal models. Families, neighborhoods, and wider communities sometimes have informal models, perhaps known on the streets or in community centres or even through informal social networks, as sources of "good advice", dispensers of wisdom, or simply effective individuals who should be emulated. Some families are fortunate to have one member, a distant aunt or a cousin who lives in an artist's commune, who is able to act as an example or occasional provide helpful chats about alternative sexual lifestyles. Social support, whether formal or informal, can be the source not only of immediate assistance when dealing with acute crises, but can provide direction when sexual choice points are presented.

10

Final Considerations

Inquiring into human sexuality is difficult. Aside from investigations into the physiology of sex, some of the difficulty is due to work that requires venturing into personal—if not extremely intimate and, possibly, sensitive—areas; and this is the case whether the investigator is a clinician, researcher, or a theorist. Another obstacle to progress in sexuality research is related to the many diverse fields in which investigators receive their training. Each of the many fields spanning the humanities, social sciences, medical sciences, and natural sciences has a unique take on training in technique, methodology, and theory. In particular, terminologies, and understandings of common language, can be unique, and can impact conceptual clarity. Clarity, or at least consistency, is certainly lacking even concerning a common terminology, as Kauth (2005) and others have noted. The lack of clarity is a problem that might prove intractable for a number of reasons beyond the diverse backgrounds of professionals interested in sex, but it is not alone there. Other issues in sexology that remain very difficult, if not impossible, to overcome include institutional, community, sexual, and personal politics that seem to cloud every discussion. Bringing everyone who works on sexuality together under any banner is a daunting, if not impossible, project.

© The Editor(s) (if applicable) and The Author(s) 2016
J. Horley, J. Clarke, *Experience, Meaning, and Identity in Sexuality*,
DOI 10.1057/978-1-137-40096-3_10

Recognizing, of course, that theory is partly political as well as personal, a further difficulty in sexology is the lack of a broad and useful theory that can unify and move thought and research forward. We have tried to address the theory issue directly within these pages. According to Johnson (2015), psychosocial theory is central to progress in sexuality studies. Individuals inhabiting a social world, as well as a personal corporeal body, that can be and typically are construed in very sexual or sensual ways represent for us the importance of PCT. The theory provides an explanation of the range of human sexual expression as well as of both stability and change of sexual identity and desires across the lifespan. Our expanded view of PCT as a psychosocial theory certainly requires empirical support. An interesting start might be a sequential study of the evolution of sexual identity from childhood to adulthood across several cultures, one that examines factors and individual experiences that influence shifts in sexual construction through the lifespan (see Lerner, Schwartz, & Phelps, 2009). Such long-term research is difficult to conduct at the best of times, let alone when funding is very limited, and research ethics boards everywhere seem driven by risk management. This could mean that the data may be a long time coming. In the meantime, the theory can be recognized and developed as a coherent account of the formation of identities and desires, or lack of desires, as well as of stability and change in sexual identity and desires. The importance of self-validation in terms of producing and reinforcing behaviors, some of which may be maladaptive and/or unpleasant from a consensus perspective, should be recognized. Broadly speaking, a psychosocial PCT can explain how sexual desires can involve opposite-sex or same-sex individuals, objects, certain kinds of activities or scenes, or even lack of desire. From a personal construct perspective, there are indeed multiple sexualities.

As Wilkerson (2007, 2009) argued so successfully, experience is the key to understanding the development of sexual desire. Experience, however narrow or varied, can explain how desire is directed via the channelization of choice and construction. Desire can be baffling, and even unwanted and disturbing, but the choices that we make while attempting to make sense of our encounters with the world have consequences with respect to mind and behavior. The notion of construct channelization, which is in effect the channelization of choice, permits an understanding of human sexual development through experience, including the active construal of events as they occur to us, around us, and within us. It allows us to make sense of ourselves, others, and our relationships to them. We argue that this view of construct stability and fluctuation can account for our relatively stable or relatively fluid sexual identities and sexual interests. We are even able to explain the lack of sexual desire without invoking a pathological state—while it may be relatively rare, there may be individuals, perhaps more than we imagine (Abbott, 1999), who do not have a personal identity that includes a sexual aspect because, for example, they have imagined a higher calling that precludes sexual interest and expression. For us, personal construct psychology represents a useful and powerful theory for understanding the range and complexity of human sexuality. It is a coherent and dynamic theory of personality that blends cognition, affect, and conation. True, it was created as a psychological theory and to a large extent remains so, but all theories are open to amendment when observations and other considerations demand such additions. As we have argued consistently here, PCT requires more concern or focus on the social aspects of people's daily experiences; however, such expansion and elaboration of the original theory does not alter the original intent of the theory. Even if additions did change the original theory significantly, such developments are perhaps well founded, because they support Kelly's (1970) view that any good theory exists to be replaced by a better one. What we suggest is a means to expand and improve PCT by acknowledging an increased role of social influences or factors in the interpretations of experience. To take this into account, we clarify and detail our suggestions in a proposal that suggests two formal additions as theoretical corollaries to potentially expand and improve PCT theory.

Sources of Constructs and Social Relations Within PCT

As mentioned in Chapter 2, Kelly (1955) presented PCT in a very formal and precise manner—as comprised of a theoretical postulate and 11 corollaries. At the end of his list of corollaries were the only two related to social relations, the commonality corollary and the sociality corollary.

We would like to think that had Kelly proceeded with his development of the theory, more social corollaries and much more psychosocial theory overall would have been the result. Since Kelly's original work, the corollaries have been fleshed out, notably by Mancuso and Adams-Webber (1982), but rarely are new ones proposed, and certainly none have been widely accepted, if given much of a second thought at all (e.g., Katz, 1984). We propose the addition of two new corollaries to expand PCT.

The first new corollary is what we have termed the "source corollary": *Constructs employed by individuals may be a unique creation of the individual or a result of an environmental experience, but are most often the result of social environmental exposure, particularly language-centred social experiences.* The question of the source or sources of personal constructs is an open one. Kelly (1955, 1970a) had little to say about this, but it has been questioned by some theorists and researchers since. Proctor and Parry (1978) and Balnaves, Caputi, and Oades (2000), for example, answered this question by pointing out that constructs appear to arise from social sources, while Katz (1984) argued that biogenetic "primordial constructs" were the earliest ones employed. The former argument, rather than the latter, makes much more sense to us for reasons and discussions covered in the preceding pages. We would, however, allow for other sources. We would not want to discount the creative aspects of humanity, although likely a select few qualify as creative enough to recreate themselves psychologically in a substantial fashion. In addition, the individual's encounters with the physical environment may provide some constructs, however imprecise or difficult to label. We argue, however, that the social world, and especially the world of human language, are major sources of constructs for the labelling and interpretation of the self and other individuals, things, and events. Early in life, we not only come to see others as good or bad depending on the judgements of those immediately around us and on social reflection and social feedback, but also develop a growing sense of our selves and our personal identities as good or not, brave or not, or beautiful or not (Mead, 1934/1977). While many of our views about ourselves and others do continue to be added to the groundwork laid down early in life, we argue that many subsequent experiences can profoundly affect our worldview and lead us to radically change the way we see ourselves and others. Certainly Balnaves, Caputi, and Oades (2000) would agree, insofar as they see corporate constructs and corporate construing, including both constructs and a style of construct usage, as relevant in some business or social situations where individual constructs are set aside or take second place to constructs promoted by a business or other larger social entity.

Kelly (1955) posited a real world that we can know only through the lens of our constructs. While this appears to reduce "knowledge" to ideas or relativistic "guesses" about the nature of the world around us, the theory is not, and was never intended to be, about the invention of ideas so much as the discovery of the reality we live in; in other words, it is not a theory steeped in idealism but in constructivism or constructive realism. As such, it needs recognition in the form of a new corollary about some aspect of the real world. We think that the social world, as the locus of much of our everyday activity and a fundamental source of our views concerning ourselves and others, requires some "solidity" in the form of a theoretical amendment concerning the nature of ubiquitous and real social conditions. We propose a PCT "relational corollary" that would express some of the points about the reality of social factors discussed in previous chapters. The corollary would read: *To the extent that an individual conducts transactions with other individuals, the course of those transactions will be influenced and directed by physical attributes, social inequalities, social power, and the broader social contexts in which the transactions occur.*

We continually gain an understanding of ourselves and discover the social world in which we live through our everyday social interactions. Far from occurring in a vacuum, these social interactions exist in people's embodied activities that are situated in specific locations within rich and layered social contexts. Often, these social interactions are mediated by rules, policies, and texts that we must somehow interpret (Smith, 1999). We need to consider constantly how the ongoing social activities individuals carry out in coordination with others within particular social contexts make explicit the intersections of physical attributes, social inequality, and social power. The physical attributes of social actors (e.g., body size, height, age, skin colour) are very real sources of influence in all interactions. They have a direct bearing on how we are perceived and treated in social interactions; additionally, these characteristics determine how we perceive and treat others. Physical attributes, however, are no more real than social power, even though they may be more obvious.

Social power is hierarchical and is a part of all our social relations at many levels, regardless of whether the setting is home (e.g., one's older sister controls access to toys, which leads to arguments), or local communities (e.g., families organize to create a shared community garden in a local park to provide a ready source of affordable and nutritious food), or the workplace (e.g., national labour laws on occupational safety dismiss an injury claim made after a fall from a ladder due to distraction by a phone call). Social inequalities too, and there are many sources, can limit access to resources and impact daily social interactions. It is not hard to imagine the following situation: when a woman who is a single parent and wearing a traditional veil for religious reasons is denied access to a housing unit without clear reasons, she interprets this event as unfair, oppressive, and based on her social class and ethnicity. To improve a personal construct perspective, not just regarding sexuality but in all areas of concern, the real characteristics of people engaged in real social actions must be formally recognized and considered in all research and clinical efforts.

Theory carries value implications and connotations in all areas or disciplines of inquiry, and this is very much the case within the social sciences. It is important and just plain fascinating to examine the value implications—or, more specifically, the ethical implications—of the theory with respect to sexuality. From its inception, PCT appears to have attracted more than its share of students who are gay (see Hinkle, 2009). Perhaps all psychological theories and subfields of the 1950s and 1960s attracted more than their share of gay postgraduate students compared to other disciplines, but a larger percentage of those working on PCT felt at ease acknowledging their sexuality. Whatever be the case, it may have been the sexual values inherent in PCT, such as equality (see Bannister, 1979; Horley, 2012), that made them feel more comfortable. An examination of PCT's values, and a consideration of values and sexual ethics more generally, appear in order here.

Ethical Stances and Sexuality

The theory of personal constructs is in a very real sense a metatheory, or a theory about theories; in other words, PCT describes and explains how various theories arise and what they are constituted of. All of us develop and use theories. Most theories are informal, limited theories (e.g., how grey is becoming the new black in fashion, why I can't lose weight), although a few informal ones may be sufficiently broad and compelling as to dominate our lives (e.g., how and why the new world order is taking charge globally). These days, with the prevalence of desktop publishing and access to the internet, we are able to distribute or publish our own informal theories easily, and thus turn them into formal ones that are open to public scrutiny and possible amendment. Many, if not most of us, have formulated some ideals or standards of acceptable behavior to govern and judge our own and others' actions, and we tend to refer to such informal collections of standards as morals or sometimes moral theories. A subset of morality is any judgement, standard, or ideal with a specific reference to sexual acts or intentions, and we wish to consider the role of PCT as a formal theory and as a metatheory in sexual morality. Prior to further discussion on ethics and sexual morality, however, some terminological clarification appears to be required, given how loose and elusive much of the terminology in this area tends to be.

Ethical or moral values can be seen as one specific type of value (Pittell & Mendelsohn, 1966). A moral value is a standard by which we evaluate human behavior, either personal (planned or enacted) or others'. Although he avoids the term, Kilmann's (1981) attempt to provide a unique definition of "value" in terms of evaluative dimensions is concerned exclusively with moral values. Kilmann consistently described his focus on values for interpersonal behavior, and he argued convincingly that interpersonal values must be seen in terms of evaluative dimensions or constructs. There are other types of dimensions, but these are not of concern in valuation. Osgood, Suci, and Tannenbaum (1957), for example, reported the use of potency (e.g., strong–weak) and activity (e.g., active–passive) dimensions in addition to evaluative dimensions (e.g., good–bad). They noted, however, that the categorization can vary as a function of the concept or, to use personal construct terminology, the element under consideration or being construed.

Personal construct theory addresses the question of the nature of ethics, insofar as PCT provides a theoretical foundation for values (Horley, 1991, 1992, 2000, 2012), with ethics or morals as one particular type or category. Kelly himself addressed the topic of morality somewhat indirectly in a number of his writings (e.g., Kelly, 1967). Values seem to refer to core constructions in PCT (for more details, see Horley, 1991, 2012). Core constructs, again, are constructs that refer to an individual himself or herself and maintain the person's sense of selfhood or identity. Core constructs provide a sense of personal identity or selfhood by serving as information on who people are and what they represent. This self-knowledge, inevitably tied to a set of roles and relationships within a given social order, allows an individual to function socially and, thus, to secure continued existence. One very important part of core construction—in a sense, the core of the core—is core role structure. All core constructs that govern social interaction (i.e., allow one to construct oneself in relation to other people) are core role constructs. Insofar as values are described in terms of the evaluation of modes of human conduct, there is clearly a similarity. In fact, to look to Kilmann's (1981) notion of interpersonal values, core role constructs are interpersonal values. Kilmann saw interpersonal values as evaluative constructs used in real or imagined interactions with others, and he saw these as the most important values. To reiterate, interpersonal values and moral/ethical values are interchangeable terms. Moral values are described typically in terms of interpersonal behavior and guilt production capability. According to Rokeach (1973), moral values refer "to those [values] that have an interpersonal focus which, when violated, arouse pangs of conscience and feelings of guilt for wrongdoing" (p. 8). It is interesting to compare this statement to Kelly's (1955) view that "perception of one's apparent dislodgment from his core role structure constitutes the experience of guilt" (p. 502). Core role constructs, however, do not exhaust the fund of core constructs, just as moral values do not constitute the universe of values. There can be constructs with a range of convenience that only includes nonrole, nonhuman events just as there can be values that concern only things and ideas (e.g., "end-states of existence"; Rokeach, 1973). Thus, core role construction in PCT corresponds to an important subset of values (viz., moral values) and not to values in general.

From a PCT position, it is definitely possible to assess values, value positions, and morality. A special rep grid designed to elicit and permit the examination of core role constructs, even select ones, could be developed, just as a particular technique has been developed and tested in order to examine the value implications of an individual's everyday activities and interactions (Horley, 2000). Such techniques tend not to be as succinct as the most popular ones available for examining values and moral values (e.g., Rokeach, 1973), but they may well prove to be useful in providing the richness and detail necessary to create valid and useful pictures of any individual's value and/or moral system.

Ethics and sexuality have been inextricably bound for millennia (Foucault, 1997). In the modern era in the Western world, commentators on sexual morality have been numerous, especially during the so-called Victorian Age. Willard (1867) attempted an ambitious project where she laid out her vision of appropriate relations between the sexes, while Ellis (1910/1913) presented a "scientific" view of sexual morality in the early twentieth century. Specific moral debates arose during this time surrounding the "proper" nature of sexual expression. Bertrand Russell (1929) presented a fine overview of the state of sexual morality in the Western world in the beginning of the twentieth century. In support of Ellis, he argued that children are better off well informed about sexuality and that women should be able to enjoy sexual activity. He also made a compelling case for abolishing all obscenity laws as well as a case for what he called "trial marriage", among other points. In short, Russell promoted sexual freedom and, in the context of British society of the 1920s, risked his own physical freedom by doing so.

Many recent forays into sexual ethics have focused on research into moral positions on sexual issues. Scott (1998) examined survey data across a number of years (i.e., roughly mid-1960s to mid-1990s) gathered in six countries (i.e., Germany, Ireland, Poland, Sweden, UK, and USA) on a variety of questions (e.g., attitudes to premarital sex, extramarital sex, homosexuality) in order to determine if sexual morals in the West were becoming more liberal or accepting. Somewhat surprisingly, only attitudes towards premarital sex were becoming more relaxed or accepting; even attitudes towards gays and lesbians, especially among male respondents, remained roughly the same over the decades. Her conclusion was that there has not been a revolutionary change in sexual morality since the so-called "Sexual Revolution" of the 1960s. Along a similar line, although on a much more limited scale, Haidt and Hersh (2001) surveyed a number of self-identified political conservatives and political liberals in the USA concerning their views on three issues relevant to sexual morality: homosexual sexual behavior, unusual masturbatory behavior, and consensual incest. The only issue that divided conservatives from liberals was their stance on gay sex, to which conservatives were very opposed. The researchers were able to make a number of recommendations (e.g., promote the view that American morality is changeable) in order to calm "the culture wars over homosexuality" (Haidt & Hersh, 2001, p. 191).

Just as PCT is not a political theory, although it has some political implications, it is neither a moral theory concerned with sexuality, although it has implications for sexual ethics. Approaching core role constructs as moral values allows us to make decisions about what is acceptable or not in terms of our own sexual behavior, although we need to be careful about generalizations concerning the messages to be inferred from the theory. A theory might support equality and egalitarian perspectives, and it may also accept non-normative perspectives, but this does not mean that it condones a *laissez faire* view of sexuality. As Raskin (1995) wrote, any constructivist theory, including PCT, makes clear that there are no ethical absolutes, but so long as an individual accepts this and has faith in their own particular system, this does not prevent ethical decision-making. As a theory that appears to promote equality and tolerance (Bannister, 1979; Horley, 2012), PCT certainly does not promote an "anything goes" view of sexuality; nor does it portray sexual relationships and sexual encounters as limitless and unrestricted. Clearly, we can all use constructs to make judgements about acceptable sexual behavior, and we would argue that we all do use our core role constructs to monitor our own and others' sexual behaviors on a daily basis. We can, for example, use a construct pair such as sexual freedom versus repression to make important decisions about sexual matters in general, but we can also use such a construct to help set sexual limits for ourselves—for example, "I can see myself doing this but not that with this type of person under these conditions". There is no doubt that we can—and regularly do—judge others according to the same standards. However, there may be some "slippage" in sexual behavior at times (i.e., some construct looseness) that may indicate that constructs, even core role constructs, require some change or replacement. It may also indicate that we tolerate a degree of looseness or just like to have it loose, perhaps owing to our view of ourselves as creative or possessing a high degree of tolerance for ambiguity. Construing oneself as straight does not necessarily mean the absence of same-sex involvement, which may be permitted under certain specific conditions, just as construing oneself as married does not necessarily prohibit extramarital sex, although both being straight and married might set very firm limits on sexual behavior. If limits are very restrictive, and we are part of a community or jurisdiction where the vast majority of members agree that it is important to reinforce sexual prohibitions (e.g., no adult–child sex, no forced sex), we may find laws in place prohibiting such acts. Unless such laws are part of a religious framework, and hence are unlikely to be viewed as arbitrary or open to change at least in the short term, they are best viewed as alterable and ultimately removable depending on social values. A good example of such change is the recent or ongoing removal of sodomy provisions that criminalized gay sex from many Western criminal codes, although decriminalization in no way means that all moral sanctions will be lifted at the same time. It appears to us that, regardless of the sexual openness of a society or community, there will always be some sexual outliers that provide some concrete meaning for a construct pole such as "sexually acceptable" (i.e., if all sexual behavior is tolerable, intolerable is meaningless). Laws and moral sanctions limiting sexual behavior will continue to exist, as long as the construing of individuals as members of larger social groups exists. If there is any message from PCT, it is that we can and should consider the perspective of any outliers to see their behavior through their constructs, not only to better understand them, but to understand their intentions and the likely outcome of their actions in terms of its impact on potential partners or "victims" and society (e.g., change in values). Not all sexual behavior should be permitted at all times everywhere, but we need to be able to understand and to justify precisely the problems of certain kinds of practices. We would, for example, as we have, use the idea of "harm" to describe a sexual offence, but we would distinguish between direct, immediate harm and indirect, distant harm in order to justify the avoidance of some sexual practices such as BDSM. This is not a discussion on whether consenting BDSM should be outlawed or not, despite the fact that we are not too sure about what consent really means when sex trade workers are coerced into such practices. We argue that it is not healthy, either personally or socially, to engage in any sexual act where a key and distinct feature is restraint, pain, or humiliation. Attempts to portray BDSM as a "spicy sexual practice" for open-minded erotophiles (see Rye, Serafini, & Bramberger, 2015), or as a therapeutic practice conducted by dominant individuals (see Lindemann, 2011), appear to betray an underlying and unstated ethical position. For us, arguments that the BDSM encounter is "pretend" or simulation (Hopkins, 1994) merely mask the underlying issue that the humiliation or pain is real, even if it is interpreted as pleasure, and we see the possible outcomes (e.g., validation of oneself as domineering, a brutal master or mistress, passive, deserving punishment) are negative ones. Harm or suffering in the course of any sexual act is not life-affirming and, thus, is unacceptable. To emphasize our point, such a position is a judgement based on sexual ethics, and it is ours to hold regardless of how many others might support or decry our position. Everyone must draw his or her own boundaries, however loose or tentative, even regarding unlawful sexual practices and taboo relationships—ethical positions do come with costs, sometimes substantial ones, as well as benefits. There may be limits or troubling cases for any secular or individual-based sexual ethical system, such as the case of the Maryland woman who arranged for her own rape–murder (Downing, 2004). Given the rarity of extreme examples, like the one presented and discussed by Downing, we can expect that most systems will hold up well in everyday sexual decision-making. Certainly for us, considering the extreme violence and harm of any form of rape and murder, the Maryland case is very much a "no-brainer" when it comes to sexual ethics.

Sexuality into the Future

Trying to predict the distant future is a bit of a mug's game, and trying to predict the direction of human sexuality requires extreme care (Hearn, 2008). It appears important, however, to consider the various possible directions sexuality and sexuality research may take in the future. We will discuss a number of related topics here, although our list is not extensive and our speculation is very tentative.

Certainly there has been plenty of recent speculation about the possibility of sexual and romantic relationships between robots, androids, or gynoids and humans. Much of this speculation comes from media depictions (Yeoman & Mars, 2012)—the futuristic Hollywood movie "Blade Runner" (1982), for example, depicts rather well an understated yet powerful sexual–romantic relationship between an advanced robot and a man—but some contributions have been made by professionals in robotics, computing, and artificial intelligence.

Levy (2008), for example, attempted to present a compelling argument in favor of increased "intimate" contact between humans and machines. He stated unequivocally that "love and sex with robots on a grand scale are inevitable" (p. 22). His case, however, is built upon suspect psychology, references to recent technological advances, and an implicit belief in the goodness of business and capitalism. More specifically, Levy picks and chooses findings and theory fragments within psychology to support his case, although he seems to fall back on the theory that instincts form the basis of human behavior. Instincts are relevant to animal behavior, but a chapter on human love for pets, as extensive as a chapter on human love, seems entirely unnecessary except that Levy admits to being a cat-lover himself. Given the thesis of his book, his unsophisticated view of people is certainly unforgiveable even if the author is a committed technophile. With respect to technology, just because technology appears to be advancing rapidly at any given point in time, there is no reason to suppose that such a trend, if indeed there is one, will inevitably continue. The case made for increasing emotional closeness and sexual encounters between humans and machines is one based on the business model of commodification. Even arguing that the use of sexbots will increase in the future requires one to make assumptions about the continued viability of a capitalist economy based on massive consumption, or at least the consumption of sexbots by a privileged elite, which may not be viable by the middle of the century, considering the rate of depletion of global resources. We grant that Levy does make a case for the use of robots for sexual surrogacy. It is quite believable that, due to the lack of trained human sexual surrogates, to say nothing of the ethics and legalities of paid sexual encounters regardless of the potential therapeutic consequences, robots could serve as sexual surrogates, through the provision of sexual training, information, and assistance to those with physical and psychosexual issues that require interventions of a psychoeducational and psychosexual nature.

Similarly, but in greater detail, Yeoman and Mars (2012) paint a rather provocative picture of Amsterdam's red-light district in 2050 inhabited by robotic sex workers servicing human clients. They argue that such a development would be driven by eight main concerns—including freedom from sexually transmitted diseases and the prevention of human trafficking—and certainly they present a compelling business case for the use of robotic sex workers. For us, however, their scenario could be better described as "nightmarish" than as a description of "perfect sex" (p. 367). From a psychosocial perspective, the idea of sexual encounters with machines, however clean and controlled, seems not only boringly predictable but damaging in the long term. Sexual relationships and encounters are, by definition, messy and chaotic in more ways than one; indeed, all human relationships contain a serious component of chaos and unpredictability. Unpredictability and a lack of control in human–human sexual encounters and relationships appear healthy for the optimal development of our personal construct systems. Not only is ambiguity a characteristic of human experience (Wilkerson, 2007) but, in a very real way, we benefit from the necessity of having to experiment with different constructs in order to construe people and events in more successful ways. By doing so, we become better human scientists in a Kellian sense, or at least acquire the potential for improvement. A world of uniform sexual encounters, which would likely spill over into many other areas precisely because of the compelling business case described by Yeoman and Mars (2012), would probably support shared, uniform manners of interpretation. While touted as ideal or "perfect", extreme predictability in sexual relations may produce expectations or demands for predictability; and total control in all relationships, and "hook-ups" with robots, either rented or owned, might become a favored means of sexual expression. Yeoman and Mars argue that this is in effect masturbation, since no humans would be penetrated during the encounter. But it is not clear to us that clients or owners of sexbots would interpret the relationship, at least over a long period of time, as autoerotic; no doubt very close and dependent relationships, possibly interpreted by human participants as love or affection, would develop between humans and machines as they have over recent decades. Individuals would possibly become more like the robots they are "intimate" with, in terms of behavior becoming conformist, programmed, nonspontaneous, and noncreative; in effect, "standardized" and unable to interpret even the simplest of human interactions or human affective experiences.

During our brief time with it, the internet has proven to be an important conduit of human sexual expression and assistance that is still rapidly changing. Long gone are the days when everyone was surprised by the revelation that both men and women in places like Sweden were using the internet for such sexual activities as "seeking partners" and "accessing erotica" (Cooper, Mansson, Daneback, Tikkanen, & Ross, 2003, p. 277). No doubt such sex-related projects will continue for Swedes and many adults accessing the internet, but the internet itself now seems to hold many more promises and problems than in its early days. Technology has advanced recently to allow everyone, including elderly adults (Adams, Oye, & Parker, 2003), access to real and virtual partners through a wide variety of sites and devices across an electronic spectrum. The internet is a new sexual space where there is anonymity, a way to escape stigmatization, and an avenue to explore different sexual identities and create one's own sexual fantasy. Experiences on the internet can be quite contradictory; and Ross (2005) notes that depending on context and one's self-perceptions, internet sex can be experienced as accelerating intimacy or as avoiding intimacy. Internet sex is also often assumed to be disembodied and experienced as such, but it may also be an experience as embodied as sexual relations in the real world. "Teledildonics" or "cyberdildonics" refers to a set of sexual devices controlled via the internet (for more details, see Levy, 2008). Whether this will replace phone sex for those individuals involved in long-distance relationships is questionable, but it certainly could add a new twist to these.

The internet has proven to be useful to tech-savvy sexual offenders in recent years. The distribution of child pornography, recruitment of potential victims, and the creation of virtual communities for sex offenders have all been documented (Taylor & Quayle, 2003); and there is reason to believe that such activities will increase in the near future. Law-enforcement agencies may have to increase technology budgets and expertise in the near future in order to pursue internet predators, but there is no reason to believe that they will be successful in slowing such illegal activities. The expansion of the "dark web", a hidden part of the internet with restricted access which caters to illegal acts, will no doubt continue, and provide sexual offenders many more options. While this may result in many more child victims in the future, it is also possible that potential victims—children and adults—may be spared because of such developments. It is possible that offenders may engage in lifelike experiences, perhaps with the aid of teledildonics, which may encourage them to skip the trouble and costs of recruiting, grooming, and stalking victims, and simply rely on "virtual abuse" or internet-based offences. Such a development may prove to be one possible advantage of androids or robots—the damage or even destruction of a robot is merely a property offence, assuming that the person destroying the robot does not own it. It is possible to imagine a specialized robot that bled red fluid and yelled loudly in ersatz pain. However distasteful such a scenario may be, it is preferable to the abuse of people.

One future use of the internet that does not involve sexual activity, at least not directly, is sexual health. This seems particularly pertinent for young people who might not get the information they need because they avoid awkward conversations with adults or get misinformation from peers. In an interesting exploratory study on teen use of the internet for sexual education and health, Jones and Biddlecom (2011) found that adolescent Americans tend to avoid the internet for sexual health information for a number of reasons, but an important one seemed to be that they did not trust the information available. Strangely, older adults do seem to be finding useful information about sexual education and health on the internet (Adams et al., 2003), so perhaps there is a lack of captivating, high-quality websites for teens. Nonetheless, accessing digital media first is not unusual for self-identified lesbian, gay, and bisexual youth, because it can be a source of information to explore one's sexual identity. In addition, coming out online can offer the security of reassuring online interactions before coming out to friends and family (Bond, Hefner, & Drogos, 2009). As Jones and Biddlecom suggested, the internet can serve as a convenient and helpful source of sex-relevant information, and their recommendation that vetted websites should be made available through schools seems like a good one. Simon and Daneback (2013) pointed out that the unique characteristics of the internet—availability, acceptability, affordability, anonymity, and aloneness—contribute to adolescents' use of the internet as a sex education resource. Brown, Keller, and Stern (2009) describe how teens and youth advocates already tend to go to digital media first for health information and later seek out health providers. Since youth are generally comfortable with different kinds of digital media, it is important to consider their interests, such as interactive games and youth-designed websites, for sex education in schools. In the future, there may be public service advertisements, no doubt topical and "catchy" in order to capture the attention of the desired audience, to refer young and old alike to sexual education and sexual health websites, some of which teens and youth advocates may even design. There is no reason, aside from possible fluctuations in advertising revenues, why such public service notices may not appear on popular future websites. Needless to say, unwanted teen pregnancy rates and sexually transmitted disease statistics across the lifespan, to name only two areas, might be positively impacted by such a development.

The future of sexuality is not simply a roll call of possible sexual technologies. One non-technological area of speculation concerns the relations between the sexes. Hearn (2008) may well be right about the future of sexual violence and conflict between men and women—the current situation might well continue, and possibly worsen, if men continue to dominate women in terms of access to political and economic power. We are both hoping and thinking that relations might well improve among the sexes for a number of reasons. First, men might well surrender more power and control due in part to women's continuing and relentless erosion of power inequities, although power and advantage may be surrendered even faster in the future if men perceive their grip loosening on their current advantages. As birth rates continue to decline in the future, and as more and more women enter and succeed in the workplace, the future may emphasize—to a greater extent—knowledge over brawn. Men may surrender more economic control in the face of more concerted and aggressive challenges by women, legal and otherwise. Increasing sexual equality may translate into much less tolerance of men's aggression, sexual and otherwise, so that perpetrators will be adjudicated more often, and more harshly. At the same time, treatment programs may be implemented to offer men a real opportunity to change by not allowing them to fall back on typical contemporary excuses (e.g., "my testosterone made me do it", "the victim made me do it by dressing provocatively"). All of this change might only occur amid the decline of global capitalism, as Hearn suggested, but such a decline is easy to foresee given declining resources and worsening environmental conditions. Of course, in the not- so-distant future, technological advances that undermine men's power position might also come into play. Slow and steady innovation in reproduction technology could undermine men, not by making men irrelevant in the future, but psychologically they may be willing to consider the possibility that, given further mistreatment of women, they could and should be replaced by nonviolent implements.

One future possibility is the end of gender. Carver (2007) made this argument relatively recently, stating that a "retreat from gendered language" (p. 131) has already begun. Carver based his views on the rise of transsexuality and, with the advance of surgical techniques, how bodies can be altered to create many new sexual variations. While this is no doubt true, it is only true to a point, because the body provides a relatively limited canvas on which to work. We suggest that the imagination is much more open and flexible, and able to create a myriad of possibilities in terms of gender. Beyond commanding media headlines, transgendered individuals appear to be taking the lead currently in redefining masculinity, femininity, and ways of sexual self-definition. Further global tolerance of sexual minorities should encourage further gender identity experimentation and the realization that virtually anything is possible. Any future consideration of gender roles will likely acknowledge more than two, a handful, and perhaps even dozens or hundreds of roles. Transgendered, two-spirited, and berdache individuals might even become a sizable sexual minority in the very near future. At some point, discussions on gender, never mind gender-inclusive signs on washroom doors, will simply refer in some general way to all variations.

Of course, what we mean here is that gender, or gender roles, will become a term that will serve so little purpose that it will fade, perhaps quickly, into disuse. At this point, we note that the end of gender is perhaps only relevant to sexuality studies or sexology. Bentley (1945) introduced the term "gender", and Money (1955) was the first to use the phrase "gender role" to signify the psychosocial aspect of an individual's biological sex. Since then, it has become common usage in the social sciences and beyond (Haig, 2004) for a very good reason—it seems to add much to our understanding and discussion on human ways of seeing and relating sexually that the notion of sex does not. Just as quickly as the construct burst into the lexicon, however, it might become unnecessary, perhaps setting the stage for its own demise by opening up the possibility that there can be countless ways of relating to others with respect to how we present ourselves and relate to others with regard to our own perceived "sexual nature". In other words, we might soon be at a point where we move from "natural" categorization into the territory of construction. With respect to gender, this is not to suggest that we will all become androgynous or look and behave exactly the same, but there will be so many possible genders, and tolerance of new and different communities will flourish so, that—for all intents and purposes—gender will not be a salient identifier when it comes to sexual identity or sexual desires.

If the direction of sexuality is difficult to determine, the direction and future of sexology is, at least in some ways, even harder to predict. Dupras (2010) called for a more integrated yet interdisciplinary study of sexuality in the near future, a proposal echoed by Johnson (2015), although he seemed less than optimistic about the acceptance of such an approach in the future. Like many disciplines, if indeed we can refer to sexology as a unitary discipline now or in the past, the formal study of sexuality appears to be fragmenting rather than coalescing about any core or approach. Such a state of affairs might well continue into the near future, as university-based researchers throughout the world compete for diminishing research resources. On the other hand, however, there may be more collaborate projects, even theoretical collaborations like our present endeavor, as researchers and clinicians are forced to do more with less. Just as physical starvation has a tendency to sharpen efforts, funding starvation might produce future sexologists who are more innovative and able to do more with less.

At the risk of succumbing to hubris, we predict that PCT or some other similar psychosocial theory will rise to unify sexuality studies. Widespread acceptance of PCT might hasten the end of gender in social science studies of sexuality, and it may even have a minor impact on sexual and gender equality in the future. As we have described in various parts of this book, especially in Chapter 3, PCT not only accepts a broad interpretation of sexuality but actively promotes it, at least in a limited sense by opening psychological vistas and promoting creativity. We need to consider how everyone views themselves with respect to sexuality, but we need not force them to choose within a limiting or a false dichotomy. Everyone will create and possibly recreate a sexual identity, or even an identity lacking a sexual component, throughout their lifespan—all the time perhaps acutely aware of the lack of a convenient, normative, prescribed, concise, descriptive term, but recognizing that such a limitation to communication does not negate identity. We can hope, if not predict, that tolerance for sexual diversity—given that a particular sexual identity does not pose potential harm to others—will continue into the future. The need is gone for boxes or Procrustean beds that might aid succinct communication and appear scientific but fail to capture the subjective reality of individuals or communities with respect to sexuality. By allowing individuals access to more and different possibilities in terms of their sexual construction, we might find psychological gridlock to be the result, where too many choices and decisions lead many to throw up their hands in confusion or become overwhelmed by choice. On the other hand, choice in and of itself is not a problem; only false choice or a choice to be made from many bad options is. If we foster creativity and the overall use of independent thought, not only in the marketplace of the future but in the home and, especially, the bedroom, people will be better able to consider and to choose how to construe themselves and others in more and better ways—life-affirming ways—and this will lead to more harmonious relationships and individual well-being.

Further Reading

Abbott, E. (1999). *A history of celibacy*. New York: Harper.
Abel, G. G., & Blanchard, E. B. (1974). The role of fantasy in the treatment of sexual deviation. *Archives of General Psychiatry, 30*, 467–475.
Abel, G. G., Becker, J. V., & Cunningham Rathner, J. (1984). Complications, consent, and cognitions in sex between children and adults. *International Journal of Law and Psychiatry, 7*, 89–103.
Adams, H. E., & McAnulty, R. D. (1993). Sexual disorders: The paraphilias. In H. E. Adams & P. B. Sutker (Eds.), *Comprehensive handbook of psychopathology* (pp. 563–579). New York: Plenum.
Adams, M. S., Oye, J., & Parker, T. S. (2003). Sexuality of older adults and the internet: From sex education to cybersex. *Sexual and Relationship Therapy, 18*, 405–415.
Adams-Webber, J. R. (1970a). An analysis of the discriminant validity of several repertory grid indices. *British Journal of Psychology, 61*, 83–90.
Adams-Webber, J. R. (1970b). Elicited versus provided constructs in repertory grid technique: A review. *British Journal of Medical Psychology, 43*, 349–354.
Adams-Webber, J. R. (1979). *Personal construct theory: Concepts and applications*. New York: Wiley.
Adams-Webber, J. R. (1989). Some reflections on the "meaning" of repertory grid responses. *International Journal of Personal Construct Psychology, 6*, 77–92.

Adams-Webber, J. R., & Davidson, D. (1979). Maximum contrast between self and others in personal judgement: A repertory grid study. *British Journal of Psychology, 70*, 517–518.

Adams-Webber, J. R., & Neff, G. (1996). Developmental trends and gender differences in construing self and parents. *Journal of Constructivist Psychology, 9*, 225–232.

Adams-Webber, J. R., & Rodney, Y. (1983). Rational aspects of temporary changes in construing self and others. *Canadian Journal of Behavioural Sciences, 15*, 52–59.

Allen, M., D'Alessio, D., & Brezgel, K. (1995). A meta-analysis summarizing the effects of pornography: Aggression after exposure. *Human Communication Research, 22*, 258–283.

American Psychiatric Association (1952). *Diagnostic and statistical manual of mental disorders*. Washington: American Psychiatric Association.

American Psychiatric Association (1968). *Diagnostic and statistical manual of mental disorders* (2nd ed.). Washington: American Psychiatric Association.

American Psychiatric Association (1973). *Diagnostic and statistical manual of mental disorders* (3rd ed.). Washington: American Psychiatric Association.

American Psychiatric Association (2013). *Diagnostic and statistical manual, 5th edition (DSM-5)*. Washington: American Psychiatric Association.

American Psychological Association (2007). *Report of the APA task force on the sexualisation of girls*. Washington: American Psychological Association.

Anderson, M. L. (2005). Thinking about women: A quarter century's view. *Gender and Society, 19*, 437–455.

Andrews, D. (2012). Towards a more adequate definition of "pornography". *The Journal of Popular Culture, 45*, 457–477.

Andrews, D. A., & Wormith, J. S. (1990). *A summary of normative, reliability, and validity statistics on the Criminal Sentiments Scale*. Unpublished manuscript, Carleton University, Ottawa, Canada.

Aries, P. (1997). Thoughts on the history of homosexuality. In P. Aries & A. Bejin (Eds.), *Western sexuality: Practice and precept in past and present times* (pp. 62–75). New York: Barnes and Noble Books (Original work published 1982.).

Armstrong, P., & Armstrong, H. (1990). *Theorizing women's work*. Toronto: Garamond Press.

Aspin, C., & Hutchings, J. (2007). Reclaiming the past to inform the future: Contemporary views of Maori sexuality. *Culture, Health, and Sexuality, 9*, 415–427.

Atkinson, M. (2002). Pretty in pink: Conformity, resistance and negotiation in women's tattooing. *Sex Roles, 47*, 219–235.

Attwood, F. (2002). Reading porn: The paradigm shift in pornography research. *Sexualities, 5*, 91–105.

Badesha, J., & Horley, J. (2000). Self-construal among psychiatric outpatients. *British Journal of Medical Psychology, 73*, 547–551.

Balnaves, M., Caputi, P., & Oades, L. (2000). A theory of social action: Why personal construct theory needs a superpattern corollary. *Journal of Constructivist Psychology, 13*, 117–134.

Bandura, A. (1986). *Social foundations in thought and action: A social cognitive theory*. Englewood Cliffs: Prentice-Hall.

Bannister, D. (1965). The rationale and clinical relevance of repertory grid technique. *British Journal of Psychiatry, 111*, 977–982.

Bannister, D. (Ed.) (1970). *Perspectives in personal construct theory*. London: Academic Press.

Bannister, D. (1979). Personal construct theory and politics. In P. Stringer & D. Bannister (Eds.), *Constructs of sociality and individuality* (pp. 21–34). London: Academic.

Bannister, D., & Agnew, J. (1977). The child's construing of self. In J. K. Cole & A. W. Landfield (Eds.), *Nebraska symposium on motivation* (Vol. 24, pp. 99–125). Lincoln: University of Nebraska.

Bannister, D., & Mair, J. M. M. (1968). *The evaluation of personal constructs*. London: Academic.

Barbaree, H. (1989). *Denial and minimization among adolescent and adult sexual offenders*. Paper presented at the Conference on the Adolescent Sexual Offender, Vancouver, November.

Barker, M. (2005). This is my partner, and this is my… partner's partner: Constructing a polyamorous identity in a monogamous world. *Journal of Constructivist Psychology, 18*, 75–88.

Barker, M. (2011). Existential sex therapy. *Sexual and Relationship Therapy, 26*, 33–47.

Barnsley, J. (1985). *Feminist action, institutional reaction: Responses to wife assault*. Vancouver: McClelland & Stewart.

Barron, M., & Kimmel, M. (2000). Sexual violence in three pornographic media: Toward a sociological explanation. *The Journal of Sex Research, 37*, 161–168.

Basson, R. (2002). A model of women's sexual arousal. *Journal of Sex and Marital Therapy, 28*, 1–10.

Baumeister, R. F. (1997). The enigmatic appeal of sexual masochism: Why people desire pain, bondage, and humiliation in sex. *Journal of Social and Clinical Psychology, 16,* 133–150.

Baumeister, R. F. (2000). Gender differences in erotic plasticity: The female sex drive as socially flexible and responsive. *Psychological Bulletin, 126,* 347–374.

Bavelas, J. B., Chan, A. S., & Guthrie, J. A. (1976). Reliability and validity of traits measured by Kelly's Repertory Grid. *Canadian Journal of Behavioural Science, 8,* 23–38.

Beail, N., & Parker, S. (1991). Group fixed-role therapy: A clinical application. *International Journal of Personal Construct Psychology, 4,* 85–95.

Beitchman, J. H., Zucker, K. J., Hood, J. E., DaCosta, G. A., Akman, D., & Cassavia, E. (1992). A review of the long-term effects of child sexual abuse. *Child Abuse and Neglect, 16,* 101–118.

Bejin, A. (1997). The decline of the psycho-analyst and the rise of the sexologist. In P. Aries & A. Bejin (Eds.), *Western sexuality: Practice and precept in past and present times* (pp. 181–200). New York: Barnes and Noble Books (Original work published 1982.).

Bell, A. P., Weinberg, M. S., & Hammersmith, S. K. (1981). *Sexual preference: Its development in men and women.* Bloomington: Indiana University Press.

Bem, D. J. (1996). Exotic becomes erotic: A developmental theory of sexual orientation. *Psychological Review, 103,* 320–335.

Benjafield, J., & Adams-Webber, J. R. (1975). Assimilative projection and construct balance in the repertory grid. *British Journal of Psychology, 66,* 169–173.

Benston, M. L. (1969). The political economy of women. *Monthly Review, 21,* 13–27.

Bentley, M. (1945). Sanity and hazard in childhood. *American Journal of Psychology, 58,* 212–246.

Berger, P. L., & Luckmann, T. (1966). *The social construction of reality.* New York: Doubleday.

Berliner, L. (1991). Clinical work with sexually abused children. In C. R. Hollin & K. Howells (Eds.), *Clinical approaches to sex offenders and their victims* (pp. 209–228). New York: Wiley & Sons.

Bernstein, E. (2001). The meaning of the purchase: Desire, demand, and the commerce of sex. *Ethnography, 2,* 389–420.

Bieri, J. (1955). Cognitive complexity-simplicity and predictive behavior. *Journal of Abnormal and Social Psychology, 51,* 263–268.

Bigras, N., Godbout, N., & Briere, J. (2015). Child sexual abuse, sexual anxiety, and sexual satisfaction: The role of self-capacities. *Journal of Child Sexual Abuse, 24,* 464–483.

Binet, A. (1887). Le fetichisme dans l'amour. *Revue Philosophique de la France et l'Etranger, 24*(143–167), 252–274.

Bivona, J., & Critelli, J. (2009). The nature of women's rape fantasies: An analysis of prevalence, frequency, and contents. *The Journal of Sex Research, 46,* 33–45.

Blackwell, C. W. (2008). Nursing implications in the application of conversion therapies on gay, bisexual, and transgender clients. *Issues in Mental Health Nursing, 29,* 651–665.

Blanchard, R., & Bogaert, A. F. (1996). Homosexuality in men and number of older brothers. *American Journal of Psychiatry, 153,* 27–31.

Blevins, K. R., & Holt, T. J. (2009). Examining the virtual subculture of Johns. *Journal of Contemporary Ethnography, 38,* 619–648.

Bloch, I. (1909). *The sexual life of our time in its relations to modern civilization.* London: Rebman Limited (Original work published 1906.).

Bogaert, A. F. (2004). Asexuality: Prevalence and associated factors in a national probability sample. *The Journal of Sex Research, 41,* 279–287.

Bogaert, A. F. (2012). *Understanding asexuality.* Plymouth: Rowman & Littlefield.

Bonarius, J. C. J. (1965). Research in the personal construct theory of George A. Kelly. In B. Maher (Ed.), *Progress in experimental personality research* (Vol. 2, pp. 1–46). New York: Academic.

Bonarius, J. C. J. (1970). Fixed role therapy: A double paradox. *British Journal of Medical Psychology, 43,* 213–219.

Bond, B. J., Hefner, V., & Drogos, K. L. (2009). Information- seeking practices during the sexual development of lesbian, gay, and bisexual individuals: The influence and effects of coming out in a mediated environment. *Sexuality & Culture, 13,* 32–50.

Bordwell, P., Gray, J. H., Thurstone, L. L., & Carlson, A. J. (1930). Academic freedom at the University of Missouri: Report on the dismissal of Professor DeGraff and the suspension of Professor Meyer. *Bulletin of the American Association of University Professors, 16,* 143–176.

Boston Women's Health Book Collective (1973). *Our bodies, ourselves.* New York: Simon & Schuster.

Boswell, A. A., & Spade, J. Z. (1996). Fraternities and collegiate rape culture: Why are some fraternities more dangerous places for women? *Gender and Society, 10,* 133–147.

Bowleg, L. (2013). "Once you've blended the cake you can't take the parts back to the main ingredients": Black gay and bisexual men's descriptions and experiences of intersectionality. *Sex Roles, 68*, 754–767.

Bowleg, L., Burkholder, G. J., Noar, S. M., Teti, M., Malebranche, D. J., & Tschann, J. M. (2015). Sexual scripts and sexual risk behaviors among black heterosexual men: Development of the Sexual Scripts Scale. *Archives of Sexual Behavior, 44*, 639–654.

Braithwaite, S. R., Coulson, G., Keddington, K., & Fincham, F. D. (2015). The influence of pornography on sexual scripts and hooking up among emerging adults in college. *Archives of Sexual Behavior, 44*, 111–123.

Braverman, H. (1974). *Labor and monopoly capital.* New York: Monthly Review Press.

Brecher, E. M. (1969). *The sex researchers.* Toronto: Little, Brown and Company.

Brickell, C. (2006). A symbolic interactionist history of sexuality? *Rethinking History, 10*, 415–432.

Brickell, C. (2009). Sexualities and dimensions of power. *Sexuality & Culture, 13*, 57–74.

Brickell, C. (2012). Sexuality, power and the sociology of the internet. *Current Sociology, 60*, 28–44.

Bridges, S., & Neimeyer, R. A. (2005). The relationship between eroticism, gender, and interpersonal bonding: A clinical illustration of sexual holonic mapping. *Journal of Constructivist Psychology, 18*, 15–24.

Brotto, L. A., Yule, M. A., & Gorzalka, B. B. (2015). Asexuality: An extreme variant of sexual desire disorder? *Journal of Sexual Medicine, 12*, 646–660.

Brown, J. D., Keller, S., & Stern, S. (2009). Sex, sexuality, sexting and SexEd: Adolescents and the media. *The Prevention Researcher, 16*, 12–16.

Brownmiller, S. (1975). *Against our will: Men, women, and rape.* New York: Simon and Shuster.

Bullough, V. L. (1994). *Science in the bedroom: History of sex research.* New York: BasicBooks.

Bullough, V. L. (1998). Alfred Kinsey and the Kinsey report: Historical overview and lasting contributions. *The Journal of Sex Research, 35*, 127–135.

Bumby, K. M. (1996). Assessing the cognitive distortions of child molesters and rapists: Development and validation of the RAPE and MOLEST scales. *Sexual Abuse: A Journal of Research and Treatment, 8*, 37–54.

Burkitt, I. (1996). Social and personal constructs: A division left unresolved. *Theory and Psychology, 6*, 71–77.

Buss, D. M. (1994). *The evolution of desire: Strategies of human mating*. New York: BasicBooks.

Buss, D. M. (1998). Sexual strategies theory: Historical origins and current status. *The Journal of Sex Research, 35*, 19–31.

Buss, D. M., & Schmitt, D. P. (1993). Sexual strategies theory: An evolutionary perspective on human mating. *Psychological Review, 100*, 204–232.

Butler, J. (1990). *Gender trouble*. New York: Routledge.

Butler, J. (2004). *Undoing gender*. New York: Routledge.

Butt, T. (2001). Social action and personal constructs. *Theory and Psychology, 11*, 75–95.

Cabeen, C. W., & Coleman, J. C. (1961). Group therapy with sex offenders: Description and evaluation of group therapy program in an institutional setting. *Journal of Clinical Psychology, 17*, 122–129.

Callis, A. S. (2009). Playing with Butler and Foucault: Bisexuality and Queer Theory. *Journal of Bisexuality, 9*, 213–233.

Callis, A. S. (2014). Bisexual, pansexual, queer: Non-binary identities in the sexual borderlands. *Sexualities, 17*, 63–80.

Cannon, M. (1998). The regulation of First Nations sexuality. *Canadian Journal of Native Studies, 1*, 1–18.

Caplan, H. L., Rohde, P. D., Shapiro, D. A., & Watson, J. P. (1975). Some correlates of repertory grid measures used to study a psychotherapeutic group. *British Journal of Medical Psychology, 48*, 217–226.

Carlson, L. (2013). Wired for interdependency: *Push Girls* and cyborg sexuality. *Feminist Media Studies, 13*, 754–759.

Carnahan, T. E. (1987). Rapists' perceptions of women: A repertory grid study. Unpublished B. A. honours thesis, University of Guelph, Guelph, April.

Carr, J., & Townes, B. (1975). Interpersonal discrimination as a function of age and psychopathology. *Child Psychiatry and Human Development, 5*, 209–215.

Carver, T. (2007). 'Trans' trouble: Trans-sexuality and the end of gender. In J. Browne (Ed.), *The future of gender* (pp. 116–135). Cambridge: Cambridge University Press.

Cass, V. C. (1979). Homosexuality identity formation. *Journal of Homosexuality, 4*, 219–235.

Chambers, W. V. (1985). Measurement error and changes in personal constructs. *Social Behavior and Personality, 13*, 29–32.

Chasin, C. J. D. (2011). Theoretical issues in the study of asexuality. *Archives of Sexual Behavior, 40*, 313–323.

Further Reading

Chasin, C. J. D. (2013). Reconsidering asexuality and its radical potential. *Feminist Studies, 39*, 405–426.

Chiang, H. H. (2010). Liberating sex, knowing desire: Scientia sexualis and epistemic turning points in the history of sexuality. *History of the Human Sciences, 23*, 42–69.

Chin-Keung, L. (1988). PCT interpretation of sexual involvement with children. In F. Fransella & L. Thomas (Eds.), *Experimenting with personal construct psychology* (pp. 273–286). London: Routledge & Kegan Paul.

Colapinto, J. (2006). *As nature made him: The boy who was raised as a girl*. New York: Harper.

Collings, S. J. (1997). Development, reliability, and validity of the child sexual abuse myth scale. *Journal of Interpersonal Violence, 12*, 665–674.

Collins, P. H. (1986). Learning from being the Outsider Within: The sociological significance of black feminist thought. *Social Problems, 33*, S14–S32.

Collins, P. H. (2000). *Black feminist thought*. New York: Routledge.

Collins, P. H. (2004). *Black sexual politics*. New York: Routledge.

Connell, R. W. (1990). The state, gender, and sexual politics: Theory and Appraisal. *Theory and Society, 19*(5), 507–544.

Connell, R. W. (2005). Hegemonic masculinity: Rethinking the concept. *Gender and Society, 19*, 829–859.

Cooper, A., Mansson, S., Daneback, K., Tikkanen, R., & Ross, M. W. (2003). Predicting the future of internet sex: Online sexual activities in Sweden. *Sexual and Relationship Therapy, 18*, 277–291.

Cordeau, D., Belanger, M., Beaulieu-Prevost, D., & Courtois, F. (2014). The assessment of sensory detection thresholds on the perineum and breast compared with control body sites. *Journal of Sexual Medicine, 11*, 1741–1748.

Cross, M., & Epting, F. (2005). Self-obliteration, self-definition, self-integration: Claiming a homosexual identity. *Journal of Constructivist Psychology, 18*, 53–63.

Cross, P. A., & Matheson, K. (2006). Understanding sadomasochism: An empirical examination of four perspectives. *Journal of Homosexuality, 50*, 133–166.

Cruikshank, M. (1992). *The gay and lesbian liberation movement*. New York: Routledge.

Cummings, W. (2003). Orientalism's corporeal dimension. *Journal of Colonialism and Colonial History, 4*, 2.

Cummins, P. (2003). Working with anger. In F. Fransella (Ed.), *International handbook of personal construct psychology* (pp. 83–91). Chichester: John Wiley & Sons.

Dant, T. (1996). Fetishism and the social value of objects. *The Sociological Review, 44*, 495–516.

Darke, J. L. (1990). Sexual aggression: Achieving power through humiliation. In W. L. Marshall, D. R. Laws, & H. E. Barbaree (Eds.), *Handbook of sexual assault* (pp. 55–72). New York: Plenum.

Davis, K. B. (1929). *Factors in the sex life of twenty-two hundred women*. New York: Harper & Brothers.

De Beauvoir, S. (1974). *The second sex*. New York: Vintage Books (Original work published 1949.).

De Block, A., & Adriaens, P. R. (2013). Pathologizing sexual deviance: A history. *The Journal of Sex Research, 50*, 276–298.

De Silva, P. (1987). An unusual case of morbid jealousy treated with role reversal. *Sexual and Marital Therapy, 2*, 179–182.

Deegan, M. J. (2003). Katharine Bement Davis (1860–1935): Her theory and praxis of feminist pragmatism in criminology. *Women and Criminal Justice, 14*, 15–40.

Demaré, D., Briere, J., & Lips, H. M. (1988). Violent pornography and self-reported likelihood of sexual aggression. *Journal of Research in Personality, 22*, 140–153.

DeMello, M. (1995). "Not just for bikers anymore": Popular representations of North American tattooing. *Journal of Popular Culture, 29*, 37–52.

DeMello, M. (2000). *Bodies of inscription: A cultural history of the modern tattoo community*. Durham: Duke University Press.

Dewey, J. (1916). *Democracy and education: An introduction to the philosophy of education*. New York: Macmillan.

Diamond, L. M. (2005). A new view of lesbian subtypes: Stable versus fluid identity trajectories over an 8-year period. *Psychology of Women Quarterly, 29*, 119–128.

Diamond, L. M. (2008). Female bisexuality from adolescence to adulthood: Results from a 10-year longitudinal study. *Developmental Psychology, 44*, 5–14.

Dines, G. (2010). *Pornland: How porn has hijacked our sexuality*. Boston: Beacon Press.

Dingman, H. F., Frisbie, L., & Vanasek, F. J. (1968). Erosion of morale in resocialization of pedophiles. *Psychological Reports, 23*, 792–794.

Doidge, N. (2007). *The brain that changes itself: Stories of personal triumph from the frontiers of brain science.* New York: Viking.

Donnerstein, E., & Berkowitz, L. (1981). Victim reactions in aggressive erotic films as a factor in violence against women. *Journal of Personality and Social Psychology, 41,* 710–724.

Downing, L. (2004). On the limits of sexual ethics: The phenomenology of autassassinophilia. *Sexuality & Culture, 8,* 3–17.

Drescher, J. (1998). I'm your handyman: A history of reparative therapies. *Journal of Homosexuality, 36,* 19–42.

Duck, S. W. (1973). *Personal relationships and personal constructs.* London: John Wiley & Sons.

Duck, S. W. (1979). The personal and the interpersonal in construct theory: Social and individual aspects of relationships. In P. Stringer & D. Bannister (Eds.), *Constructs of sociality and individuality* (pp. 279–298). London: Academic.

Dupras, A. (2010). The future of sexology. *Sexologies, 19,* 69–73.

Easton, S. D., Coohey, C., O'leary, P., Zhang, Y., & Hua, L. (2011). The effect of childhood sexual abuse on psychosexual functioning during adulthood. *Journal of Family Violence, 26,* 41–50.

Ellis, A. (1962). *Reason and emotion in psychotherapy.* New York: Lyle Stuart.

Ellis, H. (1906). *Studies in the psychology of sex: Vol. II: Sexual inversion.* Philadelphia: F. A. Davis Company (Original work published 1901.).

Ellis, H. (1913). *Studies in the psychology of sex: Vol. VI: Sex in relation to society.* Philadelphia: F. A. Davis Company (Original work published 1910.).

Ellis, H. (1920). *Studies in the psychology of sex: Vol. V: Erotic symbolism.* Philadelphia: F. A. Davis Company (Original work published 1906.).

Ensler, E. (2001). *The vagina monologues.* New York: Villard.

Epstein, R., McKinney, P., Fox, S., & Garcia, C. (2012). Support of fluid-continuum model of sexual orientation: A large-scale internet study. *Journal of Homosexuality, 59,* 1356–1381.

Epting, F. R. (1984). *Personal construct counseling and psychotherapy.* New York: John Wiley & Sons.

Epting, F. R., Gemignani, M., & Cross, M. C. (2003). An audacious adventure: Personal construct counselling and psychotherapy. In F. Fransella (Ed.), *International handbook of personal construct psychology* (pp. 237–245). Chichester: John Wiley & Sons.

Epting, F. R., Prichard, S., Leitner, L. M., & Dunnett, G. (1996). Personal constructions of the social. In D. Kalekin Fishman & B. Walker (Eds.), *The*

construction of group realities: Culture, society, and personal construct theory (pp. 309–322). Malabar: Krieger.
Epting, F. R., Suchman, D. I., & Nickeson, C. J. (1971). An evaluation of elicitation procedures for personal constructs. *British Journal of Psychology, 62,* 513–517.
Erbes, C. R., & Harter, S. L. (2005). Personal constructions in therapy with child sexual abuse survivors. In D. Winter & L. Viney (Eds.), *Advances in personal construct psychotherapy* (pp. 177–188). London: Whurr Publishers.
Escoffier, J. (Ed.) (2003a). *Sexual revolution.* New York: Thunder's Mouth Press.
Escoffier, J. (2003b). Gay-for-pay: Straight men and the making of gay pornography. *Qualitative Sociology, 26,* 531–555.
Eyerman, R. (1981). *False consciousness and ideology in Marxist theory.* Stockholm: Almqvist & Wiksell.
Eysenck, H. J. (1964). *Crime and personality.* London: Routledge & Kegan Paul.
Eysenck, H. J. (1977). *Crime and personality* (2nd ed.). London: Routledge & Kegan Paul.
Faccio, E., Casini, C., & Cipolletta, S. (2014). Forbidden games: The construction of sexuality and sexual pleasure by BDSM 'players'. *Culture, Health and Sexuality, 16,* 752–764.
Febos, M. (2010). *Whip smart: The true story of a secret life.* New York: Thomas Dunne Books.
Feixas, G., Molinder, J. L., Montes, J. N., Marie, M. T., & Neimeyer, R. A. (1992). The stability of structural measures derived from repertory grids. *International Journal of Personal Construct Psychology, 5,* 25–39.
Ferguson, C. J., & Hartley, R. D. (2009). The pleasure is momentary the expense damnable? The influence of pornography on rape and sexual assault. *Aggression and Violent Behavior: A Review Journal, 14,* 323–329.
Ferreira, V. S. (2014). Becoming and heavily tattooed young body: From a bodily experience to a body project. *Youth and Society, 46,* 303–337.
Fielding, J. M. (1975). A technique for measuring outcome in group psychotherapy. *British Journal of Medical Psychology, 48,* 189–198.
Fisher, W. A., & Barak, A. (1991). Pornography, erotica, and behavior: More questions than answers. *International Journal of Law and Psychiatry, 14,* 65–83.
Fitch, J. L., & Ravlin, E. C. (2005). Willpower and perceived behavioral control: Influences on the intention-behavior relationship and post-behavior attributions. *Social Behavior and Personality, 33,* 105–123.
Flood, M. (2009). The harms of pornography exposure among children and young people. *Child Abuse Review, 18,* 384–400.

Flugel, J. C. (1930). *The psychology of clothes*. London: Hogarth Press.
Foucault, M. (1990). *The history of sexuality: An introduction* (Vol. 1). New York: Vintage Books (Original work published 1976.).
Foucault, M. (1997). The battle for chastity. In P. Aries & A. Bejin (Eds.), *Western sexuality: Practice and precept in past and present times* (pp. 14–25). New York: Barnes and Noble Books. (Original work published 1982).
Fransella, F. (1968). Self concepts and the stutterer. *British Journal of Psychiatry, 114*, 1531–1535.
Fransella, F., & Adams, B. (1966). An illustration of the use of repertory grid technique in a clinical setting. *British Journal of Social and Clinical Psychology, 5*, 51–62.
Fransella, F., & Bannister, D. (1977). *A manual for repertory grid technique*. London: Academic.
Fransella, F., & Joyston-Bechal, M. P. (1971). An investigation of conceptual process and pattern change in a psychotherapy group. *British Journal of Psychiatry, 119*, 199–206.
Fransella, F., Bell, R., & Bannister, D. (2004). *A manual for repertory grid technique*. London: John Wiley & Sons.
Frederic, C. M., & Bradley, K. A. (2000). "A different kind of normal"? Psychological and motivational characteristics of young adult tattooers and piercers. *North American Journal of Psychology, 3*, 379–392.
Fredrickson, B. L., & Roberts, T. (1997). Objectification theory: Toward understanding women's lived experiences and mental health risks. *Psychology of Women Quarterly, 21*, 173–206.
French, J. R. P., & Raven, B. (1953). The bases of social power. In D. Cartwright & A. Zander (Eds.), *Group dynamics: Research and theory* (pp. 607–623). Evanston: Row, Peterson & Co..
Freshwater, K., Leach, C., & Aldridge, J. (2001). Personal constructs, childhood sexual abuse, and revictimization. *British Journal of Medical Psychology, 74*, 379–397.
Freud, M. (1958). *Sigmund Freud: Man and father*. New York: Vanguard Press.
Freud, S. (1955). *An outline of psychoanalysis*. London: Hogarth Press (Original work published 1940.).
Freud, S. (1962b). Fetishism. In S. Freud (Ed.), *The standard edition of the complete psychological works of Sigmund Freud* (Vol. 21). London: Hogarth Press (Original work published 1927).

Freud, S. (1962c). The aetiology of hysteria. In S. Freud (Ed.), *The standard edition of the complete psychological works of Sigmund Freud* (Vol. 3). London: Hogarth Press (Original work presented 1896.).

Freud, S. (1975). *Three essays on the theory of sexuality*. New York: Basic Books (Original work published 1905.).

Freund, K. (1990). Courtship disorder. In W. L. Marshall, D. R. Laws, & H. E. Barbaree (Eds.), *Handbook of sexual assault* (pp. 195–208). New York: Plenum.

Freund, K. (1991). Reflections on the development of the phallometric method of assessing erotic preferences. *Annals of Sex Research, 4*, 221–228.

Frisbie, L., Vanasek, F., & Dingman, H. (1967). The self and the ideal self: Methodological study of pedophiles. *Psychological Reports, 20*, 699–706.

Frith, H., & Kitzinger, C. (2001). Reformulating sexual script theory: Developing a discursive psychology of sexual negotiation. *Theory and Psychology, 11*, 209–232.

Gagnon, J. H., & Simon, W. (1973). *Sexual conduct: The social sources of human sexuality*. Chicago: Aldine.

Gaines, B. R., & Shaw, M. L. G. (1980). New directions in the analysis and interactive elicitation of personal construct systems. *International Journal of Man-Machine Studies, 13*, 81–116.

Gambescia, N., & Weeks, G. (2007). Sexual dysfunction. In N. Kazantzis & L. L'Abate (Eds.), *Handbook of homework assignments in psychotherapy: Research, practice, and prevention* (pp. 351–368). New York: Springer.

Gamson, J., & Moon, D. (2004). The sociology of sexualities: Queer and beyond. *Annual Review of Sociology, 30*, 47–64.

Gay, P. (1988). *Freud: A life for our time*. New York: Norton.

Giddens, A. (1984). *The constitution of society: Outline of the theory of structuration*. Oxford: Polity Press.

Giddens, A. (1992). *The transformation of intimacy*. Stanford: Stanford University Press.

Giles, J. (2006). Social constructionism and sexual desire. *Journal for the Theory of Social Behaviour, 13*, 225–238.

Giles, P. G., & Rychlak, J. F. (1965). The validity of the role construct repertory grid as a measure of sexual identification. *Journal of Projective Techniques and Personality Assessment, 29*, 7–11.

Goffman, E. (1959). *The presentation of the self in everyday life*. Garden City: Doubleday.

Goffman, E. (1977). The arrangement between the sexes. *Theory and Society, 4*, 301–331.
Goldberg, I. (1926). *Havelock Ellis: A biographical and critical survey.* New York: Simon and Shuster.
Goldie, T. (2014). *The man who invented gender: Engaging the ideas of John Money.* Vancouver: UBC Press.
Gramsci, A. (1971). *Selections from the prison notebooks of Antonio Gramsci.* New York: International Publishers.
Gray, C. H., Mentor, S., & Figueroa-Sarriera, H. J. (1995). Cyborgology: Constructing the knowledge of cybernetic organisms. In C. H. Gray (Ed.), *The cyborg handbook* (pp. 1–14). New York: Routledge.
Gray, N. S., Brown, A. S., MacCulloch, M. J., Smith, J., & Snowden, R. J. (2005). An implicit association test of the associations between children and sex in pedophiles. *Journal of Abnormal Psychology, 114*, 304–308.
Gueguen, N. (2012). Tattoos, piercings, and sexual activity. *Social Behaviour and Personality, 40*, 1543–1548.
Hagan, B. (2010). Killed because of lousy ratings: The Hollywood history of snuff. *Journal of Popular Film and Television, 38*, 44–51.
Hagans, C. L., Neimeyer, G. J., & Goodholm, C. R. (2000). The effect of elicitation methods on personal construct differentiation and valence. *Journal of Constructivist Psychology, 13*, 155–173.
Haidt, J., & Hersh, M. A. (2001). Sexual morality: The cultures and emotions of conservatives and liberals. *Journal of Applied Social Psychology, 31*, 191–221.
Haig, D. (2004). The inexorable rise of gender and the decline of sex: Social change in academic titles, 1945–2001. *Archives of Sexual Behavior, 33*, 87–96.
Haldeman, D. C. (2004). The practice and ethics of sexual orientation conversion therapy. *Journal of Consulting and Clinical Psychology, 62*, 221–227.
Halperin, D. M. (1989). Is there a history of sexuality? *History and Theory, 28*, 257–274.
Halperin, D. M. (2010). *How to be gay.* Cambridge: Belknap Press.
Hamilton, R. (1996). *Gendering the vertical mosaic: Feminist perspectives on Canadian society.* Toronto: Copp Clark.
Haraway, D. (1985). Manifesto for Cyborgs: Science, Technology, and Socialist Feminism in the 1980s. *Socialist Review, 80*, 65–108.
Harter, S. L., Erbes, C. R., & Hart, C. C. (2004). Content analysis of the personal constructs of female sexual abuse survivors elicited through repertory grid technique. *Journal of Constructivist Psychology, 17*, 27–43.
Hartmann, H. (Ed.) (1981). *Women and revolution: The unhappy marriage of Marxism and feminism.* London: Pluto Press.

Hauser, R. I. (1992). Sexuality, neurasthenia and the law: Richard von Krafft-Ebing (1840–1902). Unpublished Ph.D. thesis, University of London.

Hayashino, D. S., Wurtele, S. K., & Klebe, K. J. (1995). Child molesters: An examination of cognitive factors. *Journal of Interpersonal Violence, 10*, 106–116.

Hearn, J. (2008). Sexualities future, present, past…towards transsectionalities. *Sexualities, 11*, 37–46.

Helson, H. (1964). *Adaptation-level theory: An experimental and systematic approach to behavior*. New York: Harper & Row.

Henry, F., & Tator, C. (2009). *The colour of democracy: Racism in Canadian society* (4th ed.). Toronto: Nelson.

Herrn, R. (1995). On the history of biological theories of homosexuality. *Journal of Homosexuality, 28*, 31–56.

Heyl, B. S. (1977). The madam as teacher: The training of house prostitutes. *Social Problems, 24*, 545–555.

Hinkle, D. N. (1965). The change of personal constructs from the viewpoint of a theory of implications. Unpublished Ph.D. thesis, Ohio State University.

Hinkle, D. N. (2009). Reflections on the creation of a dissertation. In R. Butler (Ed.), *Reflections in personal construct theory* (pp. 319–327). Chichester: John Wiley & Sons.

Hochschild, A. (1973). A review of sex role research. *American Journal of Sociology, 78*, 1011–1029.

Holland, J. M., Neimeyer, R. A., Currier, J. M., & Berman, J. S. (2007). The efficacy of personal construct therapy: A comprehensive review. *Journal of Clinical Psychology, 63*, 93–107.

Holland, J., Ramazanoglu, C., Sharpe, S., & Thomson, R. (1998). *The male in the head: Young people, heterosexuality, and power*. London: Tufnell Press.

Holland, R. (1970). George Kelly: Constructive innocent and reluctant existentialist. In D. Bannister (Ed.), *Perspectives in personal construct theory* (pp. 111–132). London: Academic.

Honikman, B. (1973). Personal construct theory and environmental evaluation. In W. F. E. Preiser (Ed.), *Fourth International EDRA Conference* (Vol. 1, pp. 242–253). Stroudsburg: Dowden, Hutchison & Ross.

Honos-Webb, L., & Leitner, L. M. (2001). How using the DSM causes damage: A client's report. *Journal of Humanistic Psychology, 41*, 36–56.

Hooks, B. (1990). *Yearning: Race, gender and cultural politics*. Toronto: Between the Lines.

Hopkins, P. D. (1994). Rethinking sadomasochism: Feminism, interpretation, and simulation. *Hypatia, 9*, 116–141.

Horley, J. (2000). *Constructing an abnormal sexual identity: A personal construct account of perversion*. Paper presented at "Understanding the social world: Constructions and identity", Huddersfield, UK, September.

Horley, J. (1987). The units of analysis problem in psychology: An examination and proposed reconciliation. In W. J. Baker, L. P. Mos, H. V. Rappard, & H. J. Stam (Eds.), *Recent trends in theoretical psychology* (pp. 177–187). New York: Springer-Verlag.

Horley, J. (1988a). Cognitions of child sexual abusers. *The Journal of Sex Research, 25*, 542–545.

Horley, J. (1988b). The construal of events: Personal constructs versus personal projects. In F. Fransella & L. Thomas (Eds.), *Experimenting with personal construct psychology* (pp. 359–368). London: Routledge & Kegan Paul.

Horley, J. (1991). Values and beliefs as personal constructs. *International Journal of Personal Construct Psychology, 4*, 1–14.

Horley, J. (1992). A longitudinal examination of lifestyles. *Social Indicators Research, 26*, 205–219.

Horley, J. (1995). Cognitive-behavior therapy with an incarcerated exhibitionist. *International Journal of Offender Therapy and Comparative Criminology, 39*, 335–339.

Horley, J. (1996). Content stability in the repertory grid: An examination using a forensic sample. *International Journal of Offender Therapy and Comparative Criminology, 40*, 26–31.

Horley, J. (2000). Values and everyday activities. *Journal of Constructivist Psychology, 13*, 67–73.

Horley, J. (2001). Frotteurism: A term in search of an underlying disorder? *Journal of Sexual Aggression, 7*, 51–55.

Horley, J. (2003a). Forensic personal construct psychology: Assessing and treating offenders. In F. Fransella (Ed.), *International handbook of personal construct psychology* (pp. 163–170). Chichester: John Wiley & Sons.

Horley, J. (2003b). Sexual offenders. In J. Horley (Ed.), *Personal construct perspectives on Forensic psychology* (pp. 55–85). New York: Brunner-Routledge.

Horley, J. (2005a). Issues in forensic psychotherapy. In D. Winter & L. Viney (Eds.), *Advances in personal construct psychotherapy* (pp. 250–260). London: Whurr Publishers.

Horley, J. (2005b). Fixed-role therapy with multiple paraphilias. *Clinical Case Studies, 4*, 72–80.

Horley, J. (2006). Personal construct psychotherapy: Fixed-role therapy with forensic clients. *Journal of Sexual Aggression, 12*, 53–61.

Horley, J. (2008). *Sexual offenders: Personal construct theory and deviant sexual behaviour*. Hove: Routledge.

Horley, J. (2011). On the tyranny of professional labeling. *Psychotherapy and Politics International, 9*, 127–133.

Horley, J. (2012). Personal construct theory and human values. *Journal of Human Values, 18*, 161–171.

Horley, J., & Johnson, A. (2008). Meaning and change with domestic abusers. In J. Raskin & S. Bridges (Eds.), *Studies in Meaning 3: Constructivist therapy in the real world* (pp. 127–141). New York: Pace University Press.

Horley, J., & Quinsey, V. L. (1994). Assessing the cognitions of child molesters: Use of the semantic differential with incarcerated offenders. *The Journal of Sex Research, 31*, 187–195.

Horley, J., & Quinsey, V. L. (1995). Child molesters' construal of themselves, other adults, and children. *Journal of Constructivist Psychology, 8*, 193–211.

Horley, J., & Strickland, L. H. (1984). A note on Jacob Moreno's contributions to the development of social network analysis. *Journal of Community Psychology, 12*, 291–293.

Horley, J., Quinsey, V. L., & Jones, S. (1997). Incarcerated childmolesters' perceptions of themselves and others. *Sexual Abuse: A Journal of Research and Treatment, 9*, 43–55.

Houdenhove, E. V., Gijs, L., T'Sjoen, G., & Enzlin, P. (2015). Stories about asexuality: A qualitative study on asexual women. *Journal of Sex and Marital Therapy, 41*, 262–281.

Houston, J. (1998). *Making sense with offenders: Personal constructs, therapy and change*. Chichester: John Wiley & Sons.

Houston, J. (2003). Mentally disordered offenders. In J. Horley (Ed.), *Personal construct perspectives on forensic psychology* (pp. 87–120). New York: Brunner Routledge.

Houston, J., & Adshead, G. (1993). The use of repertory grids to assess change: Application to a sex offenders' group. In N. Clark & G. Stephenson (Eds.), Sexual offenders: Context, assessment, and treatment. *Issues in Criminological and Legal Psychology, 19*, 43–51.

Howe, P. D. (2011). Cyborg and supercrip: The paralympics technology and the (dis)empowerment of Olympic athletes. *Sociology, 45*, 868–882.

Howells, K. (1979). Some meanings of children for pedophiles. In M. Cook & G. Wilson (Eds.), *Love and attraction* (pp. 519–526). Oxford: Pergamon.

Howells, K. (1983). Social construing and violent behaviour in mentally abnormal offenders. In J. W. Hinton (Ed.), *Dangerousness: Problems of assessment and prediction* (pp. 114–129). London: Allen & Unwin.

Humm, M. (1990). *The dictionary of feminist theory*. Columbus: Ohio State University Press.

Husain, M. (1983). To what can one apply a construct? In J. Adams-Webber & J. C. Mancuso (Eds.), *Applications of personal construct theory* (pp. 11–28). New York: Academic.

Iuduci, A., & Verdecchia, M. (2015). Homophobic labeling in the process of identity construction. *Sexuality & Culture, 19*, 737–758.

Jackson, L. A., Bennett, C. G., & Sowinski, B. A. (2007). Stress in the sex trade and beyond: Women working in the sex trade talk about the emotional stressors in their working and home lives. *Critical Public Health, 17*, 257–271.

Jahoda, M. (1988). The range of convenience of personal construct psychology: An outsider's view. In F. Fransella & L. Thomas (Eds.), *Experimenting with personal construct psychology* (pp. 1–14). London: Routledge & Kegan Paul.

James, B. (1962). Case of homosexuality treated by aversion therapy. *British Medical Journal, 1*(1206), 768–770.

James, W. (1890). *Principles of psychology* (Vol. 1). New York: Henry Holt & Company.

James, W. (1899). *On some of life's ideals*. New York: Henry Holt & Company.

Johnson, K. (2015). *Sexuality: A psychosocial manifesto*. Oxford: Polity Press.

Johnson, P. (2004). Haunting heterosexuality: The homo/het binary and intimate love. *Sexualities, 7*, 183–200.

Johnston, L., Hudson, S. J., & Ward, T. (1997). The suppression of sexual thoughts by child molesters: A preliminary study. *Sexual Abuse: A Journal of Research and Treatment, 9*, 303–319.

Jones, J. H. (1997). *Alfred C. Kinsey: A public/private life*. New York: Norton.

Jones, R. E. (1961). Identification in terms of personal constructs: Reconciling a paradox in theory. *Journal of Consulting Psychology, 25*, 276.

Jones, R. K., & Biddlecom, A. E. (2011). The more things change…: The relative importance of the internet as a source of contraceptive information for teens. *Sexuality Research and Social Policy, 8*, 27–37.

Jordan, J. (1997). User buys: Why men buy sex. *Australian and New Zealand Journal of Criminology, 30*, 55–71.

Kaan, H. (1844). *Psychopathia sexualis*. Leipzig: Leopold Voss.

Karp, C., & Rosner, C. (1991). *When justice fails: The David Milgaard Story*. Toronto: McClelland & Stewart.

Katz, J. O. (1984). Personal construct theory and the emotions: An interpretation in terms of primitive constructs. *British Journal of Psychology, 75*, 315–327.

Katz-Wise, S. L. (2015). Sexual fluidity in young adult women and men: Associations with sexual orientation and sexual identity development. *Psychology and Sexuality, 6*, 189–208.

Kauth, M. R. (2005). Revealing assumptions: Explicating sexual orientation and promoting conceptual integrity. *Journal of Bisexuality, 5*, 81–105.

Keith, H. E. (2001). Pornography contextualized: A test case for a feminist-pragmatist ethics. *The Journal of Speculative Philosophy, 15*, 122–136.

Kelly, G. A. (1955). *The psychology of personal constructs* (Vol. 1 and 2). New York: Norton.

Kelly, G. A. (1958a). The theory and technique of assessment. *Annual Review of Psychology, 9*, 323–352.

Kelly, G. A. (1958b). Man's construction of his alternatives. In G. Lindzey (Ed.), *Assessment of human motives* (pp. 33–64). New York: Holt, Rinehart and Winston.

Kelly, G. A. (1963). *A theory of personality*. New York: Norton.

Kelly, G. A. (1967). Sin and psychotherapy. In O. H. Mowrer (Ed.), *Morality and mental health* (pp. 365–381). Chicago: Rand McNally & Company.

Kelly, G. A. (1969). The role of classification in personality theory. In B. Maher (Ed.), *Clinical psychology and personality: The selected papers of George Kelly* (pp. 289–300). New York: John Wiley & Sons.

Kelly, G. A. (1970). A brief introduction to personal construct theory. In D. Bannister (Ed.), *Perspectives in personal construct theory* (pp. 1–29). London: Academic Press.

Kilmann, R. H. (1981). Toward a unique/useful concept of values for interpersonal behavior: A critical review of the literature on value. *Psychological Reports, 48*, 939–959.

Kinsey, A. C., Pomeroy, W. B., & Martin, C. E. (1948). *Sexual behavior in the human male*. Philadelphia: Saunders.

Kinsey, A. C., Pomeroy, W. B., Martin, C. E., & Gebhard, P. H. (1953). *Sexual behavior in the human female*. Philadelphia: Saunders.

Kinsman, G. (1991). 'Homosexuality' historically considered challenges heterosexual hegemony. *Journal of Historical Sociology, 4*, 91–111.

Kinsman, G. (1996). *Regulation of desire* (2nd ed.). Toronto: Black Rose Books.

Kleese, C. (1999). Modern primitivism: Non-mainstream body modification and racialized representation. *Body and Society, 5*, 15–38.

Knight, R. A., Carter, D. L., & Prentky, R. A. (1989). A system for the classification of child molesters: Reliability and application. *Journal of Interpersonal Violence, 4*, 3–24.

Kong, T. S. K. (2006). What it feels like for a whore: The body politics of women performing erotic labour in Hong Kong. *Gender, Work and Organization, 13*, 409–434.

Krafft-Ebing, R. von (1935). *Psychopathia sexualis: A medico-forensic study* (12th ed.). New York: Physicians and Surgeons Book Company (Original work published 1886).

Laing, R. D. (1969). *Knots*. Harmondsworth: Penguin.

Landfield, A. W. (1970). High priests, reflexivity, and congruency of client–therapist personal construct systems. *British Journal of Medical Psychology, 43*, 207–212.

Landfield, A. W. (1971). *Personal construct systems in psychotherapy*. Chicago: Rand McNally.

Landfield, A. W. (1975). The complaint: A confrontation of personal urgency and professional construction. In D. Bannister (Ed.), *Issues and approaches in the psychological therapies* (pp. 2–25). Chichester: Wiley.

Landfield, A. W. (1976). A personal construct approach to suicidal behaviour. In P. Slater (Ed.), *The measurement of intrapersonal space by grid technique. Vol. 1: Explorations of intrapersonal space*. London: John Wiley & Sons.

Landfield, A. W., & Epting, F. R. (1987). *Personal construct psychology: Clinical and personality assessment*. New York: Human Sciences Press.

Langdridge, D., & Butt, T. (2005). The erotic construction of power exchange. *Journal of Constructivist Psychology, 18*, 65–73.

Lanyon, R. I. (1986). Theory and treatment in child molestation. *Journal of Consulting and Clinical Psychology, 54*, 176–182.

Laws, D. R. (Ed.) (1989). *Relapse prevention with sex offenders*. New York: Guilford Press.

Laws, D. R., & Marshall, W. L. (1990). A conditioning theory of the etiology and maintenance of deviant sexual preference and behavior. In W. L. Marshall, D. R. Laws, & H. E. Barbaree (Eds.), *Handbook of sexual assault* (pp. 209–230). New York: Plenum.

Lefebvre, V. A., Lefebvre, V. D., & Adams-Webber, J. R. (1986). Modeling an experiment on construing self and others. *Journal of Mathematical Psychology, 30*, 317–330.

Leitner, L. M., Begley, E. A., & Faidley, A. J. (1996). Sociality, commonality, individuality, and mutuality: A personal construct approach to non-dominant groups. In D. Kalekin Fishman & B. Walker (Eds.), *The construction of group realities: Culture, society, and personal construct theory* (pp. 323–340). Malabar: Krieger Publishing.

Leman, G. (1970). Words and worlds. In D. Bannister (Ed.), *Perspectives in personal construct theory* (pp. 133–156). London: Academic.
Lerner, R. M., Schwartz, S. J., & Phelps, E. (2009). Problematics of time and timing in the longitudinal study of human development: Theoretical and methodological issues. *Human Development, 52*, 44–68.
LeVay, S. (1991). A difference in hypothalamic structure in heterosexual and homosexual men. *Science, 253*, 1034–1037.
LeVay, S. (1993). *The sexual brain*. Cambridge: MIT Press.
LeVay, S. (2011). *Gay, straight, and the reason why: The science of sexual orientation*. Oxford: Oxford University Press.
Levy, D. (2008). *Love and sex with robots: The evolution of human-robot relationships*. New York: HarperCollins.
Lewin, K. (1935). *A dynamic theory of personality: Selected papers of Kurt Lewin*. New York: McGraw-Hill.
Lindemann, D. (2011). BDSM as therapy? *Sexualities, 14*, 151–172.
Little, B. R. (1972). Psychological man as scientist, humanist and specialist. *Journal of Experimental Research in Personality, 6*, 95–118.
Little, B. R. (1983). Personal projects: A rationale and method for investigation. *Environment and Behavior, 15*, 273–309.
Little, B. R. (1987). Personality and the environment. In D. Stokols & I. Altman (Eds.), *Handbook of environmental psychology* (pp. 205–244). New York: Wiley.
Little, B. R. (2006). Prompt and circumstance: The generative contexts of Personal Projects Analysis. In B. R. Little, K. Salmela-Aro, & S. Phillips (Eds.), *Personal Project pursuit: Goals, actions, and human flourishing* (pp. 3–49). Mahwah: LEA.
Little, B. R. (2014). Well-doing: Personal projects and the quality of lives. *Theory and Research in Education, 12*, 329–346.
Little, B. R., & Grant, A. M. (2006). The sustainable pursuit of core projects: Retrospect and prospects. In B. R. Little, K. Salmela-Aro, & S. Phillips (Eds.), *Personal project pursuit: Goals, actions, and human flourishing* (pp. 403–444). Mahwah: LEA.
Lorber, J. (1996). Beyond the binaries: Depolarizing the categories of sex, sex and sexuality. *Sociological Inquiry, 66*, 143–159.
Lothstein, L. M., & LeFleur-Bach, R. (2002). Group therapy treatment of sex offenders: A hybrid psychodynamic approach. In J. Magnavita (Ed.), *Comprehensive handbook of psychotherapy* (pp. 501–526). New York: Wiley.

MacCulloch, M. J., Snowden, P. R., Wood, P. J. W., & Mills, H. E. (1983). Sadistic fantasy, sadistic behavior, and offending. *British Journal of Psychiatry, 143*, 20–29.

Mackie, M. (1983). *Exploring gender relations: A Canadian perspective.* Toronto: Butterworths.

MacKinnon, C. A. (1982). Feminism, Marxism, methods and the state: An agenda for theory. *Signs, 7*, 515–544.

Mair, J. M. M. (1967). Some problems in repertory grid measurement. I: The use of bipolar constructs. *British Journal of Psychology, 58*, 261–270.

Malamuth, N. M. (1984). Aggression against women: Cultural and individual causes. In N. M. Malamuth & E. Donnerstein (Eds.), *Pornography and sexual aggression* (pp. 19–52). New York: Academic.

Malamuth, N. M., & Billings, V. (1986). The functions and effects of pornography: Sexual communications versus the feminist models in light of research findings. In J. Bryant & D. Zillmann (Eds.), *Perspectives on media effects* (pp. 83–108). Hillsdale: Erlbaum.

Mancini, E. (2010). *Magnus Hirschfeld and the quest for sexual freedom: A history of the first international sexual freedom movement.* New York: Palgrave-Macmillan.

Mancuso, J. C., & Adams-Webber, J. R. (Eds.) (1982). *The construing person.* New York: Praeger.

Marks, I. M., & Sartorius, N. H. (1967). A contribution to the measurement of sexual attitude. *Journal of Nervous and Mental Disease, 149*, 441–451.

Marshall, W. L. (1973). The modification of sexual fantasies: A combined treatment approach to the reduction of deviant sexual behavior. *Behaviour Research and Therapy, 11*, 557–564.

Marshall, W. L. (1996). The sexual offender: Monster, victim, or everyman? *Sexual Abuse: A Journal of Research and Treatment, 8*, 317–335.

Marshall, W. L. (2006). Diagnosing and treating sexual offenders. In I. B. Weiner & A. K. Hess (Eds.), *The handbook of forensic psychology* (pp. 790–818). New York: John Wiley & Sons.

Marshall, W. L., & Barbaree, H. E. (1988). An outpatient treatment program for child molesters. In R. A. Prentky & V. L. Quinsey (Eds.), *Human sexual aggression: Current perspectives* (pp. 205–214). New York: Annals of the New York Academy of Sciences.

Marshall, W. L., & Barbaree, H. E. (1990). An integrated theory of the etiology of sexual offending. In W. L. Marshall, D. R. Laws, & H. E. Barbaree (Eds.), *Handbook of sexual assault* (pp. 257–278). New York: Plenum.

Marshall, W. L., & Mazzucco, A. (1995). Self-esteem and parental attachments of child molesters. *Sexual Abuse: A Journal of Research and Treatment, 7*, 279–285.

Marshall, W. L., Marshall, L. E., Sachdev, S., & Kruger, R. L. (2003). Distorted attitudes and perceptions, and their relationship with self-esteem and coping in child molesters. *Sexual Abuse: A Journal of Research and Treatment, 15*, 171–181.

Marston, C., & Lewis, R. (2014). Anal heterosex among young people and implications for health promotion: A qualitative study in the UK. *BMJ Open, 4*, 1–6.

Martinson, R. (1974). What works? Questions and answers about prison reform. *The Public Interest, 35*, 22–54.

Maslow, A. H. (1942). Self-esteem (dominance-feeling) and sexuality in women. *Personality and Social Psychology, 16*, 259–294.

Masson, J. M. (1984). *The assault on truth: Freud's suppression of the seduction theory*. New York: Farrar, Straus, and Giroux.

Masters, W. H., Johnson, V. E., & Kolodny, R. C. (1988). *Human sexuality*. Glenview: Scott, Foresman.

May, R. (1972). *Power and innocence: A search for the sources of violence*. New York: Norton.

McCaghy, C. H. (1967). Child molesters: A study of their careers as deviants. In M. Clinnard & R. Quinney (Eds.), *Criminal behaviour systems: A typology* (pp. 75–88). New York: Holt, Rinehart, & Winston.

McCaghy, C. H. (1968). Drinking and deviance disavowal: The case of child molesters. *Social Problems, 16*, 43–49.

McCoy, M. M. (1977). A reconstruction of emotion. In D. Bannister (Ed.), *New perspectives in personal construct theory* (pp. 93–124). London: Academic.

McCoy, M. M. (1981). Positive and negative emotion: A personal construct theory interpretation. In H. Bonarius, R. Holland, & S. Rosenberg (Eds.), *Personal construct psychology: Recent advances in theory and practice* (pp. 95–104). London: Macmillan.

McIntosh, M. (1968). The homosexual role. *Social Problems, 16*, 182–192.

Mead, G. H. (1977). Self. In A. Strauss (Ed.), *George Herbert Mead: On social psychology* (pp. 199–246). Chicago: University of Chicago Press (Original work published 1934.).

Mead, M. (1935). *Sex and temperament in three traditional societies*. New York: William Morrow.

Meston, C. M., & Buss, D. M. (2007). Why humans have sex. *Archives of Sexual Behavior, 36*, 477–507.

Meston, C. M., & Buss, D. M. (2009). *Why women have sex: Understanding sexual motivations from adventure to revenge (and everything in between)*. New York: Times Books.

Meston, C. M., Rellini, A. H., & Heiman, J. R. (2006). Women's history of sexual abuse, their sexuality, their sexuality, and sexual self-schemas. *Journal of Consulting and Clinical Psychology, 74*, 229–236.

Mezey, G., & King, M. (1989). The effects of sexual assault on men: A survey of 22 victims. *Psychological Medicine, 19*, 205–209.

Millet, K. (1970). *Sexual politics*. New York: Doubleday.

Mills, C. W. (1959). *The sociological imagination*. New York: Oxford University Press.

Minton, H. L. (1967). Power as a personality construct. In B. A. Maher (Ed.), *Progress in experimental personality research: Vol. 4* (pp. 229–267). New York: Academic Press.

Mischel, T. (1964). Personal constructs, rules, and the logic of clinical activity. *Psychological Review, 71*, 180–192.

Mohr, J. W., Turner, R. E., & Jerry, M. B. (1964). *Pedophilia and exhibitionism*. Toronto: University of Toronto Press.

Money, J. L. (1955). Hermaphroditism, gender and precocity in hyper-andrenocorticism: Psychologic findings. *Bulletin of the Johns Hopkins Hospital, 96*, 253–264.

Money, J. L. (1984). Paraphilias: Phenomenology and classification. *American Journal of Psychotherapy, 38*, 164–178.

Money, J. L. (1985). The conceptual neutering of gender and criminalization of sex. *Achives of Sexual Behavior, 14*, 279–290.

Monto, M. A., & Julka, D. (2009). Conceiving of sex as a commodity: A study of arrested customers of female street prostitutes. *Western Criminology Review, 10*, 1–14.

Moradi, B., van den Berg, J. J., & Epting, F. R. (2009). Threat and guilt aspects of internalized antilesbian and gay prejudice: An application of personal construct theory. *Journal of Counseling Psychology, 56*, 119–131.

Moreno, J. L. (1960). *Who shall survive? A new approach to the problem of human interrelations*. Washington: Nervous and Mental Disease Publishing (Original work published 1934.).

Myers, J. (1992). Non-mainstream body modification: Genital piercing, branding, burning and cutting. *Journal of Contemporary Ethnography, 12*, 267–306.

Nagal, J. (2000). Ethnicity and sexuality. *Annual Review of Sociology, 26*, 107–133.
Needs, A. (1988). Psychological investigation of offending behavior. In F. Fransella & L. Thomas (Eds.), *Experimenting with personal construct psychology* (pp. 493–506). London: Routledge & Kegan Paul.
Neimeyer, G. J., Neimeyer, R. A., Hagans, C. L., & Van Brunt, D. L. (2002). Is there madness in our method? The effects of repertory grid variations on measures of construct system structure. In R. Neimeyer & G. Neimeyer (Eds.), *Advances in personal construct psychology* (Vol. 5). New York: Praeger.
Neimeyer, R. A. (1985). *The development of personal construct psychology*. Lincoln: University of Nebraska Press.
Neimeyer, R. A., Baker, K. D., & Neimeyer, G. J. (1990). The current status of personal construct psychology. In G. J. Neimeyer & R. A. Neimeyer (Eds.), *Advances in personal construct psychology* (Vol. 1, pp. 3–22). Greenwich: JAI Press.
Nelson, L. J. (2003). *Rumors of indiscretion: The University of Missouri "sex questionnaire" scandal in the Jazz Age*. Columbia: University of Missouri Press.
Nelson, M. C. (1988). Reliability, validity, and cross-cultural comparisons for the simplified attitudes toward women scale. *Sex Roles, 18*, 289–296.
Ng, S. H. (1980). *The social psychology of power*. London: Academic.
Nisbett, R. E., & Wilson, T. D. (1977). Telling more than we can know: Verbal reports on mental processes. *Psychological Review, 84*, 231–259.
Novak, J. (1988). Constructively approaching education: Toward a theory of practice. *International Journal of Personal Construct Psychology, 1*, 169–180.
Nunes, K. L., Firestone, P., & Baldwin, M. W. (2007). Indirect assessment of cognitions of child sexual abusers with the implicit association test. *Criminal Justice and Behavior, 34*, 454–475.
Nunes, K. L., McPhail, I. V., & Babchishin, K. M. (2012). Social anxiety and sexual offending against children: A cumulative meta-analysis. *Journal of Sexual Aggression, 18*, 284–293.
Oakley, A. (1972). *Sex, gender and society*. New York: Harper and Row.
Orford, J. (1974). Simplistic thinking about other people as a prediction of early drop-out at an alcoholism halfway house. *British Journal of Medical Psychology, 47*, 53–62.
Oselin, S. S. (2009). Leaving the streets: Transformation of prostitute identity within the Prostitution Rehabilitation Program. *Deviant Behavior, 30*, 379–406.
Osgood, C. E., Suci, G. J., & Tannenbaum, P. (1957). *The measurement of meaning*. Urbana: University of Illinois Press.

Palotta-Chiarolli, M., & Lubowitz, S. (2003). Outside belonging: Multi-sexual relationships as border existence. *Journal of Bisexuality, 3*, 53–85.

Palys, T. S., & Little, B. R. (1983). Perceived life satisfaction and the organization of personal project systems. *Journal of Personality and Social Psychology, 44*, 1221–1230.

Peck, B. (2015). The personal construct and language: Toward a rehabilitation of Kelly's "inner outlook". *Theory and Psychology, 25*, 259–273.

Pedersen, F. A. (1958). Consistency data on the role construct repertory test. Unpublished manuscript, Ohio State University, Columbus, Ohio.

Peele, S. (1995). *Diseasing of America*. San Francisco: Jossey Bass.

Phoenix, J. (2000). Prostitute identities: Men, money, and violence. *British Journal of Criminology, 40*, 37–55.

Pittell, S. M., & Mendelsohn, G. A. (1966). Measurement of moral values: A review and critique. *Psychological Bulletin, 66*, 22–35.

Pitts, V. L. (2003). *In the flesh: The cultural politics of body modification*. New York: Palgrave Macmillan.

Plummer, K. (1995). *Telling sexual stories: Power, change and social worlds*. Hove: Routledge.

Plummer, K. (2003). Queers, bodies and postmodern sexualities: A note on revisiting the 'sexual' in symbolic interactionism. *Qualitative Sociology, 26*, 515–530.

Prause, N., & Pfaus, J. (2015). Viewing sexual stimuli associated with greater sexual responsiveness not erectile dysfunction. *Sexual Medicine, 3*, 90–98.

Prentky, R. A., & Burgess, A. W. (1990). Rehabilitation of child molesters: A cost-benefit analysis. *American Journal of Orthopsychiatry, 60*, 108–117.

Prentky, R. A., & Knight, R. A. (1991). Identifying critical dimensions for discriminating among rapists. *Journal of Consulting and Clinical Psychology, 59*, 643–661.

Procter, H., & Parry, G. (1978). Constraint and freedom: The social origin of personal constructs. In F. Fransella (Ed.), *Personal construct psychology 1977* (pp. 157–170). London: Academic Press.

Quinsey, V. L. (1977). The assessment and treatment of child molesters: A review. *Canadian Psychological Review, 18*, 204–220.

Quinsey, V. L. (1986). Men who have sex with children. In D. N. Weisstub (Ed.), *Law and mental health: International perspectives* (Vol. 2, pp. 140–172). New York: Pergamon.

Quinsey, V. L., Bergersen, S. G., & Steinman, C. M. (1976). Changes in physiological and verbal responses of child molesters during aversion therapy. *Canadian Journal of Behavioural Science, 8*, 202–212.

Rachman, S. (1966). Sexual fetishism: An experimental analogue. *Psychological Record, 16*, 293–296.
Rada, R. T. (1978). *Clinical aspects of the rapist.* New York: Grune & Stratton.
Raskin, J. D. (1995). On ethics in personal construct theory. *The Humanistic Psychologist, 23*, 97–113.
Raskin, J. D. (2002). Constructivism in psychology: Personal construct psychology, radical constructivism, and social constructionism. In J. D. Raskin & S. K. Bridges (Eds.), *Studies in meaning: Exploring constructivist psychology* (pp. 1–25). New York: Pace University Press.
Raskin, J. D., & Epting, F. R. (1993). Personal construct theory and the argument against mental illness. *International Journal of Personal Construct Psychology, 6*, 351–369.
Rea, M. C. (2001). What is pornography? *Noûs, 35*, 118–145.
Reich, W. (1961). *The discovery of the orgone: The function of the orgasm.* New York: Noonday.
Reiter, E. (1991). *Making fast food.* Montreal: McGill-Queen's University Press.
Rich, A. (1980). Compulsory heterosexuality and lesbian experience. *Signs, 5*, 631–660.
Rieger, G., Chivers, M. L., & Bailey, J. M. (2005). Sexual arousal patterns of bisexual men. *Psychological Science, 16*, 579–584.
Ringrose, J., & Harvey, L. (2015). Boobs, back-off, six packs and bits: Mediated body parts, gendered reward, and sexual shame in teens' sexting images. *Continuum: Journal of Media & Cultural Studies, 29*, 205–217.
Ringrose, J., Harvey, L., Gill, R., & Livingstone, S. (2013). Teen girls, sexual double standards and 'sexting': Gendered value in digital image exchange. *Feminist Theory, 14*, 305–323.
Ritzer, G. (1993). *The MacDonaldization of Society.* Thousand Oaks: Sage.
Rivardo, M. G., & Keelan, C. M. (2010). Body modifications, sexual activity, and religious practices. *Psychological Reports, 106*, 467–474.
Roesch, R. (1988). Community psychology and the law. *American Journal of Community Psychology, 16*, 451–463.
Rokeach, M. (1973). *The nature of human values.* New York: Free Press.
Ross, M. W. (2005). Typing, doing and being: Sexuality and the internet. *The Journal of Sex Research, 42*, 342–352.
Rowbotham, S. (1989). *The past is before us: Feminism in action since the 1960s.* London: Penguin.
Rowe, D. (1971). An examination of a psychiatrist's predictions of a patient's constructs. *British Journal of Psychiatry, 118*, 231–244.
Rowe, D. (1994). *Wanting everything: The art of happiness.* London: Harper Collins.

Rubin, G. S. (1984). Thinking sex: Notes for a radical theory of politics and sexuality. In C. Vance (Ed.), *Pleasure and danger: Exploring female sexuality* (pp. 267–319). Boston: Routledge & Kegan Paul.

Russell, B. (1929). *Marriage and morals*. London: Allen & Unwin.

Rust, P. C. R. (2000). Bisexuality: A contemporary paradox for women. *Journal of Social Issues, 56*, 205–221.

Rye, B. J., Serafini, T., & Bramberger, T. (2015). Erotophobic or erotophilic: What are young women's attitudes towards BDSM? *Psychology and Sexuality, 6*, 340–356.

Ryle, A., & Breen, D. (1972). A comparison of adjusted and maladjusted couples using the double dyad grid. *British Journal of Medical Psychology, 45*, 375–382.

Ryle, A., & Lunghi, M. (1969). The measurement of relevant change after psychotherapy: Use of repertory grid testing. *British Journal of Psychiatry, 115*, 1297–1304.

Ryle, A., & Lunghi, M. (1970). The dyad grid: A modification of repertory grid technique. *British Journal of Psychiatry, 117*, 323–327.

Ryle, A., & Lunghi, M. (1972). Parental and sex-role identifica-tion of students measured with a repertory grid technique. *British Journal of Social and Clinical Psychology, 11*, 149–161.

Said, E. (1977). *Orientalism*. London: Penguin.

Salter, A. C. (1988). *Treating child sex offenders and victims: A practical guide*. Beverly Hills: Sage.

Sanchez, D. T., Kiefer, A. K., & Ybarra, O. (2006). Sexual submissiveness in women: Costs for sexual autonomy and arousal. *Personality and Social Psychology Bulletin, 32*, 512–524.

Sartre, J.-P. (1956). *Being and nothingness: An essay in ontology*. New York: Liveright (Original work published 1943).

Sauerteig, L. D. H. (2012). Loss of innocence: Albert Moll, Sigmund Freud, and the invention of childhood sexuality around 1900. *Medical History, 56*, 156–183.

Saunders, T. (2005). "It's just acting": Sex workers' strategies for capitalizing on sexuality. *Gender, Work and Organization, 12*, 319–342.

Schank, R. C., & Abelson, R. C. (1977). *Scripts, plans, goals, and understanding*. Hillsdale: Erlbaum.

Schildkrout, E. (2004). Inscribing the body. *Annual Review of Anthropology, 33*, 319–344.

Schilt, S., & Westbrook, L. (2009). Doing gender, doing heteronormativity. *Gender and Society, 23*, 440–464.

Schippers, M. (2007). Recovering the feminine other: Masculinity, femininity, and gender hegemony. *Theoretical Sociology, 36*, 85–102.

Scimecca, J. A. (1977). Labeling theory and personal construct theory: Toward the measurement of individual variation. *The Journal of Criminal Law and Criminology, 68*, 652–659.

Scorolli, C., Ghirlanda, S., Enquist, M., Zattoni, S., & Jannini, E. A. (2007). Relative prevalence of different fetishes. *International Journal of Impotence Research, 19*, 432–437.

Scott, J. (1998). Changing attitudes to sexual morality: Across-national comparison. *Sociology, 32*, 815–845.

Scott, J., & Marshall, G. (Eds.) (2005). *Oxford dictionary of sociology*. Oxford: Oxford University Press.

Segal, L. (1994). *Straight sex: Rethinking the politics of pleasure*. Berkeley: University of California Press.

Segal, L. (2008). After Judith Butler: Identities, who needs them? *Subjectivity, 25*, 381–394.

Segal, L., & MacIntosh, M. (Eds.) (1993). *Sex exposed: Sexuality and the pornography debate*. New Brunswick: Rutgers University Press.

Segal, Z. V., & Stermac, L. E. (1990). The role of cognition in sexual assault. In W. L. Marshall, D. R. Laws, & H. E. Barbaree (Eds.), *Handbook of sexual assault* (pp. 161–176). New York: Plenum.

Seidman, S. (2010). *The social construction of sexuality* (2nd ed.). New York: Norton.

Seto, M. (2012). Is pedophilia a sexual orientation? *Archives of Sexual Behavior, 41*, 231–236.

Seto, M., Maric, A., & Barbaree, H. E. (2001). The role of pornography in the etiology of sexual aggression. *Aggression and Violent Behavior, 6*, 35–53.

Sewell, K. W. (2005). The experience cycle and the sexual response cycle: Conceptualization and application to sexual dysfunctions. *Journal of Constructivist Psychology, 18*, 3–14.

Shapiro, D. A., Caplan, H. L., Rohde, P. D., & Watson, J. P. (1975). Personal questionnaire changes and their correlates in a psychotherapeutic group. *British Journal of Medical Psychology, 48*, 207–216.

Shidlo, A., & Schroeder, M. (2002). Changing sexual orientation: A consumers' report. *Professional Psychology: Research and Practice, 33*, 249–259.

Shorts, I. D. (1985). Treatment of a sex offender in a maximum security forensic hospital: Detecting changes in personality and interpersonal construing. *International Journal of Offender Therapy and Comparative Criminology, 29*, 237–250.

Shotter, J. (1970). Men, the man-makers: George Kelly and the psychology of personal constructs. In D. Bannister (Ed.), *Perspectives in personal construct theory* (pp. 223–253). London: Academic.

Simon, L., & Daneback, D. (2013). Adolescents' use of the internet for sex education: A thematic and critical review of the literature. *International Journal of Sexual Health, 25*, 305–319.

Simon, W. (1994). Deviance as history: The future of perversion. *Archives of Sexual Behavior, 23*, 1–20.

Simon, W., & Gagnon, J. H. (1984). Sexual scripts. *Society, 22*, 53–60.

Simon, W., & Gagnon, J. H. (2003). Sexual scripts: Origins, influences, and changes. *Qualitative Sociology, 26*, 491–497.

Sin, R. (2015). Does sexual fluidity challenge sexual binaries? The case of bisexual immigrants from 1967–2012. *Sexualities, 18*, 413–437.

Singer, B. (1985). A comparison of evolutionary and environmental theories of erotic response, Part 1: Structural features. *Journal of Sex Research, 21*, 229–257.

Skene, R. A. (1973). Construct shift in the treatment of a case of homosexuality. *British Journal of Medical Psychology, 46*, 287–292.

Slater, P. (1969). Theory and technique of the repertory grid. *British Journal of Psychiatry, 115*, 1287–1296.

Smith, D. E. (1987). *The everyday world as problematic: A feminist sociology*. Toronto: University of Toronto Press.

Smith, D. E. (1999). *Writing the social: Critique, theory and investigation*. Toronto: University of Toronto Press.

Smith, M. D., Grov, C., & Seal, D. W. (2007). Agency-based male sex work: A descriptive focus on physical, personal, and social space. *Journal of Mens' Studies, 16*, 193–210.

Smith, N. J. (2012). Body issues: The political economy of male sex work. *Sexualities, 15*, 586–603.

Smith, S. L., Moyer-Gusé, E., & Donnerstein, E. (2004). Media violence and sex: What are the concerns, issues, and effects? In J. D. H. Downing, D. Macquail, P. Schlesinger, & E. A. Wartella (Eds.), *The SAGE handbook of media studies* (pp. 541–568). Thousand Oaks: Sage.

Space, L. G., & Cromwell, R. L. (1980). Personal constructs among depressed patients. *Journal of Nervous and Mental Disease, 168*, 150–158.

Space, L. G., Dingemans, P. M., & Cromwell, R. L. (1983). Self-construing and alienation in depressives, schizophrenics, and normals. In J. R. Adams-Webber & J. C. Mancuso (Eds.), *Applications of personal construct theory* (pp. 365–377). New York: Academic Press.

Spargo, T. (1999). *Foucault and queer theory.* New York: Totem.

Sperlinger, D. J. (1976). Aspects of stability in the repertory grid. *British Journal of Medical Psychology, 49,* 341–347.

Spitzer, R. L. (2003). Can some gay men and lesbians change their sexual orientation? 200 participants reporting a change from homosexual to heterosexual orientation. *Archives of Sexual Behavior, 32,* 403–417.

Spitzer, R. L. (2012). Spitzer reassesses his 2003 study of reparative therapy of homosexuality. *Archives of Sexual Behavior, 41,* 757.

Staggenborg, S., & Ramos, H. (2015). *Social movements* (3rd ed.). Don Mills: Oxford.

Staley, C., & Prause, N. (2013). Erotica viewing effects on intimate relationships and self/partner evaluations. *Archives of Sexual Behavior, 42,* 615–624.

Stam, H. J. (1990). Rebuilding the ship at sea: The historical and theoretical problems of constructivist epistemologies in psychology. *Canadian Psychology, 31,* 239–253.

Stam, H. J. (1998). Personal-construct theory and social constructionism: Difference and dialogue. *Journal of Constructivist Psychology, 11,* 187–203.

Stein, E. (1999). *The mismeasure of desire: The science, theory, and ethics of sexual orientation.* Oxford: Oxford University Press.

Steinem, G. (1980). Erotica and pornography: A clear and present difference. In L. Lederer (Ed.), *Take back the night: Women on pornography* (pp. 35–39). New York: Morrow.

Stekel, W. (1943). *Peculiarities of behavior: Wandering mania, dipsomania, cleptomania, pyromania, and allied impulsive acts.* New York: Liveright (Original work published 1924.).

Stermac, L. E., & Segal, Z. V. (1989). Adult sexual contact with children: An examination of cognitive factors. *Behavior Therapy, 20,* 573–584.

Stermac, L. E., Segal, Z. V., & Gillis, R. (1990). Social and cultural factors in sexual assault. In W. L. Marshall, D. R. Laws, & H. E. Barbaree (Eds.), *Handbook of sexual assault* (pp. 143–159). New York: Plenum.

Storms, M. D. (1980). Theories of sexual orientation. *Journal of Personality and Social Psychology, 38,* 783–792.

Storms, M. D. (1981). A theory of erotic orientation development. *Psychological Review, 88,* 340–353.

Strachan, A., & Jones, D. (1982). Changes in identification during adolescence: A personal construct theory approach. *Journal of Personality Assessment, 46,* 529–535.

Stringer, P. (1979). Individuals, roles, and persons. In P. Stringer & D. Bannister (Eds.), *Constructs of sociality and individuality* (pp. 91–114). London: Academic.

Stryker, S. (2008). Transgender history, homonormativity, and disciplinarity. *Radical History Review, 100,* 145–157.

Taylor, L. (1972). The significance and interpretation of replies to motivational questions: The case of the sex offender. *Sociology, 6,* 24–39.

Taylor, M., & Quayle, E. (2003). *Child pornography: An internet crime.* Hove: Routledge.

Tibbals, C. A. (2014). Gonzo, trannys, and teens: Recent trends in US adult content production, distribution, and consumption. *Porn Studies, 1,* 127–135.

Tomura, M. (2009). A prostitute's lived experiences of stigma. *Journal of Phenomenological Psychology, 40,* 51–84.

Turner, B. S. (1999). The possibility of primitiveness: Towards a sociology of body marks and cool societies. *Body and Society, 5,* 39–50.

Tylka, T. L., & Van Diest, A. M. K. (2015). You looking at her "hot" body may not be "cool" for me: Integrating male partners' pornography use into objectification theory for women. *Psychology of Women Quarterly, 39,* 67–84.

Valocchi, S. (2005). Not quite queer enough: The lessons of queer theory for the sociology of gender and sexuality. *Gender and Society, 19,* 750–770.

Van Deven, M. (2014). Why diversity isn't enough: Trans theorists says feminist doors not open to all. *Herizons, 27,* 21–23.

Varble, D. L., & Landfield, A. W. (1969). Validity of the self-ideal discrepancy as a criterion measure for success in psychotherapy: A replication. *Journal of Counseling Psychology, 16,* 150–156.

Videkanic, B. (2006). You Pretend to Be a Canadian: Exploring the Work of Kinga Araya and Camille Turner. *Women and Environments, 72–73,* 32–35.

Viney, L. L., Metcalfe, C., & Winter, D. A. (2005). The effectiveness of personal construct psychotherapy: A meta-analysis. In D. Winter & L. Viney (Eds.), *Personal construct psychotherapy: Advances in theory, practice, and research* (pp. 347–364). London: Whurr.

Waldby, S. (1968). *Patriarchy at work.* London: Polity Press.

Walker, B. M., & Winter, D. A. (2007). The elaboration of personal construct psychology. *Annual Review of Psychology, 58,* 453–477.

Walker, G. (1990). *Family violence and the women's movement*. Toronto: University of Toronto Press.

Wang, B., & Davidson, P. (2006). Sex, lies, and videos in rural China: A qualitative study of women's sexual debut and risky sexual behavior. *The Journal of Sex Research, 43*, 227–235.

Ward, T., & Gannon, T. (2006). Rehabilitation, etiology, and self-regulation: The Good Lives Model of sexual offender treatment. *Aggression and Violent Behavior, 11*, 77–94.

Ward, T., Hudson, S. M., & Marshall, W. L. (1995). Cognitive and affective deficits in sexual aggression: A cognitive deconstructionist analysis. *Sexual Abuse: A Journal of Research and Treatment, 7*, 67–83.

Ward, T., Louden, K., Hudson, S. M., & Marshall, W. L. (1995). A descriptive model of the offense chain for child molesters. *Journal of Interpersonal Violence, 10*, 452–472.

Ward, T., Hudson, S. M., & France, K. G. (1994). Self-reported reasons for offending behavior in child molesters. *Annals of Sex Research, 6*, 139–148.

Ward, T., Hudson, S. M., Johnston, L., & Marshall, W. L. (1997). Cognitive distortions in sex offenders: An integrative review. *Clinical Psychology Review, 17*, 479–507.

Ward, T., Hudson, S. M., & Marshall, W. L. (1994). The abstinence violation effect in child molesters. *Behavior Research and Therapy, 32*, 431–437.

Ward, T., McCormack, J., & Hudson, S. M. (1997). Sexual offenders' perceptions of their intimate relationships. *Sexual Abuse: A Journal of Research and Treatment, 9*, 57–74.

Warr, P. B. (1971). Pollyanna's personal judgments. *European Journal of Social Psychology, 1*, 327–338.

Warren, H. C. (1921). *A history of the association psychology*. New York: Scribners.

Warren, W. (1998). *Philosophical dimensions of personal construct psychology*. London: Routledge.

Watson, J. P. (1970a). A measure of therapist-patient understanding. *British Journal of Psychiatry, 117*, 319–321.

Watson, J. P. (1970b). A repertory grid method of studying groups. *British Journal of Psychiatry, 117*, 309–318.

Watson, J. P. (1972). A possible measure of change during group psychotherapy. *British Journal of Medical Psychology, 45*, 71–77.

Weber, M. (1964). *The theory of social and economic organization*. New York: The Free Press (Original work published 1947.).

Weeks, J. (1985). *Sexuality and its discontents: Meanings, myths, and modern sexualities*. London: Routledge & Kegan Paul.

Weeks, J. (1986). *Sexuality* (2nd ed.). Hove: Routledge.
Weeks, J. (1995). History, desires, and identities. In G. P. Parker & J. H. Gagnon (Eds.), *Conceiving sexuality: Approaches to sex research in a postmodern world* (pp. 33–50). London: Routledge.
Weeks, J. (2000). *Making sexual history.* Cambridge: Polity.
Weeks, J. (2005). Fallen heroes: All about men. *Irish Journal of Sociology, 14*, 53–65.
Weeks, J. (2007). *The world we won.* New York: Routledge.
Weeks, J. (2011). *The languages of sexuality.* New York: Routledge.
Weeks, J. (2012). Queer(y)ing the 'modern homosexual'. *The Journal of British Studies, 51*, 523–539.
Weigel, R. G., Weigel, V. M., & Richardson, F. C. (1973). Congruence of spouses and reported marital success: Pitfalls in instrumentation. *Psychological Reports, 33*, 212–214.
Weitzer, R. (2009). Sociology of sex work. *Annual Review of Sociology, 35*, 213–234.
West, C., & Zimmerman, D. H. (1987). Doing gender. *Gender and Society, 1*, 125–151.
Westbrook, L., & Schilt, K. (2014). Doing gender, determining gender. *Gender and Society, 28*, 32–57.
Whitney, E. (2002). Cyborgs among us: Performing liminal states of sexuality. *Journal of Bisexuality, 2*, 109–128.
Wilkerson, W. S. (2007). *Ambiguity and sexuality: A theory of sexual identity.* New York: Palgrave Macmillan.
Wilkerson, W. S. (2009). Is it a choice? Sexual orientation as interpretation. *Journal of Social Philosophy, 40*, 97–116.
Willard, E. O. G. (1867). *Sexology as the philosophy of life: Implying social organization and government.* Chicago: J. R. Walsh.
Williams, C. (2014). Transgender. *Transgender Studies Quarterly, 1*, 215.
Willutzki, U., & Duda, L. (1996). The social construction of powerfulness and powerlessness. In D. Kalekin Fishman & B. Walker (Eds.), *The construction of group realities: Culture, society, and personal construct theory* (pp. 341–361). Malabar: Krieger Publishing.
Wilson, G. (2014). *Your brain on porn: Internet pornography and the emerging science of addiction.* Margate: Commonwealth.
Wilson, G. D., & Cox, D. N. (1983a). Personality of paedophile club members. *Personality and Individual Differences, 4*, 323–329.

Wilson, G. D., & Cox, D. N. (1983b). *The child-lovers: A study of paedophiles in society*. London: Peter Owen.

Winter, D. A. (1988). Reconstructing an erection and elaborating ejaculation: Personal construct theory perspectives on sex therapy. *International Journal of Personal Construct Psychology, 1*, 42–53.

Winter, D. A. (1992a). *Personal construct psychology in clinical practice: Theory, research and applications*. London: Routledge.

Winter, D. A. (1992b). Repertory grid technique as a group therapy research instrument. *Group Analysis, 25*, 449–463.

Winter, D. A. (2003a). The evidence base for personal construct psychotherapy. In F. Fransella (Ed.), *International handbook of personal construct psychology* (pp. 265–272). Chichester: John Wiley & Sons.

Winter, D. A. (2003b). A credulous approach to violence and homicide. In J. Horley (Ed.), *Personal construct perspectives on forensic psychology* (pp. 15–54). New York: Brunner-Routledge.

Winter, D. A. (2005). Toward a personal construct sex therapy. In D. Winter & L. Viney (Eds.), *Advances in personal construct psychotherapy* (pp. 287–295). London: Whurr Publishers.

Winter, D. A. (2007). Construing the construction processes of serial killers and other violent offenders: The limits of credulity. *Journal of Constructivist Psychology, 20*, 247–275.

Winter, D. A., & Viney, L. L. (Eds.) (2005). *Personal construct psychotherapy: Advances in theory, practice, and research*. London: Whurr.

Winter, D. A., & Watson, S. (1999). Personal construct psychotherapy and the cognitive therapies: Different in theory but can they be differentiated in practice? *Journal of Constructivist Psychology, 12*, 1–22.

Wismeijer, A. J., & van Assen, A. L. M. (2013). Psychological characteristics of BDSM practitioners. *Journal of Sexual Medicine, 10*, 1943–1952.

Worthington, R. L., Savoy, H. B., Dillon, F. R., & Vernaglia, E. R. (2002). Heterosexual identity development: A multidimensional model of individual and social identity. *The Counseling Psychologist, 30*, 496–531.

Wrong, D. (1979). *Power: Its forms, bases, and uses*. New York: Harper and Row.

Yeoman, I., & Mars, M. (2012). Robots, men and sex tourism. *Futures, 44*, 365–371.

Yorke, M. (1989). The intolerable wrestle: Words, numbers, and meanings. *International Journal of Personal Construct Psychology, 6*, 65–76.

Name Index

A
Abbott, E., 66, 69, 227
Abel, G. G., 84, 169, 177, 178, 184, 189
Abelson, R. C., 29
Adams, B., 188
Adams, H. E., 212
Adams, M. S., 240
Adams-Webber, J. R., 196, 199–202, 228
Adriaens, P. R., 16
Adshead, G., 55, 208, 218
Agnew, J., 201
Akman, D., 69
Aldridge, J., 183
Allen, M., 156
Anderson, M. L., 10
Aries, P., 16
Armstrong, H., 109–110
Armstrong, P., 109–110

Aspin, C., 79
Attwood, F., 153

B
Babchishin, K. M., 185
Badesha, J., 196
Bailey, J. M., 74
Baker, K. D., 196
Baldwin, M. W., 204
Balnaves, M., 228
Bandura, A., 157
Bannister, D., 36, 39, 50, 89, 196, 198, 200, 201, 230, 231
Barak, A., 149, 150
Barbaree, H., 156, 169, 179
Barker, M., 54, 215
Barnsley, J., 94
Barron, M., 152
Basson, R., 49

Name Index

Baumeister, R. F., 63, 64, 69
Bavelas, J. B., 199
Beail, N., 211
Beaulieu-Prevost, D., 142
Becker, J. V., 177, 189
Begley, E. A., 52, 120
Beitchman, J. H., 69
Bejin, A., 17
Belanger, M., 142
Bell, R., 12, 196
Bem, D. J., 28
Benjafield, J., 200, 202
Bennett, C. G., 162
Benston, M. L., 110
Bentley, M., 24, 242
Berger, P. L., 15
Berkowitz, L., 149
Berliner, L., 175
Berman, J. S., 211
Bernstein, E., 161
Biddlecom, A. E., 240
Bieri, J., 200
Bigras, N., 58
Billings, V., 149, 150
Binet, A., 142–4
Bivona, J., 122
Blackwell, C. W., 194
Blanchard, R., 57
Blevins, K. R., 164
Bloch, I., 21
Bogaert, A. F., 57, 66–8, 70, 155
Bonarius, J. C. J., 36, 200, 211
Bond, B. J., 240
Boston Women's Health Book Collective, 99
Bordwell, P., 17
Bond, B. J., 240

Boston Women's Health Book Collective,, 99
Boswell, A. A., 152
Bowleg, L., 29, 131
Bradley, K. A., 135
Braithwaite, S. R., 156
Bramberger, T., 63, 236
Braverman, H., 109
Brecher, E. M., 24
Breen, D., 203
Brezgel, K., 156
Brickell, C., 16, 72, 115–18, 123
Bridges, S., 54
Briere, J., 58, 156
Brotto, L. A., 67
Brown, J.D., 204, 241
Brownmiller, S., 152, 172
Bullough, V. L., 17, 22–4
Bumby, K. M., 178, 184
Burkholder, G. J., 29
Burkitt, I., 49, 50
Buss, D. M., 4, 5, 30
Butler, J., 8, 72, 106, 118, 221
Butt, T., 56, 64

C

Cabeen, C. W, 217, 218
Callis, A. S., 25, 68, 74, 77, 78
Cannon, M., 79
Caplan, H.L., 209, 210
Caputi, P., 228
Carlson, A. J., 17
Carnahan, T. E., 187
Carr, J., 201
Carver, T., 242
Casini, C., 64, 223

Cass, V. C., 32, 59
Cassavia, E., 69
Chambers, W. V., 199
Chan, A. S., 199
Charcot, J. M., 19
Chasin, C. J. D., 67, 83
Chin-Keung, L., 55
Chivers, M. L., 74
Cipolletta, S., 64, 233
Colapinto, J., 24
Coleman, J. C., 217, 218
Collings, S. J., 178
Collins, P. H., 9, 111, 112, 129–31
Connell, R. W., 108
Coohey, C., 213
Cooper, A., 239
Cordeau, D., 142
Coulson, G., 156
Courtois, F., 142
Cox, D. N., 182
Critelli, J. 122
Cromwell, R. L., 44, 202
Cross, M. C., 211
Cross, P. A., 64
Cruikshank, M., 101
Cummings, W., 132, 134
Cummins, P., 209
Cunningham-Rathner, J., 177, 189
Currier, J. M., 211

D

DaCosta, G. A., 69
D'Alessio, D., 156
Daneback, D., 241
Daneback, K., 239
Dant, T., 144

Darke, J. L., 172
Davidson, P, 155, 202
Davis, K. B., 22
De Beauvoir, S., 9, 74
De Block, A., 16
De Silva, P., 213
Deegan, M. J., 22
DeMello, M., 134, 135
Dewey, J., 35
Diamond, L. M., 5, 68, 83
Dillon, F. R., 12
Dines, G., 151
Dingman, H. F., 180, 181
Doidge, N., 157
Donnerstein, E., 149, 154
Downing, L., 236
Drescher, J., 194
Drogos, K. L., 240
Duck, S. W., 50
Duda, L., 107
Dupras, A., 243

E

Easton, S. D., 213
Ellis, A., 213, 214
Ellis, H., 18, 19, 142, 143
Enquist, M., 142, 144
Ensler, E., 99
Enzlin, P., 67
Epstein, R., 12
Epting, F.R., 36, 49, 51, 52, 64, 121, 155, 188, 194, 195, 198, 201, 203, 205, 209, 211
Erbes, C.R., 206, 214
Escoffier, J., 97, 100, 163
Eyerman, R., 53, 107, 121
Eysenck, H. J., 80

F

Faccio, E., 64, 65, 223
Faidley, A. J., 52, 120
Febos, M., 64
Feixas, G., 200
Ferguson, C. J., 149, 156
Ferreira, V. S., 134
Fielding, J. M., 210
Figueroa-Sarriera, H. J., 138
Fincham, F. D., 156
Firestone, P., 204
Fisher, W.A., 149, 150
Fitch, J. L., 45
Flood, M., 149
Flugel, J. C., 141
Foucault, M., 16, 25, 106, 119, 233
Fox, S., 12
France, K. G., 179, 183
Fransella, F., 188, 196, 198, 209, 210
Frederic, C. M., 135
Fredrickson, B. L., 126–8, 146, 151
French, J. R. P., 112, 113
Freshwater, K., 183
Freud, J. M., 19
Freud, S., 18–21, 26, 27, 56, 141, 143, 144
Freund, K., 5, 23, 24
Frisbie, L., 180, 181
Frith, H., 29

G

Gagnon, J. H., 15, 29, 156
Gaines, B. R., 197
Gambescia, N., 153
Gamson, J., 68
Garcia, C., 12
Gay, P., 19

Gebhard, P. H., 23
Gemignani, M., 211
Ghirlanda, S., 142, 144
Giddens, A., 93, 105
Gijs, L., 67
Giles, J., 59, 201
Gillis, R., 186
Godbout, N., 58
Goffman, E., 8, 10, 92, 211
Goldberg, I., 18
Goldie, T., 24
Goodholm, C. R., 200
Gorzalka, B. B., 67
Gramsci, A., 107
Grant, A. M., 216
Gray, C. H., 138
Gray, J. H., 138
Grov, C., 163
Gueguen, N., 135
Guthrie, J. A., 199

H

Hagan, B., 160
Hagans, C. L., 198–200
Haidt, J., 233, 234
Haig, D., 9, 243
Haldeman, D. C., 194
Halperin, D. M., 15, 16, 60, 223
Hamilton, R., 90, 100
Haraway, D., 138–139
Hart, C. C., 206
Harter, S. L., 206, 214
Hartley, R. D., 149, 156
Hartmann, H., 111
Harvey, L., 145
Hauser, R. I., 18

Hayashino, D. S., 178
Hearn, J., 236, 241, 242
Heffner, V., 240
Heiman, J. R., 58
Helson, H., 160
Henry, F., 111, 129
Herrn, R., 23, 30
Hersh, M. A., 233, 234
Heyl, B. S., 161
Hinkle, D. N., 203, 230
Hirschfeld, M., 17, 21, 22
Hochschild, A., 8
Holland, J., 121
Holland, J. M., 211
Holland, R., 39, 40
Holt, T. J., 164
Honikman, B., 204
Honos-Webb, L., 51
Hood, J. E., 69
Hooks, B., 131
Hopkins, P. D., 236
Horley, J., 32, 36, 39, 41, 44, 46, 48, 50–3, 55, 61, 63, 80, 114, 120, 122, 144, 160, 164, 172, 176, 178, 181–3, 188, 189, 196, 199, 203, 204, 206, 209, 211–13, 216–21, 230–3
Houdenhove, E. v., 67
Houston, J., 36, 55, 122, 187, 208, 209, 212, 218
Howe, P.D., 139, 140
Howells, K., 122, 182, 183, 187
Hua, L., 213
Hudson, S. J., 183
Humm, M., 8, 14, 126
Husain, M., 52, 120
Hutchings, J., 79

I
Iuduci, A., 58

J
Jackson, L. A., 162
Jahoda, M., 49
James, B., 118
James, W., 35, 55, 56, 125, 167
Jannini, E. A., 142, 144
Jerry, M. B., 188
Johnson, A., 122, 203, 209
Johnson, K., 226
Johnson, P., 76
Johnson, V.E., 3, 5, 55
Johnston, L., 178, 183
Jones, D., 201
Jones, J. H., 23, 55, 181
Jones, R. E., 200
Jones, R. K., 240
Jones, S., 204
Jordan, J., 164
Joyston-Bechal, M. P., 209
Julka, D., 164

K
Kaan, H., 18
Karp, C., 171
Katz, J. O., 228
Katz-Wise, S. L., 68, 83
Kauth, M. R., 12, 225
Keddington, K., 156
Keelan, C. M., 135
Keith, H. E., 160
Keller, S., 241

Kelly, G. A., 6, 14, 35–44, 46–50, 52, 55, 59, 61, 85, 89, 119, 120, 155, 181, 195–7, 202, 206, 211, 212, 216, 227–9, 231, 232
Kiefer, A. K., 122
Kilmann, R. H., 231, 232
Kimmel, M., 152
King, M., 69
Kinsey, A. C., 12, 23
Kinsman, G., 5, 11, 60, 68, 83, 101, 119
Kitzinger, C., 29
Klebe, K. J., 179
Kleese, C., 137
Knight, R. A., 187
Kolodny, R.C., 3, 55
Kong, T. S. K., 161
Krafft-Ebing, R. von., 18, 26, 84, 176, 177
Kruger, R.L., 204

L

Laing, R. D., 115
Landfield, A. W., 36, 182, 187, 188, 201, 203, 205, 206, 209
Langdridge, D., 64
Lanyon, R. I., 169
Laws, D. R., 220
Leach, C., 183
Lefebvre, V. A., 202
Lefebvre, V. D., 202
LeFleur-Bach, R., 218
Leitner, L. M., 49, 51, 52, 120, 121
Leman, G., 39
Lerner, R. M., 226
LeVay, S., 4, 30, 31, 57, 60, 63

Levy, D., 237, 239
Lewin, K., 60
Lewis, R., 159
Lindemann, D., 64, 236
Little, B. R., 39, 215, 216
Lorber, J., 72
Lothstein, L. M., 218
Lubowitz, S., 86
Luckmann, T., 15
Lunghi, M., 201, 203, 207

M

MacCulloch, M. J., 169, 204
Mackie, M., 10
MacKinnon, C. A., 127
Mair, J. M. M., 36, 137, 198, 200
Malamuth, N. M., 149, 150, 186
Malebranche, D. J., 29, 131
Mancini, E., 17, 21
Mancuso, J. C., 228
Mansson, S., 239
Marie, M. T., 200
Marks, I. M., 179, 181
Mars, M., 237, 238
Marshall, G., 9
Marshall, L. E., 182, 204
Marshall, W. L., 9, 85, 169, 178, 179, 182–4, 191, 204
Marston, C., 159
Martin, C. E., 12, 19, 23
Martinson, R., 191
Maslow, A. H., 17
Masson, J. M., 20
Masters, W. H., 3, 5, 55
Matheson, K., 64
May, R., 107, 174
Mazzucco, A., 183, 184

McAnulty, R. D., 212
McCaghy, C. H., 178, 179
McCormack, J., 183
McCoy, M. M., 43
McIntosh, M., 73, 117
McKinney, P., 12
McPhail, I. V., 185
Mead, G. H., 50, 56, 228
Mead, M., 9
Mendelsohn, G. A., 231
Mentor, S., 138
Meston, C. M., 5, 58
Metcalfe, C., 211
Mezey, G., 69
Millet, K., 8
Mills, C. W., 94
Mills, H. E., 169
Minton, H. L., 106, 107
Mischel, T., 39
Mohr, J. W., 188
Molinder, J. L., 200
Moll, A., 26, 56
Money, J. L., 10, 12, 24, 69, 243
Montes, J. N., 200
Monto, M. A., 164
Moon, D., 68
Moradi, B., 155, 195
Moreno, J. L., 211
Moyer-Gusé, E., 154
Myers, J., 136

N
Nagal, J., 111
Needs, A., 187
Neimeyer, G. J., 198, 200
Neimeyer, R. A., 35, 36, 54, 196, 200
Nelson, L.J., 17

Nelson, M. C., 182
Ng, S. H., 106
Nickeson, C. J., 198
Nisbett, R. E., 47
Noar, S. M., 29
Novak, J., 35
Nunes, K. L., 185, 204, 205

O
Oades, L., 228
Oakley, A., 8, 10
O'leary, P., 213
Orford, J., 210
Oselin, S. S., 162, 222
Osgood, C. E., 179, 180, 204, 231
Oye, J., 239

P
Pallotta-Chiarolli, M., 86
Palys, T. S., 216
Parker, S., 211
Parker, T. S., 239
Parry, G., 32, 50, 52, 228
Peck, B., 42
Pedersen, F. A., 200
Peele, S., 173
Pfaus, J., 157, 158
Phelps, E., 226
Phoenix, J., 162
Pittell, S. M., 231
Pitts, V. L., 134
Plummer, K., 25, 26, 72
Pomeroy, W. B., 12, 23
Prause, N., 153, 155–8
Prentky, R. A., 187
Procter, H., 50, 52

Q

Quayle, E., 239
Quinsey, V. L., 44, 55, 169, 178, 180, 181, 183, 185, 188, 199, 204, 206

R

Rachman, S., 143, 144
Rada, R. T., 187
Ramazanoglu, C., 105
Ramos, H., 76
Raskin, J. D., 45, 51, 234
Raven, B., 112, 113
Ravlin, E. C., 45
Rea, M. C., 150
Reich, W., 21
Reiter, E., 110
Rellini, A. H., 58
Rich, A., 11, 14, 75, 117, 118
Richardson, F. C., 210
Rieger, G., 73
Ringrose, J., 145
Ritzer, G., 109
Rivardo, M. G., 135
Roberts, T., 126–8, 146, 151
Roesch, R., 213
Rohde, P. D., 209, 210
Rokeach, M., 232, 233
Rosner, C., 171
Ross, M. W., 239
Rowbotham, S., 90, 97, 100
Rowe, D., 52, 53, 120, 121, 209
Rubin, G. S., 117
Russell, B., 233
Rust, P. C. R., 78
Rye, B. J., 63, 236
Ryle, A., 201, 203, 207

S

Sachdev, S., 204
Said, E., 131
Salter, A. C., 185
Sanchez, D. T., 122
Sartorius, N. H., 179, 181
Sartre, J.-P., 48, 53, 121
Sauerteig, L. D. H., 18, 26
Saunders, T., 161
Savoy, H. B., 12
Schank, R. C., 29
Schildkrout, E., 133
Schilt, S., 8, 79, 80
Schippers, M., 108
Schroeder, M., 194
Schwartz, S. J., 226
Scimecca, J. A., 51
Scorolli, C., 142, 144
Scott, J., 9, 71, 233
Seal, D. W., 163
Segal, L., 118, 178, 186
Segal, Z. V., 118, 178, 186
Seidman, S., 92, 117
Serafini, T., 63, 236
Seto, M., 156, 186, 190
Sewell, K. W., 55
Shapiro, D.A., 209, 210
Sharpe, S., 105
Shaw, M. L. G., 197
Shidlo, A., 194
Shorts, I. D., 186, 208
Shotter, J., 39
Simon, L., 241
Simon, W., 15, 29, 156
Sin, R., 68, 78
Singer, B., 4
Skene, R. A., 212
Slater, P., 203, 207
Smith, D. E., 111, 229
Smith, J., 204

Smith, M. D., 163
Smith, N. J., 163
Smith, S. L., 156
Snowden, P. R., 169, 204
Sowinski, B. A., 162
Space, L. G., 44, 202
Spade, J. Z., 152
Spargo, T., 25
Sperlinger, D. J., 199, 200
Spitzer, R. L., 194
Staggenborg, S., 76
Staley, C., 155–156
Stam, H. J., 15, 45
Stein, E., 194
Steinem, G., 148, 149, 152
Stekel, W., 21
Stermac, L. E., 178, 186
Stern, S., 241
Storms, M. D., 29, 30, 67
Strachan, A., 201
Strickland, L. H., 211
Stringer, P., 50, 89
Stryker, S., 72, 76, 78–79
Suchman, D. I., 198
Suci, G. J., 179, 231

T

Tannenbaum, P., 179, 231
Tator, C., 111, 129
Taylor, L., 179
Taylor, M., 239
Teti, M., 29
Thomson, R., 105
Thurstone, L. L., 17
Tibbals, C. A., 151
Tikkanen, R., 239
Tomura, M., 162
Townes, B., 210
Tschann, J. M., 29

T'Sjoen, G., 67
Turner, C., 129, 133, 188
Turner, R. E., 188
Tylka, T. L., 156

V

Valocchi, S., 77
van Assen, A. L. M., 63
Van Brunt, D. L., 198
van den Berg, J. J., 155, 194
Van Deven, M., 78
Van Diest, A. M. K., 156
Vanasek, F., 180
Varble, D. L., 206
Verdecchia, M., 58
Vernaglia, E. R., 12
Videkanic, B., 129
Viney, L. L., 205, 211

W

Waldby, S., 110, 111
Walker, B. M., 36, 160
Walker, G., 94
Wang, B., 155
Ward, T., 178, 179, 183
Warr, P. B., 202
Warren, H. C., 144
Warren, W., 36
Watson, J. P., 207, 209, 210, 214
Watson, S., 214
Weber, M., 106, 109
Weeks, J., 4, 8, 11, 13, 14, 18, 25, 55, 71–3, 75, 96–8, 101, 153, 164, 194, 199, 218
Weigel, R. G., 210
Weigel, V. M., 210
West, C., 10
Weitzer, R., 148, 160

Westbrook, L., 8, 79, 80
Whitney, E., 140
Wilkerson, W. S., 15, 31, 33, 34, 40, 48, 59, 60, 62, 226, 238
Willard, E. O. G., 17, 233
Williams, C., 13, 14
Willutzki, U., 107
Wilson, G., 157, 158
Wilson, G. D., 182
Wilson, T. D., 47
Winter, D. A., 36, 44, 45, 48, 54, 153, 174, 194, 195, 200, 201, 203, 205, 208, 211, 213–15, 218
Wood, P. J. W., 169
Worthington, R. L., 12, 32

Wrong, D., 107, 113, 115, 116
Wurtele, S. K., 178

Y

Ybarra, O., 122
Yeoman, I., 237, 238
Yorke, M., 39
Yule, M. A., 67

Z

Zattoni, S., 142, 144
Zhang, Y., 213
Zimmerman, D. H., 10
Zucker, K. J., 69

Subject Index

A

agency, 9, 45, 47, 61, 90–6, 99, 102–3, 126, 162, 163, 196
AIDS, 30, 44, 101, 102
American Psychiatric Association (or APA), 12, 67, 84, 128, 186, 188, 189
asexuality, 28, 66–70
aversion therapy, 118, 180

B

bad faith, 53, 121
biogenetic theory of sexual orientation, 31
body art, 132–7
body inscription, 128, 132, 133
body modification, 126, 132–5
body part fetishism, 126, 142–4, 146

Bondage, discipline, sadism, masochism (BDSM), 63–6, 71, 134, 137, 223, 235, 236
Boston Women's Health Book Collective

C

channelized choice, 62, 193
childhood sexuality (or sexuality in infancy), 26, 56, 89–103, 223
child molestation (or child sexual abuse), 55, 57, 58, 169, 178, 180, 183, 184, 186, 206, 213, 214
choice corollary, 46, 48, 89, 163, 227–9
civil rights movements, 96, 98
cognitive complexity, 199, 210

Subject Index

cognitive restructuring, 213–15
cognitive revolution, 36
commonality corollary, 89, 227
compulsory heterosexuality, 11, 14, 75
constricted construing, 74
construct dimensionality, 84
constructive alternativism, 37–9
constructivism, 15, 45, 229
conversion therapy (or reparation therapy), 194
credulous approach, 36, 37, 202, 214, 216
cyborg, 126, 128, 137–41

D

Diagnostic and Statistical Manual (DSM), 12, 142

E

ego-dystonic homosexuality, 12
Electra complex, 27
emerging fusion theory, 31
endocrine system (including sex hormones), 3, 22, 56, 125
erogenous zone, 27, 141, 142
erotica, 148–56, 158, 177, 239
eroticism, 54
eroticization, 28
erotic orientation theory, 29
essentialism/essentialist, 2, 11, 15, 28, 59, 79, 110, 111
eugenics, 19
evolutionary psychology, 36
exhibitionism/exhibitionist, 84, 188, 189, 209

existentialism, 39, 48, 59
existential therapy, 215
experience, 6, 9, 10, 11, 13, 19, 23, 25, 27, 31–3, 38, 40–9, 50, 55, 66, 67, 70–2, 75, 79, 81–4, 86, 89–93, 99, 109–12, 116, 117, 122, 125, 127–31, 134, 138–40, 143, 147, 151, 153–5, 159, 160, 162, 163, 164, 174–8, 185, 201, 202, 204, 208, 213, 214, 219, 221–3, 226–8, 232, 238–40
experience corollary, 48

F

false consciousness, 53, 121
family ideology, 97
feminism, 139, 140
feminist theory, 8, 9, 110, 111, 118, 127
fixed-role therapy (FRT), 211–13
fluid sexuality, 79
fragmentation corollary, 163
frotteurism, 189
fundamental postulate, 61
future of sexuality, 241

G

gay liberation, 11, 13, 101
gay (and lesbian) rights movements, 13, 74, 75
gender nonconformity, 13, 14, 79
gender role, 9, 10, 24, 98, 242, 243
gerontophilia, 190

Subject Index

Greek law of opposition, 40

H
hegemonic heterosexuality, 79
hegemony, 107, 108
heteronormativity, 11, 59, 60, 75–7, 117
homoeroticism, 29, 30
homonormativity, 76
homosexuality (including gay, lesbian), 6, 11, 12, 18, 19, 21, 22, 28, 30, 57, 58, 68, 74, 75, 79, 95, 101, 118, 212, 233, 234
hysteria, 19, 20

I
intersectionality (or intersectional analysis), 131

L
language (or language development), 1, 6, 7, 11–13, 39, 42, 45, 49, 71–4, 86, 87, 99, 119, 148, 154, 162, 164, 172, 177, 190, 197, 220, 225, 228, 242
LGBTQ (including variants), 13, 86
lovemap, 24, 69

M
Marxism (or Marxist), 53, 107, 109
masturbation, 22, 26, 56, 145, 158, 238

meaning, 5, 7–9, 11, 14, 15, 29, 31, 45–9, 51, 53, 82, 85, 90–2, 96, 97, 108, 126, 128, 129, 130, 133–7, 145, 154, 155, 162, 165, 191, 195, 205, 213–15, 235
media and sexuality, 7, 9, 10
medicalization, 11, 100
men of colour, 129–31
multiple sexualities, 71–87, 101, 226

N
necrophilia, 189
nonverbal or preverbal constructs, 55

O
objectification theory, 127, 146
objective assessment, 37
Oedipal complex, 27
orgone, 21
Orientalism, 131–3

P
paedophilia, 84, 85, 176
paedophilia erotica, 177
patriarchy (or patriarchal relations), 14, 93, 98, 110, 111, 172
penile plethysmography, 23
personal construct theory (PCT), 6, 7, 15, 32–70, 72, 73, 80, 82, 85, 89, 90–3, 102–3, 105, 106, 108, 109, 116, 119, 120, 127, 128, 131, 133, 136, 141, 146, 148–9, 153, 155, 163–6, 168–72,

188, 189, 191, 193–224,
226–32, 234, 235, 243, 244
personal projects therapy, 215–17
polymorphous perversity, 26
porn-induced erectile dysfunction
(PIED), 157, 158
pornography, 147–165, 239
poststructuralism (or
poststructuralist), 8, 25
pragmatism (or American
pragmatism), 35
Pride (or Gay Pride), 76, 77
projective assessment, 37
psychoanalysis (or psychoanalytic
theory), 20, 21, 26, 27, 37,
39, 194
psychodiagnosis, 37, 51, 179, 211
psychotherapy, 49, 153, 194, 205,
206, 208, 211–24
puberty, 28–30, 56, 60, 69

Q

queer theory, 25, 77, 116,
117, 140

R

racialization (or racialized), 111,
128–32
radical behaviorism, 35
radical feminist theory, 127
rape, 94, 122, 131, 151, 152, 154,
160, 172, 186, 236
relapse prevention, 220–22
relational corollary, 229
reproductive rights, 14, 90, 91
Role Construct Repertory Grid (or
rep grid), 37, 181, 182,
184, 187, 196, 197,
199–202, 204–10, 216, 232

S

safe sex, 102, 118, 154
seduction hypothesis, 20
self-characterization technique, 203
self-fulfilling prophesy, 85
self-validation, 34, 63, 65–70,
171, 226
sexology (or sexuality studies), 8,
15–26, 54, 108, 116, 225,
226, 242, 243
sex reassignment surgery, 13, 14
sexual activism, 18, 20, 66, 67, 135,
150, 156, 165, 171, 177,
178, 183, 189, 233, 239, 240
sexual borderland, 78
sexual commodification, 103, 147–65
sexual ethics (or sexual morality), 17,
19, 230, 231, 233, 234, 236
sexual fantasy, 20, 29, 169, 184, 239
sexual health, 99, 240, 241
sexual instinct, 4, 18, 19, 26,
59, 177
sexual inversion (or inverts), 19
sexuality history, 15–17, 79
sexuality theory, 26–31, 230
sexualization, 126–31, 137, 145, 146
sexual minorities, 17, 18, 21, 22, 31,
32, 54, 68, 69, 74, 77, 83,
85, 102, 118, 119, 123,
155, 194, 242
sexual objectification, 126, 127
sexual or gender binaries, 14, 67, 68,
72–80, 86
sexual or gender identity, 10, 14,
186, 242

sexual orientation, 4–6, 11, 12, 28, 30, 31, 60, 67, 74, 78, 186, 190, 194
sexual physiology (or reproductive organs), 1
sexual preference, 12, 28
sexual revolution, 71, 96, 100, 233
sexual script theory, 29
sexual stigmatization, 11, 73, 75, 85, 86, 101, 118, 131, 239
sexual strategies theory, 4, 30
sexual surrogacy, 237
sexual violence, 94, 95, 99, 131, 152, 156, 241
sex workers (or sex trade workers), 117, 130, 160–4, 160–5, 222, 236, 238
social class, 52, 108–10, 135
social constructionism, 14, 15, 25, 29, 59, 105
social inequality, 95, 110–12, 115, 116, 229
sociality corollary, 89, 227
socialization, 89, 227
social power (or power relations), 25, 32, 52, 105–7, 112, 113, 119–23, 229, 230
social structure, 14, 25, 75, 90–3, 102–3, 107–10, 126, 130, 181

sociological imagination, 94
source corollary, 228
subordinate construction, 38, 41
superordinate construction, 38, 41, 82, 203
symbolic interactionism, 16, 25, 29, 56, 92, 93, 195

T
Taoism, 40
teledildonics (or cyberdildonics), 239, 240
transgender (or trans), 13, 14, 72, 74, 77–9, 86
transitive diagnosis, 196
transsexual, 13, 14, 77

V
virtual reality, 138, 139
voyeurism, 189

W
women of colour, 129–31
women's movement, 97–9, 110

CPI Antony Rowe
Chippenham, UK
2016-12-27 16:38